Events That Changed Great Britain Since 1689

BOOKS OF RELATED INTERESTS

The Greenwood Press "Events That Changed America" Series
John E. Findling and Frank W. Thackeray, editors

Events That Changed America in the Twentieth Century

Events That Changed America in the Nineteenth Century

Events That Changed America in the Eighteenth Century

Events That Changed America Through the Seventeenth Century

The Greenwood Press "Events That Changed the World" Series
Frank W. Thackeray and John E. Findling, editors

Events That Changed the World in the Twentieth Century

Events That Changed the World in the Nineteenth Century

Events That Changed the World in the Eighteenth Century

Events That Changed the World in the Seventeenth Century

Events That Changed the World Through the Sixteenth Century

Events That Changed Great Britain Since 1689

edited by
Frank W. Thackeray
&
John E. Findling

GREENWOOD PRESS
Westport, Connecticut • London

Library of Congress Cataloging-in-Publication Data

Events that changed Great Britain since 1689 / edited by Frank W. Thackeray and John E. Findling.
    p. cm.
    Includes bibliographical references and index.
    ISBN 0–313–31686–4 (alk. paper)
    1. Great Britain—History—Modern period, 1485–   I. Thackeray, Frank W.
II. Findling, John E.
DA470.E94   2002
941—dc21   2002016103

British Library Cataloguing in Publication Data is available.

Copyright © 2002 by Frank W. Thackeray and John E. Findling

All rights reserved. No portion of this book may be reproduced, by any process or technique, without the express written consent of the publisher.

Library of Congress Catalog Card Number: 2002016103
ISBN: 0–313–31686–4

First published in 2002

Greenwood Press, 88 Post Road West, Westport, CT 06881
An imprint of Greenwood Publishing Group, Inc.
www.greenwood.com

Printed in the United States of America

The paper used in this book complies with the Permanent Paper Standard issued by the National Information Standards Organization (Z39.48–1984).

10 9 8 7 6 5 4 3 2 1

Copyright Acknowledgments

The editors and publisher gratefully acknowledge permission for use of the following material:

Extracts from Pearse Padraic, "The Rebel," in *The Literary Writings of Patrick Pearse: Writings in English*, collected and edited by Séamas Ó. Buachala (Dublin: Mercier Press, 1975). Reprinted with permission of Mercier Press.

Contents

Illustrations		vii
Preface		ix
Timeline		xi
1.	**The Industrial Revolution, c. 1750–c. 1850**	1
	Introduction	1
	Interpretive Essay by David Mitch	6
2.	**The Seven Years' War, 1756–1763**	19
	Introduction	19
	Interpretive Essay by Frederick M. Stowell	25
3.	**The Napoleonic Wars, 1789–1815**	37
	Introduction	37
	Interpretive Essay by S. J. Stearns	43
4.	**Pax Britannica, 1815–1914**	57
	Introduction	57
	Interpretive Essay by Lowell J. Satre	61
5.	**The Reform Act of 1832**	75
	Introduction	75
	Interpretive Essay by Thomas C. Mackey	80

6.	**The Great Exhibition of 1851**	93
	Introduction	93
	Interpretive Essay by Diana J. Reynolds	98
7.	**Sinn Fein and the Suffragettes: The Movements for Irish Independence and Women's Suffrage, c. 1880–1921**	113
	Introduction	113
	Interpretive Essay by Kenneth L. Campbell	118
8.	**World War I, 1914–1919**	133
	Introduction	133
	Interpretive Essay by Larry P. Thornton	138
9.	**World War II, 1939–1945**	153
	Introduction	153
	Interpretive Essay by George P. Blum	159
10.	**The Thatcher Era, 1979–1990**	173
	Introduction	173
	Interpretive Essay by Richard A. Leiby	179

Appendix A: Glossary — 193

Appendix B: Ruling Houses and Monarchs, 1689–Present — 201

Appendix C: Prime Ministers — 203

Index — 207

About the Editors and Contributors — 215

Illustrations

The power looms for weaving pictured here greatly accelerated the production of textiles	2
The French and Indians defeated General Edward Braddock	20
Britain's most spectacular naval victory occurred at the Battle of Trafalgar	38
The nineteenth century witnessed rapid and forceful British imperial expansion	56
Lord John Russell was for many years deeply interested in parliamentary reform	76
Six million visitors attended the Great Exhibition of 1851	94
Suffragettes adopted confrontational strategies in their struggle to win the right to vote	112
The trench warfare of World War I made for incredibly difficult conditions	134
British Prime Minister Winston Churchill surveys the ruins of Coventry Cathedral	154
Margaret Thatcher visits President and Mrs. Jimmy Carter in December 1979	174

Preface

This volume, which describes and evaluates ten of the most important events in Great Britain between 1689 and the present, is the first in a two-volume series on events that changed Great Britain. The second volume will treat events that occurred up to 1689. This volume is a kind of historical cousin to our two other series of books, Events That Changed the World, which consists of five volumes published between 1995 and 2001, and Events That Changed America, four volumes published between 1996 and 2000.

In a sense, those series and the positive response to them provided the inspiration for this series. Great Britain has loomed large in the history of the world since at least the sixteenth century, and it also, of course, played a pivotal role in the early development of the United States. As a consequence, volumes in our two other series make frequent references to British history. When Barbara Rader, our executive editor at Greenwood Press, suggested that we do a two-volume series on events that changed Great Britain, it seemed like a very good idea. We hope that this book and its companion on the earlier events that shaped British history will enable students and lay readers to place Great Britain in its proper world historical context and, also, to appreciate the fascinating history of Britain itself.

This volume is designed to serve two purposes. First, the editors provide an introduction to each chapter that presents factual material about the event under consideration in a clear, concise, chronological order. Second, each introduction is followed by a longer interpretive essay by a specialist exploring the ramifications of the event. Each essay concludes with a selected bibliography of the most important works about the event. A chronology preceeds the chapter text for ease of reference, and the ten chapters are followed by three appendixes that provide additional information useful to the reader. Appendix A is a glossary of names, events, organizations, and terms mentioned but not fully explained in the introductions and essays. Appendix B charts the ruling houses and monarchs of Great Britain, and Appendix C lists the prime ministers of Great Britain.

The events covered in this volume were selected on the basis of our combined teaching and research activities. Of course, another pair of editors might have arrived at a somewhat different list than ours, but we believe that we have assembled a group of events that truly changed Great Britain over the last three hundred years.

As with all published works, numerous people behind the scenes deserve much of the credit for the final product. Barbara Rader encouraged us to begin the project, and Kevin Ohe has been an exemplary editor through the process of turning our manuscript into a book. The staff of the Photographic Division of the Library of Congress provided genial assistance to us as we selected the photographs that appear in the book. Our student research assistant, Laura Blandford, helped us out in a number of different ways, and we are grateful for the funds that Indiana University Southeast provided to hire her and to pay other costs associated with the project. We are especially grateful to Brigette Colligan, who was always there to type or retype whatever we asked her to. Various staff members, and in particular Stacey Dean of the IUS computer center, cheerfully unscrambled disks and turned mysterious word-processing programs into something we could work with. Special thanks to Roger and Amy Baylor and Kate Lewison for making their establishment available to us, enabling us to confer with colleagues and former students in a congenial atmosphere. Among those who helped us in one way or another to make this a better book are John Newman, Sam Sloss, Sheila Anderson, Kim Pelle, Yu Shen, and Glenn Crothers. And, most important, we thank our authors, whose essays were well-conceived and thoughtful, and whose attention to both detail and scholarship was much appreciated.

Finally, we wish to express our appreciation to our spouses, Carol Findling and Kathy Thackeray, and to our children, Jamey and Jenny Findling and Alex and Max Thackeray, whose patience with us and interest in our work made it all worthwhile.

Frank W. Thackeray
John E. Findling

Timeline

1688	Glorious Revolution; William and Mary begin joint rule
1688–1697	War of the League of Augsburg
1689	John Locke publishes *Treatises on Government*
	Battle of the Boyne
1694	Mary II dies
	Bank of England established
1701–1714	War of the Spanish Succession (Queen Anne's War)
1701	William III dies; Anne ascends throne
1704	Battle of Blenheim
1707	Act of Union unites England and Scotland
1709	Abraham Darby smelts iron with coke
1713	Treaty of Utrecht
1714	Queen Anne dies; George I ascends throne
1720	South Sea Bubble
1721	Ministry of Robert Walpole begins
1727	George I dies; George II ascends throne
	Isaac Newton dies

1733	John Kay invents flying shuttle
1738	David Hume publishes *Treatise on Human Nature*
1739	War of Jenkins' Ear
1740–1748	War of the Austrian Succession (King George's War)
1742	Britain enters the War of the Austrian Succession
1745	Jacobite Rebellion
1755	General Edward Braddock's defeat
1756–1763	Seven Years' War
1756	Captured British soldiers die in "Black Hole" of Calcutta
1757	Battle of Plassey
1759	Battle of Quiberon Bay
	Britain captures Quebec
1760	George II dies; George III ascends throne
1763	Treaty of Paris
1769	James Watt perfects and patents the steam engine
	Richard Arkwright invents the water frame
1776–1783	American Revolution
1776	Adam Smith publishes *Wealth of Nations*
	Edward Gibbon publishes first volume of *Decline and Fall of the Roman Empire*
1784	Edmund Cartwright invents the power loom
	Henry Cort develops the puddling process
1788	Britain begins to send convicts to Australia
1789	French Revolution begins
1790	Edmund Burke publishes *Reflections on the French Revolution*
1791	John Wesley dies
	Thomas Paine publishes *The Rights of Man*
1792	Mary Wollstonecraft publishes *A Vindication of the Rights of Woman*
1793–1815	War with France
1796	Smallpox vaccine
1798	Rebellion in Ireland
	Thomas Malthus publishes *Essay on the Principle of Population*

Timeline

	Battle of Aboukir Bay (Battle of the Nile)
1801	Formation of the United Kingdom of Great Britain and Ireland
1802	Peace of Amiens
1805	Battle of Trafalgar
1807	Slave trade outlawed
1808–1814	Peninsula War in Spain
1811	Luddite disturbances
1812–1814	War with the United States
1814–1815	Congress of Vienna
1814	Battle of Waterloo
	Corn Laws passed
1815	David Ricardo publishes *Principles of Economics*
1819	Peterloo massacre
1820	George III dies; George IV ascends the throne
1821	John Keats dies
	Percy Bysshe Shelley dies
1822	Lord Castlereagh commits suicide
1823	Monroe Doctrine
	Jeremy Bentham dies
1824	George Gordon, Lord Byron, dies
1825	First railroad
1827	Battle of Navarino Bay
1828	Test and Corporation Acts repealed
1829	Catholic Emancipation bill passed
1830	George IV dies; William IV ascends throne
1832	First Reform Act is passed
1834	Poor Law
	Slavery abolished in the British Empire
1836–1848	Chartist movement
1837	William IV dies; Victoria ascends throne
1840	Opium War
1844	YMCA founded
1845–1851	Famine in Ireland

1846	"Repeal" of the Corn Laws
1850	William Wordsworth dies
1851	Great Exhibition opens
1853–1856	Crimean War
1857–1858	Indian Mutiny
1859	John Stuart Mill publishes *On Liberty*
	Charles Darwin publishes *On the Origin of Species*
1867	Second Reform Act
	British North American Act
1870	Charles Dickens dies
1870-1871	Franco-Prussian War
1875	Britain purchases shares in the Suez Canal
1876	Victoria crowned Empress of India
1877	General William Booth founds the Salvation Army
1882	Britain occupies Egypt
1883	Fabian society formed
1884	Third Reform Bill
1898	Battle of Omdurman
1899–1902	Boer War (South African War)
1899	Rudyard Kipling publishes *The White Man's Burden*
1900	Labour Party founded
1901	Victoria dies; Edward VII ascends throne
1902	Alliance with Japan
1903	Women's Social and Political Union established
1907	Triple Entente
1909	People's Budget
1910	Edward VII dies; George V ascends throne
	Formation of Transport and General Workers Union
1914–1918	World War I
1915	Gallipoli campaign
1916	Battle of the Somme
	Easter Rising in Ireland
1917	Balfour Declaration

Timeline

1918	Women granted vote
1919	Paris Peace Conference
	Earnest Rutherford splits the atom
1922	Irish Free State established
	James Joyce publishes *Ulysses*
	T. S. Eliot publishes *The Waste Land*
	British occupation of Egypt ends
1926	General Strike
1929	Onset of Great Depression
1931	Gold standard abandoned
	Statute of Westminster
1933	Three million unemployed
1935	Government of India Act
1936	George V dies; Edward VIII ascends throne
	Edward VIII abdicates; George VI ascends throne
	John Maynard Keynes publishes *General Theory of Employment, Interest, and Money*
1938	Munich Conference
1939–1945	World War II
1940	Battle of Britain
1942	Beveridge Report
1946	Winston Churchill's "Iron Curtain" speech
	Coal industry nationalized
1947	India granted independence
1948	National Health Service begins operation
	Britain leaves Palestine
1949	George Orwell publishes *1984*
	NATO created
1951	Steel industry nationalized
1952	George VI dies; Elizabeth II ascends throne
	Britain detonates a nuclear weapon
1956	Suez crisis
1957	Ghana granted independence

1963	France's Charles de Gaulle vetos Britain's entry into the European Economic Community
1967	Beatles record *Sgt Pepper's Lonely Hearts Club Band*
1969	Britain sends troops to Ulster
1973	Britain joins the European Economic Community
1978–1979	The "winter of discontent"
1980	Employment Act
	Housing Act
1982	Falklands War
1984	British Telecom privatized
1986	Three million unemployed
1991	Persian Gulf War
1994	Channel Tunnel opened
1996	British Rail privatized
1997	Hong Kong returned to China
1998	Good Friday agreement for Ulster
2001	War on terrorism

1

The Industrial Revolution, c. 1750–c. 1850

INTRODUCTION

The word *revolution* often conjures up images of mobs roving the streets of major cities, peasants burning manor houses, armed bands clashing with uniformed troops, and crowned heads rolling in the dust to the delight of their mortal enemies. By this standard, the Industrial Revolution could hardly be considered a revolution. It was not a sudden and violent overthrow of the prevailing status quo; rather, it was a slow, drawn-out process that proved to be by and large peaceful in nature. Nevertheless, the Industrial Revolution altered the world more profoundly than anything since the development of agriculture many thousands of years ago.

What was the Industrial Revolution? Basically, it was a transformation from the production of goods by hand to the production of goods by machine. It also included a growing concentration of machines within single structures or series of connected structures called *factories*. The Industrial Revolution began in Great Britain about the middle of the eighteenth century and gradually spread throughout the world. It continues to evolve today as nonindustrialized countries struggle to industrialize and industrialized ones adopt new and more efficient technologies.

A unique set of circumstances combined to provide fertile ground for the Industrial Revolution in eighteenth-century Great Britain. For a start, Brit-

The power looms for weaving pictured here greatly accelerated the production of textiles. Although the Industrial Revolution provided employment and a rising standard of living, factories were not as clean and orderly as this print might suggest. Reproduced from the Collections of the Library of Congress.

ain was blessed with an abundance of natural resources necessary for the industrialization process. In particular, Britain had extensive, easy to reach coal fields and numerous swift-flowing streams, which provided the energy needed to run the revolution's machines. Britain also had an adequate labor force, which turned out to be crucial as the Industrial Revolution was labor intensive. By the start of the nineteenth century, tens of thousands of British farm laborers were streaming into the towns and cities to work at the machines.

Thanks to Britain's ongoing trading activities that generated significant wealth, British enterpreneurs had access to surplus capital with which to purchase machines and erect factories. Moreover, they were accustomed to taking risks in order to reap profits. In their business endeavors they were aided by a banking system that was both mature and sound.

In the eighteenth century, Great Britain also enjoyed a high level of political stability that served to stimulate economic growth. After the bloody upheavals of the seventeenth century, eighteenth-century Britain found itself governed by a loose amalgam of Crown, landholders, and merchants. Furthermore, there was much intermarriage between the gentry and the business class. The resulting political climate not only promoted stability but also nurtured commercial and industrial initiatives.

Great Britain was also fortunate in that its large and growing colonial empire provided ready markets for British production. The demand for goods emanating from the colonies encouraged British producers to seek ways to increase their output. Furthermore, the colonies also supplied Great Britain with inexpensive raw materials such as cotton for the new machines of the Industrial Revolution.

Finally, British entreprenuers enjoyed a great deal of freedom to pursue economic goals. Unlike the European continent, where the theory of mercantilism prevailed, Great Britain in the eighteenth century embraced a more laissez-faire approach to economic life. Certainly there were taxes, and at times they were heavy, but the tax burden was not crushing and it was collected in a fair and efficient manner. Comparatively free of the tangle of governmental regulations and restrictions that mercantilism required, British merchants could rapidly adjust to the needs of a market economy, and British inventors (who were frequently little more than gifted tinkers) could direct their creative energies to the fulfillment of needs arising from the supply-demand system in the anticipation of reaping significant financial rewards.

The story of textile production perhaps best illustrates the coming of the Industrial Revolution to Great Britain. For centuries the British cottage industry, or domestic industry, had produced woolens and—to a lesser extent—linens, which were more expensive than woolens. As the name implies, production was accomplished in the cottage or at home; the name sometimes given to this was the "putting-out" system.

Under the prevailing "putting-out" system, a merchant or middleman would deliver or, "put out," raw materials to a peasant's cottage with the understanding that within a certain time period the peasant would produce a finished product. This proved to be a very useful way for country folk to supplement their meager income. Usually the entire peasant family would spend its spare time at this work; the father would weave cloth on a hand loom while his wife and children would undertake the arduous task of preparing the fibers and then spinning thread on primitive spinning wheels. Although chaotic (the peasants would sometimes fail to meet their obligations, both suppliers and producers tended to cheat each other, and upon being paid for his labor the peasant often went on a drinking binge), the putting out system worked reasonably well as long as demand and supply remained in balance.

However, the appearance of a new fiber, cotton, upset the existing equilibrium. Cotton cloth was imported from India, where Britons had begun to make significant economic inroads. It proved so popular that British manufacturers determined to produce the cloth themselves. Importing raw cotton from India and, later, the United States, they put out the fiber in the normal manner to the peasants, but the demand for the finished product outstripped the ability of the peasants to produce it. Specifically, the weaving process was too slow. Under pressure of increased demand, this bottleneck was overcome in the 1730s when John Kay invented the flying shuttle, which allowed a single weaver to operate a loom instead of the two men that had been required before. This had the effect of freeing up labor to the extent that twice as much cloth as before could now be woven.

In solving the problem of the weaving process, Kay had unintentionally created a new bottleneck: spinning, or the production of thread, was now too slow to keep up with the demands of the weavers. This lack of equilibrium stimulated attempts to speed up the spinning process, and about 1765 James Hargreaves, a carpenter, invented the spinning jenny, a hand-operated multiple spindle device that spun a fine thread. A few years later, one-time barber Richard Arkwright went one step further when he invented the water frame, a water-powered machine that contained several hundred spindles that spun a tough, coarse thread. The water frame was too large to fit into the tiny cottages occupied by the weavers; moreover, it had to be located near a stream and housed in a large building. This led to the construction of factories. The production of cotton began to leave the cottage for the factory. A decade later, Samuel Compton, son of a Lancashire yeoman, invented the spinning mule. This device merged the most advantageous features of Hargreaves' spinning jenny and Arkwright's water frame. Experts estimate that the introduction of these machines increased the amount of cotton thread produced between 1770 and 1800 by more than 1,000 percent.

The production of so much thread once again destroyed the spinning-weaving balance. When the scales tipped so clearly in favor of thread production, efforts to modernize the weaving process began. In 1784, Anglican churchman Edmund Cartwright invented the power loom, which provided for weaving by machine. By 1833 there were more than one-hundred thousand power looms in England and the days of both the cottage based spinner and the hand weaver were over.

Together with the new machines, power—or physical force or energy—led to this spectacular rise in the output of cotton thread and woven cloth as well as increased production in almost every imaginable field. The ancients knew something about the power of steam, and something akin to a modern steam engine had been constructed by Hero of Alexandria during the Greco-Roman era; but Hero's engine found no practical application and it soon faded into oblivion. Nothing resembling this ancient machine appeared on the scene again until the early eighteenth century. At that time, English coal and tin mine operators sought some way to pump excess water from their mines in order to increase productivity and profits. Responding to this demand, Thomas Newcomen, an engineer and ironmonger, designed an engine powered by steam to pump out the mines. By 1730 more than one hundred of Newcomen's engines were in operation. However, the Newcomen engine had several important shortcomings that limited its practical value. It was wildly inefficent, virtually immobile, and quite large.

During the 1760s, James Watt, an instrument maker at the University of Glasgow, began to experiment with a Newcomen engine then under repair. Eventually Watt introduced several modifications that made Newcomen's engine significantly more efficient and practical. In 1769 Watt acquired a patent for what was to become the modern steam engine. Shortly thereafter he joined forces with Matthew Boulton, a toy and button manufacturer from Birmingham, to manufacture his steam engine. Initially used in the iron and coal industries, in 1785 Watt's steam engine was employed to provide power for the textile machines. It gradually replaced water power, allowing for a concentration of machinery in a single place—in an urban factory—rather than alongside swiftly running streams. Further alterations to Watt's basic idea led to the steamship and the locomotive, thereby creating a veritable revolution in transportation as well as manufacturing.

Because it enabled more coal to be mined, Watt's steam engine replaced Newcomen's engine at England's coal mines. In turn, Watt's engine was fueled by coal, thereby raising the demand for that mineral and stimulating its production. Well into the twentieth century, the industrial world relied upon coal to fuel its various engines.

Iron proved to be as important as coal. Machines of all sorts including locomotives and ships were constructed from iron, and iron has rightly been called one of the building blocks of the Industrial Revolution. For centuries, England produced iron. However, by the beginning of the eighteenth century England's iron industry was in danger. Oak trees, which had supplied the charcoal used to smelt iron ore, were rapidly disappearing. Luckily for England, coal appeared to be an attractive substitute for charcoal. However, mineral impurities present in coal tended to be absorbed into the molten iron during the smelting process, thereby weakening the final product. In 1709 Abraham Darby, an ironmaster, partially solved this problem when he smelted iron ore with coke, or coal whose impurities had been burned off in a bakinglike process.

Still, problems remained. In particular, the coke failed to generate enough heat to melt the iron ore thoroughly. By midcentury, an engine was devised that blasted jets of air into the cooking ore. This caused more impurities to burn off. Nevertheless, the resulting pig iron contained 2 to 5 percent carbon, which made it quite brittle. A better solution surfaced in 1784, when Henry Cort invented the puddling process. Cort discovered that by stirring, or puddling, the molten mass even more impurities could be burned off. The resulting product, wrought iron, proved stronger and easier to work than pig iron. Cort also invented the rolling mill, a device similar to the rollers of an old-fashioned wringer washer that squeezed even more impurities from wrought iron and turned it into sheets and other shapes that fit the demands of industry. As a building block of the Industrial Revolution, iron would remain dominant until it was replaced by steel in the middle of the nineteenth century.

INTERPRETIVE ESSAY
David Mitch

In 1750 Britain was a major world power both militarily and economically. Through its preeminent navy, it had gained control over world trade routes from such rival powers as France, Holland, Portugal, and Spain. It possessed either colonies or effective control or was soon to gain such over much of the earth's surface from North America to India. London had long achieved status as one of the world's preeminent cities, and provincial cities such as Bristol, Liverpool, Edinburgh, and Glasgow had also recently emerged as significant centers of commerce and culture. Moreover, by this date England had already experienced several major self-styled political and economic revolutions. Administrative arrangements in government had been transformed during Tudor times, with increased centralization of standards in such areas as poor relief enacted during the reign of Elizabeth I (1558–1603). The civil war of the seventeenth century and the subsequent Glorious Revolution (1688) boosted the authority of Parliament relative to that of the Crown. This in turn provided the foundation for the establishment of the Bank of England in the late seventeenth century and the so-called financial revolution of the early eighteenth century, which established new markets in government debt. Meanwhile, a commercial revolution was underway, establishing increasingly regular and profitable international trade routes. And an agricultural revolution involving both new crop-rotation methods and the enclosure of commonly farmed fields into private plots had by many accounts already been completed. This substantially increased food productivity of the English land area, thus releasing labor for other activity. Already by 1760 half of the English labor force was employed in activities other than agriculture.

Nevertheless, it seems evident that changes in the economy in the century between 1750 and 1850 produced a far more profound transformation in the nature of British society and economy than any that had gone before. In this spirit, historian Peter Laslett's influential account of English society prior to 1750 was titled *The World We Have Lost*. These changes between 1750 and 1850 have been labeled the Industrial Revolution, indicating that they were driven by developments in the manufacturing sector. The most evident change is in the marked redeployment of resources from agriculture to manufacturing that occurred during these hundred years. The percentage of the male labor force engaged in agriculture and industry approximately reversed during this period, the former falling from about 50 percent to 25 percent; the latter moving from 25 percent to 50 percent. The most evident consequence associated with this redeployment was the increase in output per capita. In 1850 the British economy produced over half as much again per person as it did in 1750. The possibility of long-term improvements in output at a faster rate than population growth went counter to many expectations at the time. Whether this is unprecedented in world history, or indeed, whether the British lead in output per person dates to this period or occurred earlier are matters of controversy, as is the degree of acceleration. Still, the prospect of these increases in economic productivity are at the heart of why the Industrial Revolution is viewed as changing so fundamentally the nature of British society.

Although profound, economic change between 1750 and 1850 was also gradual. The economy of Great Britain in 1850 was similar in many basic respects to that of 1750. The population of Britain in 1850 was still substantially rural, with about half the people living in rural areas. Although, as already noted, just under half the labor force in 1850 was engaged in manufacturing and about a quarter was still engaged in agriculture, a large percentage of those engaged in manufacturing activities were working in traditional workshop and artisan trades such as construction and shoemaking.

From the perspective of the working classes, it was not clear that their living standards in 1850 were much improved from those of 1750. The degree of continuity is suggested by the fact that some of the most astute economic and social observers of the time were unaware of any degree of change. Leading economists of the day such as Adam Smith, David Ricardo, and Thomas Malthus saw the economic foundations of Britain as rooted in agriculture and trade. Malthus in particular emphasized the tendency for population to increase faster than food production. That Malthus's views on the limits to improvements in agricultural productivity were shared by most economists of the early nineteenth century is suggested by contemporary historian and essayist Thomas Carlyle's labeling of economics as the "dismal science," reflecting the pessimistic expectations of the discipline for improved living standards. Novelists in the early nineteenth century such as Jane Austen still depicted a largely rural, landed society. Although later in the nineteenth century the novelist George Eliot was to show more awareness of manufacturing activity, as in her classic *Silas Marner, Weaver of Raveloe*, or in her depiction of the manufacturer Nicholas Bulstrode in *Middlemarch*, rural and agrarian themes are still pervasive in her work. However, despite the gradual nature of the change, economic developments between 1750 and 1850 were fundamentally transforming Great Britain in a wide range of dimensions, politically and socially as well as economically.

According to one influential view, the underlying force for economic change in the British economy was a marked acceleration in the pace of technological advance. In the oft-cited words of the examination answer of an English schoolboy, "About 1760 a wave of gadgets swept over England." New and improved inventions such as the steam engine and the power loom, the mechanization of cotton spinning, and the puddling process for making iron and steel have often been seen as laying the foundation in the late eighteenth century for subsequent British economic growth. Due to the combination of new energy sources such as steam and mechanization of production, the price of a yard of cotton cloth in 1840 was only one-third of what it had been in 1770. It remains a source of controversy how pervasive the acceleration in technological advance was. By some accounts, it was broadly based throughout the economy including such traditional sectors as agriculture and construction; by other accounts, it was concentrated in a few modernizing sectors such as textiles and metal production. Nevertheless, it does appear that the industries that experienced technological advance were diverse in character, ranging from textiles to iron and steel production to ocean shipping. This in turn leads to the issue of whether there is some common underlying factor behind technological advance or whether the factors were diverse. The economist Arnold Harberger has suggested that the sources of technological advance can be viewed either as equivalent to the workings of yeast, a homogeneous substance at work throughout its environment, or, alternatively, as equivalent to the sprouting of mushrooms in scattered locations, with diverse sources at work diffused throughout the economy.

One underlying "yeast" factor to which much attention has been paid is the development of new energy sources, in particular the development of steam power and with it the increased importance of coal as an input. This meant that the location of economic activity became less tied to the location of energy sources. Moreover, the seeds for further change were sowed when the steam engine was used as the locomotive power behind the railway. This had the result less of lowering transportation costs over a given distance than of dramatically lowering the time required to travel or haul a load a given distance. A trip from London to Manchester that would have taken over eighty hours by the fastest stagecoach in 1750 could be completed by railway in under eight hours by 1845. With improvements in transportation came improvements in communications that were greatly accelerated with the invention of the telegraph in 1837. Information that formerly took days to travel could now be communicated in a manner of minutes. In 1805 it took seventeen days for news of the battle of Trafalgar to reach England from Spain's southern coast via ship and horseback messengers. In 1845 use of the telegraph enabled the police to arrest the suspected murderer John Tawell after he was seen boarding a train in Slough bound for London. This increased speed of communication transformed many aspects of everyday life. For example, it heightened interest in racing and other sporting events. The outcome of a horse race that formerly would have taken days to be known throughout England could now be known in a matter of minutes and diffused in newspapers throughout the country, in turn leading to the proliferation of betting pools based on the outcome.

It is sometimes claimed that the Newtonian revolution in science provided the foundation for inventiveness in the British Industrial Revolution.

But inventions during this period seem based on trial-and-error tinkering rather than on formal application of scientific principles. This would tend to favor the mushroom over the yeast view of the nature of technological advance. More generally, monocausal explanations of technological advance and the British Industrial Revolution would seem problematic. Britain's educational system was mediocre. Britain was blessed with important natural resource endowments in the form of abundant coal and iron deposits, and access to water transport provided by its island situation lowered transportation costs. Nevertheless, it relied on critical imports of raw cotton for one of its most visible rising industries, cotton textiles. However, a variety of key developments noted above did lay the foundation by the mid-eighteenth century for subsequent British economic growth. British merchants had been setting up extensive overseas commercial networks during the seventeenth and eighteenth centuries. These provided broad markets that British manufacturers could employ both for obtaining key inputs for production and for selling their finished products. The Glorious Revolution of the late seventeenth century established that the power of the monarchy was balanced by that of the legislature. This in turn reduced the chances of onerous taxes being levied on commercial and manufacturing activity. The emergent toleration of diverse religious views allowed for a greater pool of engineering and commercial talent for the development of enterprise. In any event, expectation of ongoing innovation came to be sufficiently anticipated that some labeled this period in England the Age of Improvement, a change from former times when little or no technological change was contemplated.

The Industrial Revolution should be seen not only as involving technological advance but also as involving change to a variety of institutional and social relationships. One prominent development that points to this complexity is the rise of the factory. The spread of the factory was an evident but dramatic physical change in the overall landscapes of both city and countryside in Britain, as the factory could be located in either setting. Elizabeth Gaskell provides the following description of the arrival of the Hale family in the fictional northern manufacturing town of Milton from a southern rural village in her novel *North and South*:

> For several miles before they reached Milton, they saw a deep lead-coloured cloud hanging over the horizon in the direction in which it lay. It was all the darker from contrast with the pale gray-blue of the wintry sky ... Nearer to the town, the air had a faint taste and smell of smoke; perhaps, after all, more a loss of the fragrance of grass and herbage than any positive taste or smell. Quick they were whirled over long, straight, hopeless

streets of regularly built houses, all small and of brick. Here and there a great oblong many windowed factory stood up, like a hen among her chickens, puffing out black, 'unparliamentary' smoke, and sufficiently accounting for the cloud which Margaret had taken to foretell rain.

Increasingly, production in key manufacturing industries occurred in factories. The factory has been defined in both technological and institutional/organizational terms. The defining technological feature of the factory was its use of a central energy source to power machinery, most typically in this period water as well as steam. At the beginning of the nineteenth century, steam engines were still predominantly associated with mine drainage. By 1850 use of steam had become widespread in textile factories. In 1850, 86 percent of cotton textile factories made use of steam. But the percentage was lower in other activities: 72 percent of other textiles made use of steam, and iron production was the only other manufacturing activity to make significant use of steam power at this point.

However, the distinctive economic function of the factory has been defined by some as the centralized control and monitoring of work. Nineteenth-century scholar Andrew Ure's classic account of the rise of the factory links the use of new energy sources and resultant mechanization with enhanced diligence in work effort and dexterity by the factory worker: "The principle of the factory system . . . is to substitute mechanical science for hand skill. . . . The grand object . . . of the modern manufacturer is, through the union of capital and science, to reduce the task of his work-people to the exercise of vigilance and dexterity." However, still other accounts placed more emphasis on the increased discipline that factory work would require compared with more traditional workplace settings. Workers had to keep regular hours and maintain the pace of the machinery in order to achieve adequate utilization of capital and to get full return on the large overhead investment required. Increased work discipline and the modification of people's habits is one basic change in the British way of life often associated with the factory. Workers could no longer celebrate "St. Monday"; that is, take Mondays off after wild weekend carousing, as sometimes alleged in rural life. In Friedrich Engels's account of factory work:

> The supervision of machinery, the joining of broken threads, is no activity which claims the operative's thinking powers, yet it is of a sort which prevents him from occupying his mind with other things . . . this work affords the muscles no opportunity for physical activity . . . Moreover, he must not take a moment's rest; the engine moves unceasingly; the wheels, the straps, the spin-

dles hum and rattle in his ears without a pause, and if he tried to snatch one instant, there is the overlooker at his back with the book of fines.

It should be noted that more traditional forms of work organization persisted. The 1851 census of England and Wales indicates that such traditional craft and manufacturing activities as building, tailoring, and shoemaking employed more male workers than industries such as cotton, wool, or iron manufacture where the factory method was more predominant. However, when female workers are taken into consideration, the balance shifts toward the factory.

One might think that the rise of the factory and other forms of visible fixed investment such as the spread of railway networks would be associated with dramatic shifts in methods of finance. The term *capitalism* itself draws attention to the centrality of investment sources as capital for modern industry. This point is highlighted in Karl Marx's eponymous *Capital*, which emphasizes the demands for these investment sources as defining the underlying dynamic of modern social and economic change. But in fact, there is little evidence of dramatic shifts in sources of finance during the Industrial Revolution. It is important here to distinguish between fixed capital—investments in buildings, machinery, and transportation network improvements that implied a commitment of years if not decades to the activity in question—and circulating capital—funds tied up in immediate inventory and payroll that implied a commitment of only a matter of weeks or months. The sources of fixed capital for the growth of manufacturing enterprise during Britain's Industrial Revolution seem to have been largely based on reinvestment of earnings from the enterprise in question rather than investment funds drawn from outside the enterprise. Thus the construction of factories and investment in machinery does not seem to have depended critically on developing new sources of funds.

Sources of funds for circulating capital were more critical. However, financial networks for these purposes were already well developed. Fluctuations in markets and inability to repay debts could lead to bankruptcy and the foundering of new manufacturing enterprises. As with the so-called new economy of the late twentieth and early twenty-first centuries with its dot-com enterprises, the new manufacturing enterprises of late eighteenth and early nineteenth-century Britain were subject to considerable volatility and cycles of decline as well as prosperity. There is some debate as to whether England was too restrictive and conservative in the development of its banking system compared with Scotland, where more competition and expansion were present. Nevertheless, during the initial stages of the

Industrial Revolution there were no dramatic changes in methods of finance. All the same, the gradual accumulation of fixed capital in industry through retained earnings does appear to have led to very substantial changes in the composition of Britain's capital stock between 1760 and 1850. In 1760, 39 percent of British fixed capital formation was in agriculture and only 13 percent in mineral based industries. Other activities claimed 48 percent. By 1850 agriculture's share in fixed capital formation had fallen to 16 percent, while the share of mineral-based industries such as coal, gas, iron, and railways had risen to almost 60 percent. This shift in fixed capital formation clearly indicates Great Britain's transformation from a landed society to an industrial one.

The period of industrialization was associated more generally with the evolution of changing institutional forms and social relationships. There was a growing pull of labor into urban and manufacturing areas, and this had important consequences for the nature of cities and rural areas alike.

One basic change was a shift from personal ties to a cash nexus as the basis of social relationships. It is telling in this regard that the now legendary Ebenezer Scrooge was brought into the world by Charles Dickens during the mid-Victorian period. Historians ranging from Arnold Toynbee to E. P. Thompson and Harold Perkin have suggested that industrialization transformed British society from one based on hierarchical orders with some sense of patriarchal responsibility of more privileged orders for those lower down the social scale to one based on conflict between classes defined in terms of economic interests. There was particular concern that provisions for poor relief dating from Elizabethan times discouraged efforts of the poor to find work and support themselves. Under the new Poor Law of 1834, able-bodied males seeking poor relief were required to move into workhouses. It was the nineteenth century that witnessed the development of labor unions. Marx and some labor leaders saw the organization of workers as leading to the overthrow of the existing social order. Yet it has been striking to many that in the most advanced manufacturing country of the world the labor movement was not more revolutionary. Nevertheless, the spread of labor activity and labor unionism did set the stage for the emergence of the Labour Party as a central force in twentieth-century and current British political life.

During the Industrial Revolution, the accelerated pace of urbanization changed British society fundamentally. Although London remained dominant as the country's political, cultural, and commercial center, at the outset of the Industrial Revolution in 1760 only a fifth of the overall British population resided in cities; by 1840 this proportion had risen to one-half. This implies that agrarian habits were still widespread in British society. Nevertheless, for much of the British population the change in environment would have been profound. Instead of the bucolic English countryside of meadows, hedgerows, and streams, more and more Britons would have encountered the oppressive setting described by Engels in *The Condition of the Working Class in England* (1844):

> If we briefly formulate the result of our wanderings, we must admit that 350,000 working-people of Manchester and its environs, live, almost all of them in wretched, damp, filthy cottages, that the streets which surround them are usually in the most miserable and filthy condition, laid out without the slightest reference to ventilation, with reference solely to the profit secured by the contractor ... Here are long, narrow lanes between which run contracted, crooked courts and passages, the entrances to which are so irregular that the explorer is caught in a blind alley at every few steps, or comes out where he least expects to, unless he knows every court and every alley exactly and separately ... When the sanitary police made its expedition hither in 1831 ... they found in Parliament Street for three hundred and eighty persons, and in Parliament Passage for thirty thickly populated houses, but a single privy.

A variety of both legislative and medical efforts over the last two-thirds of the nineteenth century acted to improve sanitation and health conditions in cities. The activities of reformers such as Edwin Chadwick and John Simon are usually credited with calling attention to the importance of clean water supplies in suppressing the spread of contagious disease and in turn leading to improvements in sewage and drainage.

Eventually, the redeployment of resources from agriculture to manufacturing did facilitate improvement in living standards. The typical British household at the end of Victoria's reign at the turn of the twentieth century had a level of purchasing power more than double that of its counterpart at Victoria's accession to the throne in the late 1830s. But gains in working-class living standards over the previous seventy years were much less pronounced; indeed, by some accounts living standards deteriorated over this period. This conclusion is based on a variety of measures including life expectancy, real-wage trends, and estimates of food and other consumption of basic goods. By many measures, wealthier groups gained while those of more modest means improved far less surely. There were widespread concerns about whether the employment of women and children was excessive. And as noted above, the gains in earnings to be had by moving to industrial areas came at the expense of worsened health conditions.

Nevertheless, it is notable that despite the eventual formation of a labor movement there was never any serious prospect of overturning the existing political order in Britain.

Despite the shrinkage of Britain's agriculture sector to well under half of its overall economy by 1840, the landed elite continued to have a powerful influence in Parliament at this point even as this basic phase of British industrialization was coming to an end. But by the early 1830s, pressure had grown to reform Parliament so that, if still elitist, it became more representative of the growing nonagrarian interests present throughout Britain. This became manifest in the growing support in Parliament for promotion of free trade. Under the influence of landed interests, tariffs on imports of grain from abroad had actually risen during the late eighteenth and early nineteenth centuries. Manufacturers had an interest in reducing or eliminating these tariffs because cheap grain would mean cheap bread, implying that factory workers could be attracted at lower wages with a resulting increase in manufacturers' profits. Industrialists paid subsistence wages; food was the greatest expense for the workers. Cheaper bread (food) allowed the industrialists to pay lower wages and still keep the workers alive. Finally, in 1846 the tariffs on grain imports were repealed. The politics involved were more complicated than a simple matter of manufacturing interests in Parliament predominating over agricultural interests. But industrial interests were advocated forcefully by the Anti–Corn Law League, an especially visible faction lobbying for repeal of these tariffs. These measures, generally favored by industrialists, were followed by others—less popular with manufacturers—during the middle third of the nineteenth century in which Parliament attempted to come to terms with the increasing perception of the darker side of industrialization.

Industrialization's aftermath brought increased efforts by Parliament and concerned civic groups to investigate and ameliorate a range of social problems ranging from crime to lack of schooling. Some of the earliest investigations and legislation concerned working conditions in factories, and a series of legislation was passed restricting hours of work and employment of children in factories. The scope of these investigations was subsequently extended to mining and to agriculture. The rise of national funding for and administration of schooling that began in the 1830s and continued over the course of the nineteenth century was in part seen as a way of reducing crime and improving morality in the population. The general improvement in the country's educational level was reflected in a rise in the proportion of brides and grooms able to sign their names at marriage from around 60 percent in 1840 to almost 100 percent by 1900.

The Industrial Revolution began in Britain through the development of new technologies in manufacturing. Although the influence of agriculture still remained strong by the time this revolution was over, Britain had been changed in profound and irreversible ways. The continual improvement in the productivity of the overall British economy was decided. The unprecedented prospect of ongoing advancement in working-class living standards was established in the mid-nineteenth century. The rise of the industrial sector, which overturned the previous agrarian and landed basis of the British political system, ultimately led to the rise of the Labour Party and direct involvement by working-class representatives in twentieth-century Britain's political leadership. Coping with the social consequences of industrialization led to the proliferation of government regulation of Britain's economy and society in pervasive ways. In obvious but also profound ways, the sensations of daily life in Britain were transformed. The clip-clopping sounds of horses' hooves and the scent of manure gradually gave way to the whistle, soot, and smoke of the railroad and eventually to the honking horns and exhaust fumes of the automobile and the lorry (truck).

SELECTED BIBLIOGRAPHY

Ashton, T. S. *The Industrial Revolution, 1760–1830*. London: Oxford University Press, 1948. An especially influential overview by a noted British economic historian of the fundamental changes brought on by the British Industrial Revolution.

Berg, Maxine. *The Age of Manufactures: Industry, Innovation, and Work in Britain, 1700–1820*. London: Fontana Press, 1985. Argues for the importance of traditional craft, cottage, and workshop forms of production during the Industrial Revolution.

Brown, John C. "The Condition of England and the Standard of Living: Cotton Textiles in the Northwest, 1806–1850." *Journal of Economic History* 50 (1990): 591–615. Finds that higher wages paid in textile-manufacturing districts of England compensated for higher mortality rates and other hardships of life.

Clark, Gregory. "Factory Discipline." *Journal of Economic History* 54 (1994): 128–163. Highlights the organizational and supervisory features of the factory as compared with its technological aspects.

Collier, Frances. *The Family Economy of the Working Classes in the Cotton Industry, 1784–1833*. Manchester: Manchester University Press, 1964. Considers the organization of the working-class family in cotton-manufacturing areas during the Industrial Revolution.

Crafts, N. F. R. *British Economic Growth during the Industrial Revolution*. Oxford: Oxford University Press, 1985. An important quantitative history of the Industrial Revolution.

Daunton, M. J. *Progress and Poverty. An Economic and Social History of Britain, 1700–1850*. Oxford: Oxford University Press, 1995. Provides a careful

Industrial Revolution

overview of central themes and issues in economic and social change in Great Britain during the Industrial Revolution.

Evans, Eric. *The Forging of the Modern State. Early Industrial Britain: 1783–1870.* London: Longman, 1983. A useful general history of Britain during the Industrial Revolution.

Floud, R., and D. McCloskey, eds. *The Economic History of Great Britain since 1700.* Vol. 1, *1700–1860*, 2nd ed. Cambridge: Cambridge University Press, 1994. Essays by economists on specific aspects of the British Industrial Revolution.

Himmelfarb, Gertrude. *The Idea of Poverty: England in the Early Industrial Age.* New York: Knopf, 1984. An intellectual history of the efforts of eighteenth- and early nineteenth-century British social commentators and policy makers to address the problems of poverty associated with the British Industrial Revolution.

Landes, D. *The Unbound Prometheus: Technological Change and Industrial Development in Western Europe from 1750 to the Present.* Cambridge: Cambridge University Press, 1969. A very influential survey of the role of technological change in Western European economic development.

Mantoux, Paul. *The Industrial Revolution in the Eighteenth Century.* Rev. ed. New York: Harper Torchbooks, 1961. A classic early history of the Industrial Revolution with particular emphasis on the impact of the factory and the role of organizational changes in the British economy.

Mokyr, J., ed. *The British Industrial Revolution: An Economic Perspective.* 2nd ed. Boulder, CO: Westview, 1999. Contains surveys of technology, macroeconomic trends, agriculture, and human capital as well as a comprehensive overview by the editor.

Morris, R. J. *Class and Class Consciousness in the Industrial Revolution, 1780–1850.* London: Macmillan, 1979. A concise survey of the literature on the formation of social classes during the Industrial Revolution.

Perkin, Harold. *The Origins of Modern English Society.* London: Routledge, 1969. An important formulation of the changes in social class structure that occurred in England in the aftermath of industrialization.

Roberts, D. *Victorian Origins of the British Welfare State.* New Haven: Yale University Press, 1960. An examination of the rise of bureaucratic administration in British government that ensued in the aftermath of the British Industrial Revolution.

Samuel, Raphael. "The Workshop of the World: Steam Power and Hand Technology in Mid-Victorian Britain." *History Workshop Journal* 3 (1977): 6–72. Argues for the persistence and pervasiveness of traditional methods of work organization in manufacturing in the mid-nineteenth century.

Temin, Peter. "Two Views of the British Industrial Revolution." *Journal of Economic History* 57 (1997): 63–82. A cogent analysis of whether technical change during the British Industrial Revolution was concentrated in a few leading sectors or was diffused throughout the economy.

Thompson, E. P. *The Making of the English Working Class.* New York: Vintage, 1963. A classic study of the English working-class movement during the Industrial Revolution.

Toynbee, Arnold. *Lectures on the Industrial Revolution in England.* 1884. Reprint, New York: A. M. Kelley, 1969. One of the earliest and most influential statements of the profound economic and social consequences stemming from industrialization in England.

Williamson, J. G. *Did British Capitalism Breed Inequality?* London: Allen and Unwin, 1985. A quantitative history of trends in income inequality in Britain in the eighteenth and nineteenth centuries.

2

The Seven Years' War, 1756–1763

INTRODUCTION

The immediate origins of the Seven Years' War extend back to at least 1740. In that year the Habsburg ruler Charles VI died without a male heir. Charles had spent much of his reign promoting the Pragmatic Sanction, an exception to tradition that would allow his lands to pass in their entirety to his daughter, Maria Theresa, upon his death. However, the new Prussian king, Frederick II—later "the Great"—stymied Charles's plans when he seized Austria's rich Habsburg province of Silesia in eastern central Europe from Maria Theresa in December 1740. Frederick's aggressive act brought about the War of the Austrian Succession, which lasted until 1748.

The war soon escalated into a major conflict involving the most important European countries. Great Britain, although it had no direct interest in the struggle, entered the fray in 1742 in order to counter its traditional rival France, who had entered the war on Prussia's side. During the course of the war, a British expeditionary force to the Continent found little success. In 1745 French sponsorship of a Stuart restoration in Britain failed ignominiously, permanently ending the Stuart threat to the Hanoverian dynasty. In India France made gains at British expense, while in North America Britain eventually captured the important French post of Louisbourg. However, these respective gains were undone by the 1748 Treaty of Aix-la-Chapelle

The French and Indians defeated General Edward Braddock. Braddock was killed in battle near present-day Pittsburgh during the North American phase of the Seven Years' War. Reproduced from the Collections of the Library of Congress.

that—except for Silesia—largely restored the status quo ante bellum, or the prewar state of affairs. Thus, after several years of fighting and at a cost of £80 million, Britain had accomplished nothing; however, the war brought into sharper relief Britain's colonial rivalry with France and set the stage for their crucial colonial struggle.

Following the Treaty of Aix-la-Chapelle, although Great Britain and France were nominally at peace, they continued to skirmish in India and North America. Only in May 1756 was a state of hostility declared. A few months later, Frederick II invaded Saxony, an independent and fairly important state at this time, and the Seven Years' War—or the French and Indian War, as it is known in American history—was truly underway. However, this time there was one major change in the lineup of combatants. Thanks to what is called the Diplomatic Revolution, France now allied with its ancient enemy Austria, whereas Britain in early 1756 signed the Convention of Westminster, which placed it at Prussia's side.

Even before the formal declaration of hostilities, things had been going badly for Great Britain; now the defeats increased in number and severity. In 1754 the English colonist George Washington had led a band of colonials over the Appalachian Mountains to the site of present-day Pittsburgh only to be captured by the French, who had erected Fort Duquesne at that location. The following year the British sent regular troops under General Edward Braddock to dislodge the French. The French were traders and the British were settlers. The Indians feared the loss of their land or British encroachment and for that reason they allied themselves with the French. The French and their Indian allies ambushed and annihilated Braddock and his redcoats. The French also took the Mediterranean island of Minorca from England, a defeat so shameful that the British court-martialed and executed John Byng, the luckless admiral assigned to defend the island.

Once the Seven Years' War was officially underway, the French made progress toward capturing Hanover, the ancestral home of Great Britain's Hanoverian dynasty and still an important part of that family's possessions. Moreover, in North America a British attempt to seize Louisbourg failed, and English settlements along the frontier faced French and Indian attacks. The French also captured Britain's Fort Oswego on Lake Ontario.

In July 1757 word also arrived in London of a severe British setback the previous year in India. By 1756 the ongoing British-French rivalry in the great subcontinent had shifted to Bengal in the northeast. There the native prince, Surajah Dowlah, objected to the encroachments of the British and overran the British garrison at Calcutta. The captured British were placed in a small, dark room where during a night of imprisonment 122 out of 145 of them died of suffocation. These deaths in the "Black Hole of Calcutta" left an indelible mark on the collective British memory.

Further reversals occurred in 1757. In North America the French captured Fort William Henry in New York, and the Duke of Cumberland, one of King George II's younger sons who was fighting on the Continent, lost the Battle of Hastenbeck, allowing Hanover to fall temporarily to the French.

Despite these setbacks, Great Britain's fortunes were about to turn around. The source of Britain's renewed hope was William Pitt, who together with the Duke of Newcastle formed a very successful war ministry in 1757. Pitt was the grandson of Thomas "Diamond" Pitt, who had made the family fortune when, as governor of Madras, he purchased a magnificent diamond that he later sold for a huge profit. The Pitt family was active in British politics throughout the eighteenth century, and a seat in Parliament was purchased for William in 1735 shortly after he left Oxford University.

Pitt was a difficult person—aloof, acerbic, irascible, arrogant, moody, and probably manic-depressive. He also suffered from debilitating bouts of gout. However, he was also intellectually brilliant, a marvelous orator, a superb organizer and administrator, scrupulously honest, an inspirational leader, and a patriot of the first magnitude who saw clearly that the Seven Years' War offered Great Britain an unusual opportunity to build a global empire at the expense of the hated French. Pitt never doubted his abilities, declaring in the face of British defeats, "I am confident that I can save the country and that no one else can."

Upon taking office as secretary of state and, thus, shouldering the responsibility for conducting the war, Pitt moved aggressively. He cashiered a number of mediocre admirals and generals, filling the vacated posts with vigorous and competent replacements. As Pitt moved Britain to a wartime footing, its army grew to 100,000 and its navy to 70,000. Realizing the navy was the key to success, Pitt expanded the British fleet so that by 1759 it was twice the size of its French rival. Pitt the dynamo was everywhere: developing strategy, dictating tactics, expanding Britain's military-industrial capacities, rallying the nation.

Pitt's decision to subsidize generously the continental forces that opposed France paid enormous dividends. In supporting France's enemies on the Continent, Pitt ensured that France would devote the bulk of its efforts and its resources to the European conflict at the expense of its colonial interests. This would allow Great Britain to seize France's colonies with considerably less difficulty than might otherwise have been the case. There is much truth to Pitt's boast that "America [was] conquered in Germany."

By 1758 Pitt's prodigious energy was evident and British forces began to show some success. In North America the British captured the great French fortress at Louisbourg that guarded the mouth of the Saint Lawrence River, and General John Forbes avenged Braddock's defeat by conquering Fort Duquesne and renaming it Fort Pitt.

The victories of 1758 proved mere prelude for the triumphs of 1759, that "Glorious Year" for British arms. In North America, Great Britain seized the strategic French outpost of Quebec. Sitting high upon a bluff commanding the Saint Lawrence, Quebec appeared inpregnable. General James Wolfe, who had triumphed at Louisbourg the previous year, approached Quebec from the river. However, the terrain afforded him no relief and it seemed that his mission would fail. Luckily for Wolfe, he discovered an unguarded but narrow path leading from the river to the Plains of Abraham, a long, flat piece of ground that stretched out before the city. Taking the initiative, Wolfe unloaded his redcoats and hustled them up the path before the French could detect them. Upon arriving at the plains, Wolfe encountered the main French force under the Marquis de Montcalm. A ferocious battle ensued during which both commanders were killed. However, the British captured Quebec. One year later Montreal fell too, and New France belonged to Britain.

The French also suffered defeat at sea. Concluding that the best way to counter Great Britain in the colonial realm was to launch an attack on the British Isles, the Duke of Choiseul, France's chief minister, ordered preparations to be made for a cross-Channel invasion. To that end, Choiseul ordered France's Mediterranean fleet to rendezvous with the Atlantic fleet on the northern Atlantic coast at Brest. However, in August 1759 an English squadron under Admiral Edward Boscawen surprised this flotilla as it passed by Gibraltar. A few months later, Admiral Edward Hawke smashed the French Atlantic fleet at the Battle of Quiberon Bay, also on France's northern Atlantic coast, thereby ending any threat of a French invasion and securing the seas for Britain.

Great Britain—or at least the East India Company, which was fast becoming synonymous with the British state—also won a huge victory in India. Robert Clive, at one time an East India Company clerk, had recaptured Calcutta in early 1757 and he next challenged Surajah Dowlah. Although badly outnumbered, Clive managed to suborn Dowlah's second in command, Mir Jafar. With Jafar supporting the British, in 1757 Clive won a major victory at the Battle of Plassey that assured British domination of Bengal. Farther south, along the Coromandel Coast, a British squadron lifted the French siege of Madras in 1759 and proceeded to bring the entire coast under British control. In 1761 Pondicherry, France's most important outpost in India, fell to Britain.

Great Britain even won a major victory on the Continent. Intially Pitt had opposed subsidizing Hanover, a position that earned him the enmity of King George II. However, over time Pitt changed his mind. By 1759 there were 20,000 British soldiers stationed in Europe and Pitt was pouring money into Germany. He paid Frederick the Great an annual sum of £670,000 and hired at least 50,000 mercenaries to protect Prussia's western flank and to guard Hanover. In August 1759 this Anglo-German force dealt the French a stunning defeat at the Battle of Minden, thereby forcing France to abandon its designs on Hanover.

Further buttressed by smaller but nonetheless important victories including the captures of Guadeloupe, the important sugar colony in the Caribbean, and Ile de Gorée, the French slave-trading outpost in West Africa, the year 1759 was indeed a victorious one for Great Britain. Horace Walpole, son of the great English politician Sir Robert Walpole, did not miss the mark when he noted that in 1759 "the church bells were worn threadbare from ringing victories."

Although Great Britain now enjoyed the upper hand, Spain entered the conflict in May 1762 on the side of France. Pitt, however, was no longer present to lead Britain to victory over this new foe. Having run afoul of George III, the new king, and victimized by his own haughtiness, Pitt had been forced from office in 1761. Yet even without this remarkable leader, Britain continued to triumph. British naval forces soon captured both Havana, Cuba, and Manila, in the Philippine Islands. They also took additional French islands in the Caribbean including Martinique, Grenada, and Saint Lucia.

Shortly thereafter, peace negotiations opened that resulted in the 1763 Peace of Paris. By the terms of this treaty, Great Britain effectively ousted France from North America. With France's departure, Britain extended its North American domain to include all of Canada, including Cape Breton Island where Louisbourg was located, and all the land lying between the Appalachian Mountains and the Mississippi River. Furthermore, Spain ceded Florida to Britain and in return received New Orleans and "Louisiana" west of the Mississippi River from France. Havana and Manila were also returned to Spain.

France retained its presence in India and even regained control of Pondicherry. However, French power there was permanently broken, especially since it was no longer permitted to fortify its outposts. By the terms of the Treaty of Paris, France pledged to neither challenge the British directly nor stir up the "natives" against the British.

France returned the Mediterranean island of Minorca, and Great Britain received the Caribbean islands of Grenada, St. Vincent, Dominica, and Tobago from France. Britain also acquired the slave-trading outpost of Senegal in West Africa from France. With the conclusion of the Seven Years' War, Britain held a dominant global position.

INTERPRETIVE ESSAY
Frederick M. Stowell

Most students of United States history are more familiar with the name and events of the French and Indian War than with those of the Seven Years' War. From the standpoint of the English people, the French and Indian War was merely one arena within the larger, global Seven Years' War. Regardless of the name given the conflict that raged from 1756 to 1763 and included the major powers of Europe, the impact of the war was significant and long lasting, both for the participants and for future generations.

The Seven Years' War, which officially began on August 29, 1756, was the last of four wars fought between the English and their allies and the French and their allies between 1689 and 1763. These were wars of empire that were intended to provide the victor with commercial domination of world trade, especially in North America. For this reason, the English historian Lawrence H. Gipson has termed the Seven Years' War the Great War of the Empire.

The first of the four wars was the War of the League of Augsburg, or King William's War (1688–1697). It was fought by King William III of England and his allies against King Louis XIV of France. Louis had been attempting to increase his influence in Europe through aggression but ended up calling forth a coalition led by England against him. Despite a number of victories on land, in 1692 France lost the naval Battle of La Hogue. With this defeat, any possibility that Louis could successfully invade England disappeared. After several more years of inconclusive struggle, the 1697 Peace of Ryswick ended the war. It also confirmed William as king of England, a development that Louis had been eager to contest. This war had little effect on the North American colonies of either nation.

The second war was the War of Spanish Succession, or Queen Anne's War (1701–1713). At the outset of this war, France was in a strong military position, with troops holding strategic positions in Europe and a fleet capable of dominating the western Mediterranean. France was allied with Spain, Savoy, Bavaria, and Cologne. Facing France was the Grand Alliance made up of England, Holland, Austria, Denmark, Prussia, Hanover, and some lesser German states. Success for the Grand Alliance would depend on the various participants' maintaining good relations among themselves. The French were successful during the first two years of the war, holding the English at bay in the Netherlands and at sea.

In 1704 English fortunes began to improve greatly. Portugal and Savoy had both joined the alliance. John Churchill, the Earl of Marlborough, attacked along the Rhine River into Bavaria, defeating both French and Bavarian armies at the decisive Battle of Blenheim. This ended France's hope of expanding into territories east of the Rhine. In the Mediterranean, the English fleet defeated the French at Malaga and captured Gibraltar off the southwestern tip of Spain. Between 1704 and the end of the war in 1713, the French were cleared from the Spanish Netherlands and were placed on the defensive to protect Paris from an English advance. The Treaty of Utrecht in 1713 resulted in French territorial and commercial losses. Great Britain gained important colonial concessions in North America including Hudson Bay, Acadia (Nova Scotia), and Newfoundland along with Saint Kitts in the Caribbean. However, France retained Cape Breton Island at the mouth of the Saint Lawrence River. From Spain, the British received Gibraltar and the island of Minorca in the Mediterranean. In addition, England was granted the monopoly on supplying slaves to the Spanish colonies in the Americas. England emerged from the war with a strong navy and a commercially active and prosperous colonial empire. The war left France both exhausted and bankrupt, elements that would start to erode the monarchy and plant the seeds of revolution.

The third war, the War of the Austrian Succession, or King George's War (1740–1748), in part grew out of a colonial dispute between Great Britain and Spain in 1739, sometimes referred to as the War of Jenkins' Ear. The Treaty of Utrecht had given the British trading rights that included—in addition to the monopoly on supplying slaves to the Spanish colonies—land within Spanish colonies for the "storage" of slaves and the right to have their ships repaired in any Spanish port. The British used these rights to cover a very large smuggling operation in Spanish America. The Spanish, in turn, established a coast guard force that stopped British ships approaching Spanish territories, searched them, and confiscated the ships and their cargoes on the slightest pretext. In 1731 an incident occurred during one of these search and seizures that resulted in the Spanish cutting off the British ship captain's ear. By 1739 the continuing conflict between the two nations led to a declaration of war by Britain.

The War of Jenkins' Ear did not amount to much in North America. Each side made raids on the other's colonies with little success. This conflict eventually merged into a larger one involving the question of Austrian suc-

The Seven Years' War

cession. When Emperor Charles VI of Austria died in 1740 he was succeeded by his daughter, Maria Theresa. Because females could not inherit the Habsburg crown, Charles had spent much of his later life convincing the various European states to accept the Pragmatic Sanction, an exception to this traditional law that would allow Maria Theresa to ascend the throne. At Charles's death, several countries reneged on their commitment. The most egregious was Prussia; its ruler, Frederick II (the Great), took the opportunity to seize the rich Habsburg province of Silesia. A European-wide war ensued. Holland, Russia, Savoy, and Great Britain joined to protect the young monarch from France, Spain, and Prussia. Britain was already at war with Spain and was the first to commit to the protection of Austria. British monetary subsidies helped support Austria and paid for Hessian and Danish troops to protect Austrian holdings in the Netherlands. When France threatened to invade Germany, Britain's King George II declared the neutrality of his dominion of Hanover and convinced Maria Theresa to cede Silesia to Prussia, reducing the threat from that quarter.

In 1742 the British again threw their support behind Maria Theresa with subsidies, an end to Hanoverian neutrality, naval pressure against Spain, and a combined army to defend the Austrian Netherlands. At the Battle of Dettingen in 1753, an army led by George II defeated a French army. Unfortunately for the British, in 1744 and 1745 victories were few and far between. By the end of 1745, most British forces were withdrawn from the Continent to face the threat of an uprising in Scotland. Bonnie Prince Charlie, with support from the French, planned an invasion of Great Britain that he hoped would take him to the throne he believed was his. Although French aid evaporated, Charlie proceeded with his ill-planned invasion and was defeated at the Battle of Culloden in 1746. As a consequence of this battle, the English severely punished the Scots, banning the wearing of kilts and tartans and disarming the people. The rest of the war went poorly for the British on the Continent. However, in North America the British fared better, capturing the French fort of Louisbourg on Cape Breton Island. Operations by the British navy against French fishing fleets in North America and French trading vessels at sea finally forced France to request a peace treaty.

In the Treaty of Aix-la-Chapelle, the French regained Louisbourg in exchange for Madras, in India. France also gave up land it had captured in Holland and Austrian Netherlands, recognized George II as the rightful king of Great Britain, and withdrew all support for the Catholic Stuarts in Scotland. The issues of smuggling, the Spanish coast guards, and New World trade and territorial rights were never addressed. The primary result of the war was to establish future rivalries and alliances in Europe. Prussia continued to increase in power and influence and to oppose Austria. Britain and France continued their commercial and colonial rivalry, one that would extend into the next century.

The Seven Years' War has been considered by some historians to be the first true global, or world, war. It involved the major powers of Europe and featured combat on four continents. While the cause of the war in Europe was the rivalry between Prussia and Austria for control of Silesia, the dominant theme of the conflict between Great Britain and France was control of commerce and trade with the colonies overseas in India, Africa, and North America. Of particular importance to these two nations was the highly profitable Atlantic trade triangle. Trade routes carried slaves from West Africa to the Americas to provide labor in the production of sugar, rice, cotton, lumber, fish, and other agricultural products. The raw materials were then shipped to New England or Europe for processing and sale. Finished products that were not sold in Europe were transported back to Africa and the American colonies for consumption or further trade. While France dominated the Caribbean sugar production, Britain controlled the material harvested in the North American colonies. A similar rivalry between the two countries existed in India for tea, spices, and cotton.

The Anglo-French economic rivalry in North America served to open the Seven Years' War. As early as 1753 French colonists began settling in the Ohio River Valley south of the Great Lakes. The French had a good relationship with the Native Americans and hoped to increase trade with them. The British colonists, who did not want to be confined to the Atlantic coastal regions, viewed this French move as a threat to westward expansion and reacted with force. The governor of Virginia dispatched a force of militia led by George Washington to establish a British presence in the Ohio River Valley and to challenge the French expansion. Building a small stockade fort near present-day Pittsburgh, Washington's forces unsuccessfully attacked the French at Fort Duquesne. The British militia was repulsed and forced to withdraw to their stockade, where the French laid siege to them. After the loss of one-third of his force, Washington was forced to surrender. This battle is considered to be the first of the French and Indian portion of the Seven Years' War.

In Canada, France reinforced the fort at Louisbourg while Great Britain fortified Halifax, Nova Scotia. In 1755 the British relocated all French colonists in Nova Scotia to other communities along the southern Atlantic seaboard. At the same time, the British sent a force commanded by General Edward Braddock into the Ohio River Valley to capture Fort Duquesne. Nearing the French fort, the British column, made up of both colonial militia and British regular soldiers, was surprised by a mixed force of French soldiers and Indian warriors. The British attempted to fight in traditional

European style, formed in ranks with controlled firing. The French and Indians used the forest for cover and fired at will into the exposed British ranks. Two-thirds of the British and colonial soldiers were killed or wounded, including Braddock. This defeat marked the beginning of two years of British military disasters in North America. The Native Americans, armed and directed by the French, subjected the western frontier of the British colonies to devastating raids.

With battle joined in North America, the conflict developed rapidly in Europe. In January 1756, by the so-called Convention of Westminster, Great Britain allied itself with Prussia. The French immediately joined in alliance with Austria. The alliances of the War of Austrian Succession were now reversed, with Britain and Prussia opposing France and Austria. This reversal of partnerships is known as the Diplomatic Revolution. Russia and Sweden later joined the Franco-Austrian association.

While forging this alliance in Europe, the British experienced political turmoil at home. The secretary of state, Thomas Pelham-Holles, Duke of Newcastle, who was responsible for the foreign alliances, subsidies, and the war in general, was losing support in the House of Commons. The threat of an invasion by the French in 1756 led him to request and implement the stationing of Hessian and Hanoverian troops in Great Britain. Criticism of this policy and the military defeats in the colonies led to a change of government in early 1757, with Newcastle becoming first lord of the treasury and William Pitt, the first Earl of Chatham, becoming secretary of state. Under Pitt's leadership, a consistent and successful prosecution of the war began.

Pitt's first decision was to return the Hessian and Hanoverian troops to the Continent. This act won the approval of the British people and helped to gain their support for the war effort. To replace the German troops, Pitt began strengthening the militia, or home guards. This included raising Scottish regiments for the defense of the home islands. In North America he established more colonial militia under colonial officers rather than British regulars, giving the colonials a greater stake in the fighting and freeing up the regulars for service in other areas.

Pitt was aware that the war would have to be fought on many fronts and that resources, alliances, and strategy would need to be coordinated. He established his primary goal: destroying France's colonial empire and capturing its commerce. To accomplish this goal, he kept the French occupied on the European continent with the minimal use of forces while chipping away at the colonies. Frederick the Great of Prussia received subsidies from London to help him fight the Austrians, French, and Russians. An army of Hessian and Hanoverian soldiers commanded by a British general was sent to defend Hanover. Raids, some successful others not, were made on the French coastline. These tactics tied up large numbers of French soldiers who were then spread widely throughout the Continent. The financial burden for France was significant.

At sea Pitt used the Royal Navy effectively in a similar manner. The British navy blockaded the French in their ports of Brest and Toulon, causing a decline in French morale and combat efficiency. In both Canada and India the British used their navy to support army operations. Battles occurred between the two navies, although the outcome was not always favorable for the British.

By the summer of 1756 Austria had been ready to invade Prussia. To prevent this, Frederick the Great launched a preemptive invasion of Saxony, which had sided with the French and Austrians. In the Mediterranean that year, the French had forced the British out of Minorca. Even after Pitt took office in 1757, the tide of war did not change until the end of the year, when the Prussians defeated the French and the Austrians in two major battles. The British-led Hanoverian army was reorganized and a new commander placed at its head.

During 1758 the British succeeded in stopping two French supply convoys headed for Canada with reinforcements. Louisbourg was finally captured, opening the Saint Lawrence to British ships, while two French forts between the Great Lakes and the Saint Lawrence Valley were captured, cutting the French off from supplies from the Continent. This forced the French to abandon Fort Duquesne, opening the Ohio River Valley to British and colonial access. On the European continent, the British retook Emden from the French and made successful raids on the French coast.

The year 1759 would prove decisive for the war. Prince Ferdinand, leading a German army, defeated the French at Minden, in northwestern Germany, thereby taking pressure off of Frederick the Great after his defeat at Kunersdorf. The French again threatened the British with an invasion until the French fleets at Toulon and Brest were defeated by the British navy. In North America, Pitt directed his commanders to take Canada from the French. This operation called for one army to attack up Lake Champlain while the other came down the Saint Lawrence. The attack from the south failed, but the operation from the north was successful. Supported by the Royal Navy, the British army under General James Wolfe defeated the French on the Plains of Abraham and captured the city of Quebec. The following year the remainder of the French army and the city of Montreal surrendered, effectively ending all French influence in North America. The French and Indian War was the bloodiest conflict fought on North American soil in the eighteenth century, costing more lives than the American Revolution.

The clash between Great Britain and France in India found its roots in the commercial competition between the British East India Company and its French counterparts. The British East India Company was a private concern that handled all commercial trade with the Indian colonies and, at the same time, helped to fund the British government through loans and credit. While Britain and France were at peace in Europe, their two commercial interests were at war in India. By backing local princes, each side sparred for control over the Indian trade. By 1754 the British East India Company had gained a position of power. When the Seven Years' War began in Europe the French dispatched the Compte de Lally, an accomplished soldier, to India to organize their Indian allies against the British. He laid siege to the British colony of Madras in 1758 only to be forced back a year later with the arrival of a British fleet. At the Battle of Wandiwash, on the east coast of India, the French were defeated in 1760. The British followed up this victory with the siege of the French forces at Pondicherry the following year. The final surrender of the French in 1761 marked the end of the war in India.

Having lost their colonies in North America and India, and facing a steady and seemingly endless drain on their manpower and revenue, the French were ready to sue for peace in 1761. Hoping to acquire more colonial possessions to trade at the negotiating table, Pitt opted to continue the war in the West Indies. However, the British cabinet would not support him even though the French signed a treaty with Spain that would bring that country into the war. Frustrated by the internal politics of the cabinet, Pitt resigned in October 1761. He was replaced by Lord Bute, the King's confidant. Spain did enter the war the following year but proved ineffective. Instead of helping the French cause, Spain managed to lose both Havana, Cuba, and Manila, in the Philippines, to British forces.

The year 1762 saw the withdrawal of Russia and Sweden from the war as a result of Empress Elizabeth of Russia's death. Her successor, Peter III, who was an admirer of Frederick the Great, quickly signed a peace treaty with the Prussian monarch.

The Peace of Paris, which officially ended the Seven Years' War, was concluded in 1763. The British gained the greatest amount, leaving France with very little. In North America Britain retained the areas she had won in the war—French Canada and Cape Breton Island. In the Caribbean, Grenada, Dominica, Tobago, and Saint Vincent became British possessions. Minorca, in the Mediterranean, was returned to British rule. In West Africa, Senegal became a British colony and Britain gained control of the slave trade to the Americas. In India the British retained Madras and gained the right to intervene in French possessions at any time. Although the French retained some colonies in India, this effectively ended their influence in that country.

The Spanish ceded Florida to the British in return for Havana and Manila. In addition, Spain temporarily received the Louisiana Territory from France to compensate for the cost of the war. The French possessions in the West Indies—Guadaloupe, Martinique, Saint Lucia, and Marie-Galante—along with the Ile de Gorée in Africa were restored to France. In Newfoundland, France retained fishing rights and territory for processing the fish for shipment. The Peace of Paris, however, ignored most of the concerns of Prussia, England's ally.

The Treaty of Hubertusburg, signed on February 15, 1763, addressed Prussia's concerns. It confirmed Prussia's possession of Silesia, the main point of contention between Prussia and Austria, and indirectly established Prussia as a leading power in Europe. At this point, the British-Prussian alliance ended and effective political contact between the two nations did not resume until the end of the century.

The impact of the Seven Years' War, like the war itself, was global. The war's impact was also long lasting, with its effects still apparent in the twenty-first century. Control of all the lands east of the Mississippi, including the Canadian territories, gave Great Britain the raw materials and markets for its expanding colonial empire. The islands of the West Indies also brought economic opportunities and bases for naval control of the Caribbean, where both the French and the Spanish still held colonies. The African colony of Senegal provided the English with slave labor for their North American and Caribbean agricultural operations. Control of the Atlantic trade routes and the growth of the British navy to protect them would benefit Britain well into the next century.

In India, Great Britain did not just gain trading colonies, she gained what would amount to full governmental control over the Indian subcontinent and its people. India remained a colony of Britain until the late 1940s. This dominance stunted the social and cultural growth of the Indian people, whose lives were molded in the image of the British. The Indians, like all people that were part of the British colonial empire, were considered "little brown brothers" or "the white man's burden." This attitude of white superiority became ingrained not only in the British themselves but also in the colonists of North America and Australia and their descendants. The results of this worldview continue to create social and economic problems today. Another result of British colonialism in India was the increased diversity within Britain after the demise of its empire in the last half of the twentieth century. As former colonies gained their independence, Britain granted British citizenship to anyone living in the former colonies. People from Pakistan, India, Kenya, and other former colonies relocated to Britain, bringing with them their unique cultures. The result has been cultural, social, ethnic, and economic conflict in Britain as unskilled immigrants struggle for jobs, housing, and economic equality.

To manage such diverse and far-flung colonial possessions, the British government created an efficient administrative system. The establishment of the Colonial Office with responsibility for trade, emigration, and management of the colonies provided the first step toward a consistent policy. This office increased in size and responsibility well into the Victorian era.

British cultural patterns affected all the colonies acquired by Great Britain during its wars of empire. The English language spread throughout the world, as did the Anglican faith. Today more Anglicans live in the former colonies than in Britain itself. Also, British models of government, law, education, and economics are still used in most of these now independent countries.

Funding the Seven Years' War had significant and disastrous consequences for Great Britain, however. The British believed that the colonists in North America should help to pay for the cost of defending themselves from the French and the Native Americans. But the colonists resented the manner in which the war was financed. British taxes imposed on them resulted in boycotts, demonstrations, and, eventually, revolution. In the end, Britain lost the very colonies Pitt had fought so hard to gain. By 1783 the Atlantic seaboard colonies had established their own nation and Britain retained only Canada from the settlement of the Treaty of Paris. Ultimately, the cost of the Seven Years' War was paid by the British themselves.

The American colonists resented not only the British attempt to have them pay for the war but also other heavy-handed policies imposed by the British government. For example, the quartering of British regular soldiers in colonial homes and public buildings outraged the colonists. Discontent increased in the period following the war as the colonists felt estranged from Britain. The lack of representation in Parliament and the attitude of British governors sent to control the colonies exacerbated tensions and sped the colonists on the road to revolution.

The American colonists gained military experience from the Seven Years' War as they learned from their Native American adversaries. The methods of ambush, attacking from concealed positions, and operating in small groups would provide them with an advantage against the stiff and formal tactics of the British. In addition, leaders of the revolution such as George Washington learned the art of fighting in the wilderness from the French and Indian War.

The impact the British had on the Native Americans was even more devastating than the effects on the people of India. In North America, contact between the Native Americans and the European colonists resulted in the spread of fatal diseases for which the Native Americans had no immunity. Unknown thousands died from smallpox, measles, and other diseases, wiping out whole tribal groups. Furthermore, the animosity between the colonists and the Native Americans continued into the nineteenth century, resulting in mass relocation, open warfare, and the application of social reforms to "convert the savages" into civilized people.

The war's impact on France was the opposite of its impact on Great Britain. France was weakened by the loss of commerce and overseas colonies and the drain on its resources. By 1760 the potential for revolution grew dramatically as the lower classes were drastically overtaxed to support the war effort. The government was out of touch with the people, but it continued to hold power until the French Revolution began in 1789. This monumental upheaval resulted from more than a century of inefficient government, social unrest, and the example provided by the American Revolution. The animosity between the French and the British would rekindle open conflict in the Napoleonic Wars.

In Canada, the resentment of the descendants of the French colonists toward British rule is still creating tension today. Periodically, the largely French province of Quebec considers seceding from Canada and forming a new nation. In a step toward independence, Quebec has made French the official language of government.

The alliance between Great Britain and Prussia that helped to win the Seven Years' War came to an immediate end with the Treaty of Paris. Prussia's increased importance in Europe helped lead to the growth of the German state in the nineteenth century and the subsequent world wars of the twentieth that proved so ruinous for Great Britain.

One of the war's delayed but crucial consequences occurred in the late 1800s. The United States naval historian Alfred Thayer Mahan analyzed the importance of naval power during the period 1690 to 1783. The publication of his *Influence of Sea Power on History, 1690–1783*, in 1890 had a dramatic effect on military strategy throughout the twentieth century. Mahan cited the need to project sea power to protect colonies and commercial trade routes, the need for overseas bases to support such power, and the necessity for a large navy. British naval leaders followed Mahan's advice. The British navy was structured to fit Mahan's views, as were the navies of the United States and Japan, among others.

Like the proverbial stone thrown into the still pond, the ripples set in motion by the Seven Years' War are still being felt around the globe. The legacy of the war can be found in the governments, the languages, and the legal, educational, and economic systems of countries around the world. The Seven Years' War guaranteed that Great Britain and its empire would become the world's dominant military, naval, and commercial power. Until the end of the nineteenth century, Britannia truly ruled the waves.

SELECTED BIBLIOGRAPHY

Anderson, Fred. *Crucible of War: The Seven Years' War and the Fate of Empire in British North America.* New York: Knopf, 2000. The most recent account of the Seven Years' War, focusing on the British experience in North America.

Anderson, M. S. *The War of the Austrian Succession, 1740–1748.* New York: Longman, 1995. The author, an expert on eighteenth-century military and diplomatic history, surveys the inconclusive War of the Austrian Succession.

Ayling, Stanley. *The Elder Pitt, Earl of Chatham.* London: Collins, 1976. This sympathetic if less-than-adulatory biography of the architect of victory sees Pitt's role in the Seven Years' War as one of his few real achievements.

Black, Jeremy. *The Rise of the European Powers, 1679–1793.* New York: E. Arnold, 1990. The complex and sometimes confusing story of eighteenth-century international relations receives a lucid and enlightening treatment.

Brewer, John. *The Sinews of Power: War, Money, and the English State, 1688–1783.* New York: Knopf, 1989. Includes an insightful discussion of Great Britain's ability to finance the Seven Years' War.

Brown, Peter Douglas. *William Pitt, Earl of Chatham.* London: Allen and Unwin, 1978. A lively but somewhat uneven effort, this volume sheds light on Pitt's psychological instability.

Corbett, Julian Stafford. *England in the Seven Years' War.* 2 vols. 1907. Reprint, London: Greenhill Books, 1992. A dated and opinionated detailed account of the Seven Years' War.

Dann, Uriel. *Hanover and Great Britain, 1740–1760: Diplomacy and Survival.* Leicester: Leicester University Press, 1991. Discusses the role Hanover played in Great Britain's involvement in the Seven Years' War.

Dorn, Walter L. *Competition for Empire, 1740–1763.* New York: Harper and Row, 1940. Although dated, this volume presents a comprehensive overview of the mid-eighteenth century's wars.

Gipson, Lawrence H. *The British Empire before the American Revolution.* 15 vols. New York: Knopf, 1939–1970. This is a monumental series on the British Empire up to the nineteenth century. Volumes 6–8 provide a detailed description of the Seven Years' War.

Jennings, Francis. *Empire of Fortune: Crowns, Colonies, and Tribes in the Seven Years' War in America.* New York: W. W. Norton, 1988. This subjective revisionist account challenges the accepted version of events.

Mahan, Alfred Thayer. *The Influence of Sea Power on History, 1690–1783.* 1890. Reprint, New York: Hill and Wang, 1957. An analysis of the use of naval power during the wars of empire, this is one of the most influential books of the twentieth century.

Middleton, R. *The Bells of Victory: The Pitt-Newcastle Ministry and the Conduct of the Seven Years' War.* Cambridge: Cambridge University Press, 1985. Perhaps the best available general account of Great Britain's role in the Seven

Year's War. Middleton views Pitt's role as less decisive than the authors of earlier works have.

Peters, Marie. *Pitt and Popularity: The Patriot Minister and London Opinion during the Seven Years' War*. Oxford: Clarendon Press, 1980. Provides background on the public service of this wartime secretary. This examination of Pitt's public service features a close look at his wartime image as created by the London press.

Plumb, J. H. *Chatham*. Hamden, CT: Archon, 1965. This short, readable biography of Pitt is probably the best place to start for those wishing to know more about one of Great Britain's most famous leaders.

Riley, James C. *The Seven Years' War and the Old Regime in France: The Economic and Financial Toll*. Princeton, NJ: Princeton University Press, 1986. This detailed study of the economic and financial impact of the war on the French monarchy provides a good overview of the cost of the war to the losing belligerent.

Schwartz, Seymour L. *The French and Indian War, 1754–1763: The Imperial Struggle for North America*. New York: Simon and Schuster, 1994. Heavily illustrated with maps, drawings, portraits, site plans of forts, and engravings, this volume is quite helpful when used with a good narrative.

Schweizer, Karl W. *Frederick the Great, William Pitt, and Lord Bute: The Anglo-Prussian Alliance, 1756–1763*. New York: Garland, 1991. An expanded doctoral thesis that provides a comprehensive study of the alliance between England and Prussia during the war.

Sherrard, O. A. *Lord Chatham: Pitt and the Seven Years' War*. Westport, CT: Greenwood Press, 1975. A detailed account of Pitt's public career from 1755 to 1761, with emphasis on the North American campaigns.

Speck, W. A. *Stability and Strife: England, 1714–1760*. Cambridge, MA: Harvard University Press, 1977. The development of England's political, social, and religious institutions in the period of the Seven Years' War.

3

The Napoleonic Wars, 1789–1815

INTRODUCTION

In the summer of 1789, France—continental Europe's wealthiest and most important state—dissolved into revolution. The overthrow of the French regime led to twenty-six successive years of turmoil, chaos, and bloodshed. Great Britain was swept into the maelstrom of the French Revolution and the Napoleonic period that followed despite its island status and its great reluctance to become involved in continental events.

Initially, many Britons viewed the first stages of the French Revolution with guarded optimism. They were pleased and somewhat flattered that the French seemed to be modeling their future after Britain's Glorious Revolution of the previous century. Other Britons were even more enthusiastic. Fired by the revolution's inspirational rhetoric, they hoped for the dawning of a new era grounded in "liberty, equality, and fraternity." The young British poet William Wordsworth captured this sentiment when he wrote of the revolution:

> Bliss was it in that dawn to be alive,
> But to be young was very Heaven!

Others were even more effusive. Thomas Paine, of American Revolution fame and then living in Great Britain, published *The Rights of Man* in 1791. This popular work praised the French Revolution in extravagant terms.

Britain's most spectacular naval victory occurred at the Battle of Trafalgar. On October 21, 1805, Horatio Lord Nelson, whose flagship HMS Victory is shown in the foreground, annihilated a combined French and Spanish fleet, thereby assuring that Great Britain would maintain naval supremacy for the remainder of the Napoleonic Wars. Reproduced from the Collections of the Library of Congress.

Citing the French experience, Paine urged the abolition in Britain of both the monarchy and the House of Lords, and proposed a thoroughly republican reform of British society.

However, even before the appearance of Paine's radical pamphlet, more conservative elements in Great Britain were beginning to have second thoughts about the French Revolution. Their concerns were best articulated by Edmund Burke, who published *Reflections on the Revolution in France* in late 1790. Burke argued that it is in the natural order of things for societies to evolve, and that disruptions to this evolutionary process such as the French Revolution do infinitely more harm than good by indiscriminately destroying the foundations upon which a well-ordered society rests. Burke's condemnation of the revolution and defense of the British status quo found many supporters among Britain's propertied and influential classes.

Burke's analysis seemed even more valid when in 1792 the French Revolution entered its most radical phase. The Reign of Terror, the execution of King Louis XVI in January 1793, and the radical revolutionaries' decision to spread their ideas beyond France's borders turned British public opinion decisively against the revolution. The result was something akin to panic in Great Britain as a series of harsh, repressive measures were implemented: habeas corpus was suspended from 1794 to 1801; in 1795 the Treasonable Practices Act severely restricted free speech and the Seditious Meetings Act drastically limited the right to assemble; stamp duties curtailed the free press; the Combination Acts outlawed trade unions. Government spies and agents provocateurs abounded, and arrests and rigged trials resulted in the imprisonment and/or exile of thousands.

It was, however, the decision of the French radicals to extend their experiment beyond the borders of France that brought Great Britain into direct conflict with the revolution. Having declared itself a republic in September 1792, France soon overran the Austrian Netherlands (present-day Belgium) and threatened Holland. French aggression alarmed Great Britain since it had been British policy for centuries to make certain that no strong nation controlled the Low Countries, an obvious jumping-off point for any potential invasion of the British Isles. When France showed no interest in addressing Britain's concerns but, instead, executed the king and announced its intention to expand at the expense of the balance of power on the Continent, the two countries drifted into war in February 1793.

For Great Britain, conduct of the war fell to Prime Minister William Pitt the Younger, son of Britain's successful prime minister during the Seven Years' War. However, Pitt's expertise was finance, not war. At first Pitt was successful in creating an anti-French alliance. This First Coalition included not only Britain but also Prussia, Austria, Holland, Spain, and Sardinia.

Copying his father, Pitt hoped to avoid sending large numbers of British troops to Europe. Rather, Britain would retain its mastery of the seas while generously subsidizing continental armies that would defeat—or at least tie down—France. Britain thus would once again become the "paymaster of the Allies."

The Europeans had no trouble accepting British subsidies; however, they spent as much time and energy quarrelling amongst themselves and engaging in peripheral activities such as the destruction of Poland as they did fighting France. Furthermore, when they did fight the French they usually lost. The end result was a string of French triumphs that left it in control of Belgium, Holland, northern Italy, and the left bank of the Rhine River. By 1797 the First Coalition had collapsed. For Britain, naval victories provided the only bright spot. In 1797 the British defeated a Franco-Spanish fleet (by this time Spain had switched alliances) at the Battle of Cape St. Vincent, off the southwest coast of Portugal, thereby thwarting a planned invasion of England.

It was during the struggles of the First Coalition period that Napoleon Bonaparte made a name for himself. Known as "the Little Corsican," he helped to drive a British fleet from Toulon in 1793 and a few years later won a series of stunning victories over Sardinia and Austria in northern Italy. Napoleon's 1798 invasion of Egypt appeared in part to be an attempt to threaten indirectly Great Britain's position in India. Although Napoleon won the Battle of the Pyramids, he was far from his European base, and the weak French navy that had transported him to Egypt found itself exposed to superior British naval forces. In August the British squadron under Horatio Nelson caught and destroyed the French fleet at the Battle of Aboukir Bay, or—as it is sometimes known—the Battle of the Nile. Nelson at sea was every inch the equal of Bonaparte on land. However, Napoleon managed to escape from Egypt and return to France, where he misrepresented his Egyptian adventure as he overthrew the existing government and laid the foundation for his subsequent dictatorship.

Meanwhile, a French attempt to take advantage of rising discontent in Ireland proved futile. Because of poor weather, the French failed to land a small military force and an Irish rebellion was brutally crushed. The only major casualty of the Irish imbroglio was Pitt, whose attempt to find an equitable solution to the Irish problem ran into opposition from King George III, thereby causing Pitt to resign in 1801. However, Henry Addington, his successor, proved inept and in 1804 Pitt was back as prime minister.

One consequence of Napoleon's uncontrollable ambitions and his defeat in Egypt was to revive the alliance of European states that challenged him. By spring 1799 Great Britain had succeeded in enlisting Austria, Russia, and Turkey in the Second Coalition. However, despite a new outpouring of "Pitt's gold," the Second Coalition fared no better than its predecessor. After some initial victories, Russia withdrew from the alliance in a huff and Napoleon pounded the Austrians at the Battle of Marengo. By late 1800 the Second Coalition was defunct. Again, Britain's naval forces provided the only bright spot. With the Royal Navy controlling the sea, France was unable to mount a cross-channel invasion of the home islands. The British naval blockade of France also gained greater credence. Finally, France had to yield her position in the Mediterranean to the British, and when France sponsored a League of Armed Neutrality, including Russia, Denmark, Prussia, and Sweden, designed to deny the British access to the Baltic Ocean, a squadron with Nelson second in command destroyed the Danish fleet at Copenhagen.

In March 1802 Great Britain and France signed the Peace of Amiens; it was a sham, however, and in May 1803 the two rivals were once again at war. This time it appeared certain that Napoleon would invade Britain as he assembled a 100,000-man army at Boulogne. Once again, however, Britain's navy came to the rescue. In order for Napoleon's cross-channel invasion to succeed, he needed to achieve at least temporary control of the English Channel. To that end, units of the French fleet embarked upon a series of complicated voyages designed to draw Britain's naval forces away from the channel. Napoleon's scheme ended in ignominious failure on October 21, 1805, when Nelson attacked a combined France-Spanish fleet off Cape Trafalgar. There the British achieved one of the greatest naval victories in history, marred only by the death of Nelson.

Unknown at the time of Trafalgar was that Napoleon had already concluded that an invasion of Great Britain was not feasible and that the French emperor had moved his army toward central Europe. Once again Pitt had been at work, this time creating the Third Coalition—Britain, Austria, and Russia. And once again Britain would pay subsidies while Austrian and Russian troops would do the fighting.

Napoleon moved quickly to destroy the Third Coalition and in a stunning series of victories at the Battles of Ulm, Austerlitz, Eylau, and Friedland he achieved his objective. (Napoleon also defeated Prussia at the Battles of Jena and Auerstadt after the German kingdom ill-advisedly entered the war against him.) By 1807 the Third Coalition was dead, as was Pitt, who had died in January 1806. Napoleon occupied Berlin, controlled Austria, and by the Treaty of Tilsit converted Russia from opponent to ally. Napoleon stood triumphant and Great Britain stood alone.

Up to then, the Napoleonic Wars had proven to be quite a drain on Great Britain's finances. The national debt had more than doubled, inflation continued to soar, and tax rates went through the roof. Pitt had even introduced an unpopular graduated income tax.

Because Napoleon's army could not defeat Great Britain's navy, the French emperor resorted to economic warfare. He initiated the Continental System, a comprehensive program that barred any European country from trading with Britain. Napoleon hoped that the Continental System would deprive Britain of its lucrative markets on the Continent and easy access to cheap food and raw materials. In turn, this would trigger an economic disaster that would bring Britain to its knees. Britain responded by implementing its own economic blockade of the Continent.

While Britain's economy did suffer, Napoleon's attempt to shut off continental Europe from English goods proved to be a hopeless task. For one thing, it was almost physically impossible; the French could not police every harbor and every port. Furthermore, many Europeans craved the products of Britain's empire and its domestic industry, and they resented the French attempt to keep them from satisfying their desires. Finally, many European producers—people of wealth and power in their own right—endured real economic hardship because they could not sell their grain, timber, and naval stores to the British. As their profits decreased, their dislike of Napoleon grew.

One consequence of the Continental System was Napoleon's decision to invade Iberia because he feared that British goods would penetrate Europe through Portugal and Spain. The Portuguese royal family escaped to Brazil under the protection of the English fleet, but in 1808 Napoleon forced the king of Spain to abdicate and replaced him with his (Napoleon's) brother Joseph. The Spanish rebelled against the French, waging a protracted guerrilla war. They also appealed successfully to the British for help. The ensuing Peninsular War, 1808–1814, so greatly damaged France that Napoleon subsequently compared it to an ulcer sapping the French nation's health.

At this juncture, the British army found a figure equal to that of the navy's Nelson. Arthur Wellesley, later the Duke of Wellington, commanded the British force in Iberia with exceptional vigor and intelligence. On the defensive, Wellington held the French army at bay, and when the time came for him to attack, he moved swiftly to exploit French weaknesses such as their propensity to live off the land.

As successful as Wellington was—he defeated large French forces at the Battles of Salamanca and Vitoria—Russia was chiefly responsible for Napoleon's downfall. In the summer of 1812 Napoleon invaded his erstwhile ally with an army of six hundred thousand men. Despite capturing Moscow, Napoleon failed to destroy the Russian army and Tsar Alexander I refused to sue for peace. Meanwhile, disease, hunger, cold, and marauders exacted a horrible toll. By the time a confused Napoleon retreated from Russia, he had lost at least 80 percent of his army. A year later, in October 1813, he lost the pivotal Battle of Leipzig (sometimes called the Battle of the Nations) and in 1814 he abdicated the French throne. In 1815 Napoleon returned from exile in Elba for his last fling. This "Hundred Days" came to an end in June of that year when Napoleon's old nemesis, the Duke of Wellington, defeated him at the Battle of Waterloo.

After his defeat, Napoleon sought the protection of the victorious British, who subsequently exiled him to Saint Helena, a small island in the south Atlantic. He died there in 1821. The job of restoring the shattered Continent fell to the participants at the Congress of Vienna, in which the British foreign minister, Viscount Castlereagh, played a prominent role.

INTERPRETIVE ESSAY
S. J. Stearns

The Napoleonic Wars, growing out of the French Revolution, were a titanic European-wide struggle that eventually reached across the globe including North America, the Caribbean, and Africa. As seen at the time, they were carried on with unprecedented ferocity. Over nearly a quarter of a century of continuous fighting, the wars left their mark on all the societies that were drawn into them. Great Britain played a leading role in opposing, first, the ideological hopes of revolutionary France to establish a radical democracy and, then, the vaulting ambitions of the dictator Napoleon Bonaparte. Following their traditional strategy, the British confronted a dominant threatening power on the European continent by organizing a series of unstable coalitions, subsidizing their allies, and hiring foreign mercenaries to supplement their own armies. Militarily they responded to Napoleon militarily much as they had to Louis XIV a century earlier. By the time France was defeated after more than two decades of exhausting warfare, Britain had armed the greatest force in its history.

The impact of the Napoleonic Wars on British society needs to be disentangled from the effects of the preceding century of warfare. Before the outbreak of the struggle with revolutionary France, Great Britain had been so frequently at war both in Europe and across its growing global empire that historians have referred to these conflicts collectively as the "second Hundred Years' War." On numerous occasions between 1689 and 1783 Britain had fought many states; but it always found itself ranged against France, the most powerful monarchy in Europe. All these wars had a cumulative effect on Britain's civil and military institutions, and upon British society. In assessing the consequences of the Napoleonic Wars, care should be taken to distinguish significant changes that had already taken place before the wars' outbreak from those that occurred later and were caused by the wars.

Historians of warfare have frequently seen in the Napoleonic Wars a radical change in both the scale of the conflict and the unrestrained character with which it was waged. Compared to the wars of the early and mid-eighteenth century, usually described as "limited" in their goals and objectives, the Napoleonic Wars were thought to prefigure the "total war" of modern times. The wars of the eighteenth century frequently reflected economic considerations. They were waged for concrete objectives, such as a piece of territory, and their costs could be weighed against the value of the objective.

Napoleon's style was markedly different. His brutal tactics showed that enemy armies might be crushed decisively; utterly overthrown by massing unprecedentedly large numbers of men and cannons against decisive points in their defensive positions. If a commander like Napoleon had no scruples about risking heavy casualties, maneuvered quickly, and acted decisively, success against the cautious generals of the old order tended to follow. Napoleon's aim was to annihilate armies that opposed him. After such victories, not mere slices of territory but rather whole governments might fall.

In fact, military forces had been increasing in size for some time in the eighteenth century. Whether Napoleon was more ruthless or cynical than Prussia's Frederick the Great is debatable at best. On the British side, Horatio Nelson matched Napoleon in daring and determination. Though only a subordinate commander, Nelson destroyed two of Napoleon's great fleets at the Battles of the Nile (1798) and Trafalgar (1805). Nelson had none of Napoleon's ideological baggage but did share his desire to triumph completely over the enemy and capture the lion's share of the glory.

After the war, the Prussian officer and military theorist Karl von Clausewitz provided some theoretical justification for this behavior. He argued that successful wars must be waged in this extreme fashion. Whether considering theory or practice, war between great powers seemed to most onlookers at the time far bloodier and more vicious than the norm. When the truth of this became clear in retrospect, only transcendent political goals such as democracy or nationalism—or resistance to them—seemed able to justify this escalation in military ruthlessness.

British generals were slow to change their thinking about the conduct of war, despite their lack of success against Napoleon. It was not until the later stages of the war that the British found in the Duke of Wellington a commander who could succeed in the new environment. Wellington's methods, however, were the traditional ones used by his predecessors, much as the weapons he employed were essentially unchanged. The standard infantry muskets in 1814–1815 were not very different from those used in 1660. The same was true of artillery, except perhaps for the fact that many more guns were employed. Despite the "revolutionary" change in the political character of warfare; Napoleon's tactical innovations; and the greater size of the new armies, which made them much harder for a general to control, little else had changed. Above all, troops still moved as they always had from ancient times—on their own feet at about twelve to fifteen miles a day.

Moreover, in larger strategic terms the Napoleonic Wars did not inspire any substantial changes in British thinking, nor did they require any. The country's essential conception of how to defend itself had been worked out long before. As an island kingdom undivided since 1603, it had been clear that the British navy was its crucial first line of defense. So long as its "wooden walls" were unbreached, no continental enemy—no matter how strong—could conquer the kingdom. Great Britain therefore enjoyed the luxury of maintaining a relatively small peacetime army. Low military spending was a key to funding a powerful navy, the crucial element of national strategy. There was nothing new in this.

Threatened by Napoleonic invasion in 1803–04, the cabinet remembered and identified with Queen Elizabeth I's success in 1588. Although British governments during the Napoleonic Wars could not be secure about dominating the global seas, their island was successfully protected from invasion throughout the period and, after 1805, was never seriously threatened. The more complex issue of grand strategy—whether a sea-based power could prevail against a state that dominated the entire European continent—would not be answered in Britain's favor until the war's conclusion.

The restless, captive, Catholic island of Ireland provided an exceptional area of vulnerability in Great Britain's long-held defensive strategy. Whenever a foreign war distracted Britain, the possibility of an Irish rebellion arose. Two years after a failed French attempt at invasion, London shut down Ireland's three-hundred-year-old parliament sitting in Dublin. Its functions and some token representatives were transferred to the Westminster Parliament. This is the only major permanent alteration in British constitutional arrangements that can be attributed to the war. Ireland did not rise in revolt afterward, but the problem of how to govern Ireland would haunt British governments into the twentieth century.

Great Britain's ability to finance the Napoleonic Wars proved to be another element of continuity with past practices. War imposed a very serious strain on the British treasury, as it did on all early modern states. As the size of wars grew, so did their costs. Wartime expenses often drove the great European states to the brink of bankruptcy. Nevertheless, Britain's development of increasingly effective measures to pay for war was a major factor in its success during the century of warfare beginning in 1689.

The British learned early from the Dutch how to manage war's financial concerns effectively and prudently without damaging the country's foreign trade. The government established a system of finance that combined relatively efficient taxation on both trade ("the excise," in modern terms a sales tax) and land with extensive borrowing from the population. The creation of the Bank of England in 1694 had encouraged an increasingly prosperous society to lend funds to its government, which, for the first time, could be counted on to repay its debts in a timely fashion. This made readily available the massive sums of money needed to wage war.

Bank

Despite frequent financial difficulties, Great Britain managed to pay for its share of the Napoleonic Wars without immobilizing interruptions. Without money, armies were paralyzed when they did not break down entirely. Soldiers who were not fed tended to desert, and armies melted away. Even for Britain, which limited its commitment to making war on the European continent as much as possible, the sums involved were enormous by the standards of the day.

One estimate is that the Napoleonic Wars cost Great Britain over £860,000,000. Although payment of the government's debts in gold was suspended and lenders had to be content with paper money—traditionally regarded with the gravest suspicion—the government continued to meet its obligations. Financial strength proved to be a significant weapon. It allowed the government to defend the island from the ravages of war, to fund its allies, and to pay for mercenary troops.

As prime minister, the younger William Pitt was as thoughtful a manager of the kingdom's resources in the first half of the war as he had been earlier in peacetime. He had come to prominence politically as a young man when a major issue had been how to handle the long-term debt left over from the disastrous lost war with the American colonies. Prime minister throughout most of the early years of the Napoleonic Wars, he put government funding of the conflict on as sound a basis as that age could imagine. Necessity obliged him to risk imposing an income tax, a highly unusual step that he took boldly if reluctantly.

Effective war finance was a crucial factor in Great Britain's success against Napoleon. However, despite Pitt's innovations and refinements, the fundamentals of the fiscal system itself reflected earlier experience in war going back to Walpole and his predecessors in the reigns of Queen Anne and William III.

To contemporary observers, what the Napoleonic Wars represented above all and in the most dramatic fashion possible was a massive increase in the scale of warfare. It was the extraordinary growth in the size of the forces engaged that made these wars so expensive. The British navy at its peak in 1809 had just slightly fewer than one thousand ships in service, nearly three times as many as a half-century earlier. The army, with some three hundred thousand men, had also tripled in size since the American Revolution. All told, in 1809 the country's land and sea forces, including the militia and volunteers—part-time soldiers kept at home to defend the island from invasion—amounted to some eight hundred thousand men. The population of England and Wales at this time—the areas providing roughly 80 percent of the men in the military—was roughly ten million. For an essentially agricultural society, this represented a very high level of mobilization of manpower.

Figures for the losses of men have not been calculated as satisfactorily, but approximately more than two hundred thousand soldiers and sailors died in service during the war. In proportional terms, this seems to be a higher ratio of men lost to those who served than Great Britain suffered in the course of World War I, albeit over a much longer period. Most of these military deaths in the Napoleonic Wars were not due to battle but to disease, in the age-old pattern that had been true since ancient times. Not until the terrible losses of World War I would deaths caused by combat exceed the mortality caused by infectious disease. Compared to the wars that preceded them, however, the Napoleonic Wars seemed to those in Britain who experienced them extraordinarily bloody and destructive.

Beyond the stunning increase in the price of war paid in human lives, the staggering economic costs need to be acknowledged. Though it can be argued that Great Britain's traditional financial practices were as successful as its traditional military and naval strategies against Napoleon, it is still necessary to estimate the unprecedented financial burden war imposed on the country. A little past the middle of the eighteenth century, the Seven Years' War had cost the government £160 million a year, roughly triple the expense of war in the early years of the century. In comparison, the Napoleonic Wars cost roughly £1,600 million annually, a rate some ten times higher than at midcentury, barely a generation earlier.

To pay for these huge and accelerating costs, the bulk had to be borrowed and the bill left for the nation to repay, spread out over future peacetime years. By the war's end, the national debt had tripled. Because some part of the war's expense had to be paid for currently, taxes increased sharply, despite the growth of the national debt. By 1815 the government was raising £60 million a year annually in taxes, five times as much as it did toward the end of the American Revolution a long generation earlier. That represented an increase of thirty times the amount that had been collected in 1690. It is worth noting that the British paid taxes during the Napoleonic Wars at rates two or three times those the French imposed. Surprisingly, British taxpayers paid without significant protest.

If the taxpaying class accepted the heavy financial burdens of the war, the general population felt its direct impact unhappily in other ways. The war interrupted foreign trade, especially after 1806, when Napoleon implemented the Continental System in an effort to exclude all British commerce from Europe. While Napoleon's effort to bring Great Britain to its knees economically failed in the end, it was the source of considerable economic difficulty and dislocation. The Continental System prevented the importation of grain, which worked ultimately to the advantage of British farmers by pushing up domestic prices for their wheat. As this also necessarily drove up the price of bread, the staple food of the poor, the result was public disturbances. There were widespread bread riots in the 1790s when a combination of poor harvests at home and the war-driven interruptions in the importation of grain drove up prices significantly. Later, a persistent general inflationary pressure caused by the war drove up most prices, including bread, faster than worker's wages increased. This squeeze on the subsistence of the working poor and their families imposed the most serious and unendurable hardships. The result was hardly a surprise—more bread riots and a considerable threat to public order.

Chronic underemployment among casual farm laborers had been a growing problem for some time. As the war rapidly drove up basic food prices, local governments concerned themselves with the well-being of more than the unemployed. They were now obliged to subsidize the wages of their rural working poor (the "Speenhamland system"). Relief payments to the working poor—not just to the indigent wretches in the poorhouse—seemed a particularly dangerous idea to the proponents of the new, market-based political economy. However, the national government accepted the spread of the new system as the temporary price of public order and social safety.

The war also had negative effects on the smaller but rapidly growing nonagricultural sector of the economy. It interrupted foreign trade in goods, including both exports of British manufacturers and the re-export trade of foreign-made goods and raw materials carried in British shipping. Unemployment rose significantly among urban laborers whose work depended on foreign sales. The government responded to the complaints of urban workers by passing legislation against "combinations"; that is, rudimentary labor unions, which were understood as workers "conspiracies" to drive up wages. In the absence of regular police forces—an invention of the future—the government called upon its troops to control large threatening crowds and to break up their demonstrations.

The volunteers and the local militia, whose ranks were full of more prosperous members of society than the regular army of ruffians fighting in Europe, were used to put down public disturbances as firmly as the government dared. Those who could be identified as the leaders of riots or other threats to the public peace might be "transported" to the new penal colony in far-off Australia, or even hung for sedition.

While harsh tactics may have contained violent protests from the under class, it did not stop them. Late in the war, industrial workers who lost their jobs or saw their wages sharply reduced reacted angrily by smashing the machines that made their labor overpriced or took their jobs away. However violent these "Luddites" were, they were unable to stop the development of mechanized production.

British governments during the Napoleonic Wars were fortunate that the public tended to support them. Public opinion had not been uniformly hostile to the earliest stages of the French Revolution, and some voices were initially raised in its favor. Edmund Burke's fierce attack, *Reflections on the Revolution in France* (1790), was seen as extreme at first. Thomas Paine's answering *Rights of Man* (1791) was widely read and stirred anxiety in government circles that the propaganda in favor of democracy would carry the day. While the great aristocratic leaders of the Whigs such as Charles James Fox might celebrate their commitment to "liberty," "democracy" was dreaded by virtually all respectable people as the rule of the mob. As time went on, and especially after the execution of the French king, public opinion turned against the radicalism in Paris. What had earlier seemed hysteria in Burke now seemed to be statesmanlike prophecy. When Pitt reluctantly led the country into war against revolutionary France, he did not face massive protests. However, he could not rely on any vast natural reservoir of support. That had to be cultivated.

The government systematically suppressed groups that took a favorable view of the revolution in order to encourage popular reaction against radical politics. This was convenient in that it also helped choke off all demands for domestic political reform, a movement that had been gaining momentum since the 1780s. By the late 1790s, the political climate had darkened considerably. There was widespread repression, and those who expressed sympathy for the revolution or even reform found themselves under popular attack. Whatever popular sympathy there had been initially in Great Britain for the French revolutionary cause had largely disappeared by the time Napoleon came to power. The British government enjoyed great success in mobilizing opinion against Bonaparte, though most ministers continued to be regularly alarmed by reports of small and ineffectual radical groups opposing the government's anti-Napoleon stance. If the government won the propaganda war, there were always exceptional resisters such as the essayist William Hazlitt, who continued to defend Napoleon both during and after the war. The crucial political fact was that the split in Parliament within the Whig Party—the self-styled party of liberty—meant that there was no effective opposition to a conservative government at home. After the death of Fox, the Whigs' most eloquent spokesman, there were few voices in Parliament to present the Whig position.

Across the course of the eighteenth century, a common bond among "the British people" was created and a common national identity forged among English, Scots, Welsh, and perhaps even the much-abused Irish. British identity was defined in that series of struggles against foreign enemies. The ancestors of the Scots in 1814–1815 had risen in 1715 and 1745 against the "German kings," the Hanoverians George I and George II. Now Highland regiments fought and died for George III without hesitation. Whether the response was due to mere xenophobia or, more positively, the new force of patriotic nationalism, the Napoleonic Wars seem to have played a significant part in this process.

Though the war against "Boney" (never "Napoleon"), the foreign tyrant and bogeyman, certainly encouraged nascent patriotism, the domestic economic hardships imposed by the war generated sufficient difficulty for the government that it felt obliged to develop a number of harsh repressive measures and strengthen other, older ones designed to keep "the lower orders" in check by force if necessary. The legal guarantees against arbitrary government imprisonment provided by the habeas corpus act were suspended; treason was redefined to make prosecutions easier; harsh legislation was adopted against aliens. If popular opinion generally supported the war against "Boney," toward its end there was a sufficient revival of religious skepticism about the efficacy of slaughter as national policy to see the creation of the first organized pacifist groups. It would be a long time before these would find a hearing from serious statesmen. One exception to

Parliament's ultraconservative or reactionary cast was a group of evangelical Christians led by William Wilberforce who succeeded in passing legislation that abolished slavery in Great Britain; however, the institution itself remained untouched in the West Indies, where it had far greater economic significance.

Despite the vast increase in size and cost of the Napoleonic Wars, in many respects they were not so very different in character from the wars that had preceded them. To the extent that the Napoleonic Wars were the final part of the eighteenth-century's "second Hundred Years' War" and waged with the same technology as earlier wars, we should perhaps expect that they would not differ greatly. However, looking back at Great Britain with the perspective of lengthy hindsight, the country that emerged victorious after 1815 was clearly beginning to be a very different one from the country that had entered the contest against revolutionary France. How much those differences were due to the war in some direct fashion and how much to other more diffuse causes remains a matter of contention among historians.

Victory in 1815 left Great Britain for the first time essentially unchallenged as the great financial center of Europe and the dominant power in international trade. Over the following decades, to this commercial and financial success was added the extraordinary transformation that has been labeled since the 1880s the Industrial Revolution. The roots of British industrialization lay deep in the eighteenth century, but its profoundly transformative consequences became obvious to a great degree only after 1815, with the development of the steam engine, the locomotive, and the railway.

In the late nineteenth and the twentieth centuries, the connection between industrial development and the conduct of warfare became an obvious one. However, the Napoleonic Wars, despite their increase in scale compared with earlier wars, were waged largely with eighteenth-century technologies that had changed little, if at all, over time. Experiments with canned foods, aerial balloons for observational purposes, submarines, and rifled firearms (too expensive to issue to common soldiers) were all on the margins of warfare. The reality of military experience for vast numbers of men was that they still marched on foot, as soldiers always had. Cannons and muskets were not so different from the ones used a century earlier; nor were the wooden ships that, with their batteries of guns, were still the most formidable application of existing military technology.

When later historians, writing in the aftermath of World War I, reconsidered the impact of the Napoleonic Wars, they were impressed by the ferocity and destructiveness of both conflicts. Understandably enough, their analysis focused on the negative consequences of war. Many of their British and American predecessors, writing from the vantage point of nineteenth-century liberalism, assumed the truth of its theory that free trade would be a guarantor of international peace. All states would be drawn by economic self-interest into the marketplace, eventually producing universal peace and prosperity. By the end of World War I's murderous fighting, this theory seemed thoroughly discredited.

In similar fashion, economic historians trying to work out the relationship between the Napoleonic Wars and the origins of the Industrial Revolution in Great Britain made the case that the war had diverted economic activity and capital away from productive enterprise into the futility and wastefulness of massive slaughter and destruction. In the view of such historians, the Napoleonic Wars should have shown, as World War I did, that the wholesale economic irrationality of war between great states must have retarded economic growth and development.

More recent historians, however, influenced by the economic theories of John Maynard Keynes published during the Great Depression of the 1930s, concluded that however reckless and destructive wars might be they also provide economic stimulus and encourage basic technological change and development. If the debate among economic historians has not been settled, it has left a rough consensus that the Napoleonic Wars did not slow economic growth in Great Britain. In fact, it has left room for the argument that the wars may have promoted some development, contributing to the country's early industrialization.

Another long-term but crucial issue raised by the Napoleonic Wars was the matter of democracy. British political institutions had changed little over the eighteenth century. For example, the traditional tension between Crown and Parliament continued. However, Great Britain's defeat in the American War of Independence raised the issue of its system of government's effectiveness. In the 1780s the response was "administrative reform"—repair the machinery of government, rationalize its functions, and eliminate the accumulated anomalies of the past.

The American experiment with democracy represented a far more basic challenge to the British political system. With its relatively open franchise, "popular government" in America proved not to be mob rule, as the pessimistic critics of democracy had expected. British "representative" government, on the other hand, was clearly dominated by its great landed families.

The French Revolution raised the issue for all European societies of whether they ought to be democracies, though, given the Reign of Terror, the question was put far more ambiguously than by the more benign American experiment. Whether Napoleon was seen as a revolutionary democrat seeking justice and opportunity for anyone of talent or as a traditional tyrant and opportunistic usurper, he was easily understood to be a danger to the existing social order. The conservative powers were obliged to coalesce, putting aside their ancient rivalries to defeat him if they hoped to survive. In Great Britain this empowered those who were fiercest about resisting any basic changes in Britain's own political order.

However, the British system, which prided itself on its representative character, had in fact drifted very far from that. Burke's casuistry to the contrary notwithstanding, most of the king's subjects were not represented by or in Parliament. Burke's argument that all the country's interests were "virtually" represented could not satisfy the vast majority who had no voice in government and whose interests were often ignored by it. The first halting steps to deal with that problem were not taken until 1832 with the passage of the First Reform Bill, and then only after an enormous uproar that deeply divided the political elites. It was only in the hope of avoiding a revolution of the kind France had suffered that Great Britain gradually began to reform its political order in the 1830s, piecemeal and with the greatest possible caution.

The Napoleonic Wars had been an era of considerable political repression in Great Britain. Thought of change in the system had been ruled out as too subversive; democracy was labeled an ideology that, whatever it promised, could only give aid and comfort to the nefarious doctrines of a dangerous enemy. The Napoleonic Wars froze the old aristocratic political system in place and prevented its rationalization or even the most modest gestures toward democratization for a long generation.

In the long run, however, the world that Burke looked back upon would not stay unchanged. Industrialization, and ultimately, democratization loomed on the horizon. In the short run, the principal British beneficiaries of the Napoleonic Wars were the agricultural landlords, who enjoyed a period of considerable prosperity, and, far more unevenly, parts of the merchant community, especially those nimble enough to respond to the loss of European markets by smuggling or switching to the newly opened Latin American markets. Most of the country's "lower orders" had to pay the price of readjustment to the rapidly changing economy; at least for the moment, their standard of living was under siege.

Above all, those who had governed Great Britain during the conflict coped with challenges of unprecedented size and found themselves at war's end in charge of a country that was no longer merely one of a number of major European states. Britain had entered a period of great power, wealth, and influence. London was becoming the financial capital of the world, Britain its first industrial workshop, and the country's statesmen the masters of a global empire greater than ancient Rome's. Having survived a military challenge that might have conquered their island kingdom, Britain's political elites felt comfortably prepared to exercise their newly gained influence on all they surveyed. If they could withstand the potential challenge to their rule posed by the forces calling for democracy, they could govern the island for some time. That was their reward for a great military and naval victory in the "great war" of their time.

SELECTED BIBLIOGRAPHY

Best, Geoffrey. *War and Society in Revolutionary Europe, 1770–1870.* New York: St. Martin's Press, 1986. A general survey of the European context of civil-military relations.

Bowen, H. V. *War and British Society, 1688–1815.* New York: Cambridge University Press, 1998. This brief survey examines the recent literature on the domestic impact of the eighteenth-century's wars.

Brewer, John. *The Sinews of Power: War, Money, and the English State, 1688–1783.* New York: Knopf, 1988. A close study of eighteenth-century British practices of state finance for war. Develops the concept of the "fiscal-military state."

Brown, Richard. *Revolution, Radicalism, and Reform: England, 1780–1846.* Cambridge: Cambridge University Press, 2000. An introductory survey of political developments before and after the Napoleonic Wars.

Chandler, David, ed. *The Oxford Illustrated History of the British Army.* Oxford: Oxford University Press, 1994. A recent collection of essays. Particularly relevant to this period is D. Gates, "The Transformation of the Army, 1793–1815," which makes the case for discontinuity.

Christie, Ian. *Wars and Revolutions: Britain, 1760–1815.* Cambridge: Harvard University Press, 1982. An excellent general survey emphasizing issues relevant to the problem of state management of war.

Colley, Linda. *Britons: Forging the Nation, 1707–1837.* New Haven: Yale University Press, 1992. A study of the formation of British national identity.

Cookson, J. E. *The Friends of Peace: Anti-War Liberalism in England, 1793–1815.* Cambridge: Cambridge University Press, 1982. A careful monograph.

Deane, Phyllis. "War and Industrialization." In *War and Economic Development,* edited by J. M. Winter, 91–102. Cambridge: Cambridge University Press, 1975. Argues the case that the Napoleonic Wars did not interrupt Great Britain's economic development.

Dickinson, H. T., ed. *Britain and the French Revolution, 1789–1815.* New York: St. Martin's Press, 1989. A wide-ranging collection of scholarly articles usefully surveying recent scholarship.

Emsley, Clive. *British Society and the French Wars, 1793–1815.* Totowa, NJ: Rowman and Littlefield, 1979. A careful study of the domestic response of Great Britain to the French Revolution.

Evans, E. J. *William Pitt the Younger.* New York: Routledge, 1999. The most recent brief treatment of the most important British political figure, from the early 1780s to his death in 1806.

Kennedy, Paul. *The Rise and Fall of the Great Powers: Economic Change and Military Conflict from 1500 to 2000.* New York: Random House, 1987. A detailed

The Napoleonic Wars

comparative work examining the relative strengths and strategies of the Great Powers since 1500. Useful tables.

Mitchell, L. G. *Charles James Fox*. New York: Cambridge University Press, 1992. A recent study of the most important political figure of the period after Pitt.

Sherwig. J. M. *Guineas and Gunpowder: British Foreign Aid in the Wars with France, 1793–1815*. Cambridge: Harvard University Press, 1969. A study of the financial inducements on which Britain based its coalitions.

Stevenson, John. *Popular Disturbances in England, 1700–1832*. 2nd ed. London: Longman, 1992. An authoritative account.

Stone, Lawrence, ed. *An Imperial State at War: Britain from 1689 to 1815*. London: Routledge, 1994. A collection of essays focused on historian John Brewer's concept of the fiscal-military state.

Thompson, E. P. *The Making of the English Working Class*. New York: Vintage Books, 1963. Studies sympathetic to any socio-economic class are always regarded as controversial. There will always be someone to raise a fuss.

The century of Pax Britannica (1815–1914) was also the century of rapid and forceful British imperial expansion into places such as India, as this political cartoon shows. Reproduced from the Collections of the Library of Congress.

4

Pax Britannica, 1815–1914

INTRODUCTION

Between the end of the Napoleonic Wars in 1815 and the outbreak of World War I in 1914, there were no major world wars. During that time Great Britain, by virtually any index or standard, was the leading nation in the world, and as a consequence the period has often been referred to as the *Pax Britannica*, the "Peace of Britain." (In a similar way, the period since 1945 has sometimes been referred to as the *Pax Americana*.)

In 1815 the British navy controlled the seas, and Great Britain no longer needed fear that any nation would come to dominate continental Europe. To maintain the *Pax Britannica*, British policy aimed to continue Britain's naval supremacy and worked to maintain the balance of power among the European states, primarily through diplomacy and, occasionally, the threat of force. British naval supremacy was acknowledged, and since at this time Britain was more interested in acquiring markets for its industrial goods than adding to its roster of colonies, the foreign secretary from 1815 until 1822, Lord Castlereagh, was able to work effectively with other European governments to moderate the peace settlement with France, check Prussian aggressions, and dampen Spain's ambitions to recover its American empire.

Great Britain also benefited from being nationally unified and economically strong when its rivals were politically divided, as Germany and Italy were, or recently defeated in war, as France had been. Standing in Britain's path to even greater profits and international authority were the conservative monarchies of the Continent, who had little use for the kind of free-trade international marketplace that British business owners sought. Under Castlereagh, Britain broke away from the loose alliance created at the Congress of Vienna that had made peace with France in 1815 and set out on an independent foreign policy course for the rest of the century.

At home after 1815, the cause of free trade became an important adjunct of international policy. The new business elite believed that the restrictive trade regulations left over from the eighteenth century were major impediments to their own profit margins and to the nation's prosperity in general. The movement for free trade aimed to rid Great Britain of these regulations. When in 1842 the Tory government of Sir Robert Peel introduced the first income tax since 1816 as a source of national income, the door was opened for lowering or eliminating tariffs, which had been an important revenue source for the government. By 1845 Parliament had lowered tariffs on more than 750 items and abolished duties on most raw materials that were important to British industry. The principal remaining obstacle was the Corn Laws, a set of duties on agricultural products (especially corn) designed to protect British farmers. By the 1840s they no longer served their purpose, and the free-trade campaign focused on repealing them. Thanks in part to the Irish potato blight and resulting famine, and to a bad corn harvest in England, Peel was able to drastically lower (but not completely repeal) the duties on imported corn in 1846. In the generation after the "repeal" of the Corn Laws, British exports rose by a factor of four, from £47 million to £200 million.

The most prominent mid-Victorian politician was Lord Palmerston—indeed, the period between about 1850 and 1865 is sometimes called the Age of Palmerston. A Conservative Party leader who served twice as prime minister (1855–1858; 1859–1865), he was also keenly interested in foreign policy and was foreign secretary on three occasions. Under Palmerston and Benjamin Disraeli, who followed very similar policies, Great Britain between the 1850s and 1870s was at the height of its prestige and power, and managed to maintain them while staying out of all of Europe's wars except the Crimean War (1853–1856). Palmerston handled British diplomacy with less tact than his predecessors, adopting the attitude that British friendship was available but only to those who were willing to dance to Britain's tune. He saw no need for Britain to go out and court the affections of others. At times this made British policy appear inconsistent and even impulsive, but it did keep others on their guard and enabled Palmerston to maintain the balance of power on the Continent. This commitment led to British involvement in the Crimean War, which was undertaken to prevent Russian expansion that would upset the balance of power in Russia's favor.

In the case of the American Civil War (1861–1865), British public opinion was sharply divided. The upper class saw the South's secession as another example of national self-determination, not unlike that of Italy at the same time, while the working class sympathized with the antislavery forces of the North. Some political leaders wanted to grant diplomatic recognition to the South, which would have been a major boost to its chances of winning the war, but Palmerston opted to wait until the war took a significant turn in favor of the South. It never did, and British recognition never came. Thus, a complete rupture (and possibly war) with the North was averted, and the substantial commercial ties that had developed remained intact.

In the 1860s, the British Empire consisted of India, several white-populated colonies such as Canada, Australia, and New Zealand, and an array of smaller colonies in the Caribbean, Africa, Asia, and the Pacific. Much more expansion occurred in the 1880s and 1890s, although Britain never formulated a long-range plan of imperial growth, and some prominent politicians were very skeptical about colonial expansion in general and the responsibilities empire entailed. Although Disraeli flattered Queen Victoria in 1876 by making her empress of India, he also referred to British colonies as "millstones around our neck."

Imperial growth veered off in several directions in mid-Victorian Great Britain. Some colonies were acquired through the efforts of ambitious governors-general wanting to extend their domain and their authority; others were added to augment trade routes or to serve as military outposts. The history of the American colonies served as a reminder that the colonial grip need not be too firm; Canada and the Australian states were given internal self-government and moved toward federation, and enlightened governors such as Lord Ripon in India encouraged more native Indian participation in the government of that large and diverse colony.

Beginning with the second Disraeli government in 1874, British imperial policy accelerated. White demands for land led to trouble with Zulus in South Africa; conflict with Russia involved the British in Afghanistan; and economic imperatives contributed to the establishment of protectorates over the Gold Coast in West Africa, the Malay states in Southeast Asia, and Fiji in the Pacific. In the 1880s and 1890s, international rivalries created the so-called scramble for Africa, in which Great Britain's prizes included Egypt, Nigeria, the Rhodesias, Kenya, and—after the Boer War—the Transvaal and the Orange Free State.

Although much of the rationale for American territorial expansionism at the end of the nineteenth century was grounded in economics and the search for foreign markets, Martin Pugh argues that this was not the case with Great Britain. Most political leaders had reservations about colonial acquisitions, and most foreign investment went to older, more established colonies or to the United States. Those enterprises, such as the British East Africa Company, that did attempt to exploit the newer colonies economically were not very successful. Pugh notes that to politicians such as Conservative prime minister Robert A. T. Gascoyne-Cecil, Lord Salisbury, colonies were useful as pawns in an international chess game; to retain the goodwill of Germany, for example, Britain gave Germany a parcel of land in East Africa.

By the end of the nineteenth century, cracks began to show in the Pax Britannica, most notably in present-day South Africa. There the Boers, Dutch-descended settlers who lived under a system of self-government in the Orange Free State and the Transvaal, were threatened by the discovery of gold in 1886, which made the British in neighboring Cape Colony more anxious to involve themselves in the Boer territories. In 1895 the so-called Jameson Raid was a failed British attempt to seize control of the Transvaal. This incident contributed to a gradual deterioration in Boer-English relations. The British governor-general, Alfred Milner, and the president of the Transvaal, Paul Kruger, tried to negotiate a settlement in June 1899, but when they were unsuccessful the Boer War broke out.

Britain won this difficult war in 1902 but in doing so showed the inadequacies of the British military as well as Britain's growing isolation from the rest of Europe. (It is worth noting that Britain received the most support from the United States, then involved in its own colonial war in the Philippines.) There were no offers of assistance from other European nations, but there was a good deal of internal political dissension in Parliament, about both the apparent lack of principle in the war and the treatment of native people, many of whom were herded into unhealthy detention camps, where significant numbers died. One consequence of the war was that Britain recognized its isolation and in 1902 began to craft a series of alliances, first with the Japanese and then with the French, that would be an essential element in the course of events leading to World War I in 1914.

Yet the British Empire remained very popular among the British people. Magazines made heroes of colonial explorers, novels and travel accounts set in exotic places were best-sellers, and philatelists enjoyed collecting the wide variety of stamps issued by far-flung outposts of the empire. World's fairs with a focus on imperial achievements were very popular, not only in Britain but also in France, Belgium, and even the United States, and vaudeville houses attracted large enthusiastic audiences with songs and skits glorifying the empire. Occasionally there was criticism—the Boer War, for instance, dragged on too long and left a residue of higher taxes but no obvious gains.

Imperial expansion also served as an outlet for emigration for those looking for greater economic opportunities than they could find in the crowded cities and towns of England. Well over ten million people left Great Britain between 1870 and 1914. Many went to the United States, but others sought new futures in Canada, Australia, and New Zealand. Because of the emigration, many families had relatives living in distant parts of the empire, which created bonds of loyalty and solidarity that help explain the ready response to the war in 1914.

INTERPRETIVE ESSAY
Lowell J. Satre

The expansion and development of empire that transformed the United Kingdom of Great Britain and Ireland during the nineteenth century traditionally is dated from 1815 to 1914. The empire expanded at the rate of about one hundred thousand square miles per year (equivalent to the areas of Ohio, Pennsylvania, and Maryland combined, plus a bit more) during the century. This total addition of approximately ten million square miles helped to make it the largest empire in world history, which reached its greatest extent shortly after World War I. This era of dramatic empire-building is often referred to as the *Pax Britannica*, the "Peace of Britain," implying that peace and prosperity reigned throughout the empire, as they had in ancient Rome during its Pax Romana. The use of the term *pax*, "peace," is misleading in both instances. In the case of the Pax Britannica, the use of military force, either in the form of the army or the navy, was common. The exercise of military power was enhanced by the wealth and the weapons of war generated by another great transforming event of nineteenth-century Britain, The Industrial Revolution.

No one institution was responsible for governing the huge empire. Authority was spread throughout a myriad of agencies, including the monarch and Parliament, the War Office and the Admiralty, the India Office and the Foreign Office, the Treasury and the Board of Trade. Great Britain's formal empire consisted of the white dominions of Canada, Australia, New Zealand, and South Africa, which were colonies extensively settled by Europeans that had gained considerable rights of self-government in the period from the 1860s to 1914. Most of the formal empire, however, was made up of colonies populated by non-Europeans who enjoyed no self-government but were governed by representatives from Britain. These colonies are often collectively referred to as the "dependent empire," of which India was the largest and most important part. In addition to the formal empire, there existed an informal empire. Britain, through its military prowess and trading power, effectively controlled or influenced the economic and political fortunes of many other areas of the world, notably nations in Latin America, without bearing the heavy cost of direct government. The informal empire flourished until the 1870s, when Britain and several European nations began engaging in an orgy of land-grabbing, especially in Africa and south Asia. This aggressive scramble for colonies, which lasted from about 1880 to 1914 and which historians term the *New Imperialism*, focused the attention of the British on the empire.

India, which England acquired piecemeal through the East India Company between 1757 and 1842, was the jewel of the empire. In 1857 many sepoys (Indian soldiers in the East India Company army) rose in revolt, marking the beginning of the Indian Mutiny, an event marked by brutal conduct on both sides. In response to the uprising, Great Britain restructured its government in India, abolishing the East India Company and instituting direct control through an appointed viceroy and a new cabinet officer, the secretary of state for India. Britain's control of India had a direct impact on its diplomatic relations with other nations. Russia, because of its close proximity to India, had long been deemed a threat. In both the 1840s and the 1870s, fear of Russian intrigue in an unsettled Afghanistan on India's northwest frontier led to two British invasions of Afghanistan. Benjamin Disraeli's Conservative government purchased 44 percent of the shares in the Suez Canal in 1875 to ensure control of this strategic waterway to India. When Russia invaded the Ottoman Empire in 1877 in response to Turkish atrocities in Bulgaria, Disraeli came to the defense of Constantinople to help restrict Russian power in the eastern Mediterranean and India. This confrontation with Russia led to the emergence of jingoism, a mindless enthusiasm for war expressed most notably in the large British music halls.

Public support for an aggressive empire was not consistent in the nineteenth century. As Great Britain's industries required ever greater raw materials and markets, reformers called for a dismantling of the old mercantile system of regulations and tariffs, which were seen as hindering competition. In the second quarter of the nineteenth century, free traders and advocates of fewer government regulations often turned a critical eye to the colonies, which they associated with the closely regulated empire. While free trade triumphed by 1850, few critics or responsible leaders had advocated the breakup of the empire. Rather, they wished to make the white settler colonies more self-governing and hence more efficient. To a certain extent, they looked upon those particular colonies as part of an extended family that would remain loyal to the parent, even after reaching political maturity.

In the 1870s Disraeli attempted to wrap his party in the mantle of empire, by arranging for Queen Victoria to become empress of India in 1876. He perceived a growing public enthusiam for the empire, and he sought to capitalize on it for political gain. This public support, however, was fleeting, as a significant portion of the public turned against Disraeli after his aggressive, bloody colonial wars in Afghanistan and against the Zulus in South Africa in the late 1870s. Actually, both political parties supported the empire. In 1882 William Gladstone's Liberal government conducted an invasion of Egypt, where a nationalist movement threatened British investment interests. Gladstone decided that temporary occupation of Egypt was necessary to bring about significant reform and to protect property. This temporary commitment lasted until 1922; for the forty years following 1882 Egypt was a central factor in Great Britain's diplomatic activities.

The greatest imperial impact on British politics involved Ireland. While Ireland is often treated as a domestic issue, since it was governed directly as a part of the United Kingdom after the Act of Union of 1801, it can also be viewed as England's oldest colony, dating to the twelfth century. No other "colony" occupied as much time of the cabinet or Parliament as Ireland. In the 1820s Daniel O'Connell led a successful movement to seat Roman Catholic members of Parliament (M.P.s) in London. The Irish potato famine of the 1840s led to a staggering death toll, an ineffective government relief program, and the migration of millions of Irish. The home rule movement, led first by Isaac Butt and more dramatically by Charles Stewart Parnell, forced various Liberal and Tory governments after 1870 to address Ireland's outstanding political and economic problems. While the Home Rulers wanted direct local control over Ireland, except for defense and foreign policy, governments were reluctant to admit such power, fearing that granting home rule to Ireland would lead to the same demand by other parts of the empire. Landowners and political administrators were harassed and killed; the term *boycott* entered the English language after Irish peasants refused to deal with Captain C. C. Boycott, a land agent. Parnell, who disavowed violence, used filibustering tactics to bring business in Parliament to a standstill. Governments used both coercive measures and ameliorating land acts in attempts to buy peace. Gladstone, who became a convert to the Irish cause, introduced home rule bills in both 1886 and 1893 and in the process helped to divide the Liberal Party, which was politically powerless for two decades. A home rule bill finally passed in 1914, but it was not implemented because of the onset of World War I.

Many British leaders perceived the empire as a source of strength for the nation. Trade, notably in raw materials and foodstuffs, flourished between Great Britain and its colonies; colonial ports protected and supplied the navy; colonies occupied strategic routes, including the Suez Canal and the Cape of Good Hope in South Africa; and possession of a huge empire brought diplomatic respect and power. The government of India maintained, at no cost to Britain, a very large Indian army that the mother country could use at a moment's notice in military conflict, such as the two Afghanistan wars and the South African (Boer) War of 1899–1902. But difficulties in the empire also caused concern and pessimism within the public mind and amongst the leaders.

Joseph Chamberlain, colonial secretary in Lord Salisbury's Conservative government, reluctantly supported the war against the South African Republic, which was fought to ensure British economic and political control over all of South Africa. Chamberlain, earlier a leader of the Liberal Party, had broken with Gladstone in 1886 over home rule for Ireland. As colonial secretary after 1895, he advocated developing all parts of the empire through trade and investment. He was one of the New Imperialists, who believed that British power would be preserved and enhanced through a more unified and well-defined empire. Most political and military leaders anticipated that the war in South Africa, which began in October 1899, would be a brief and easy task against the numerically inferior Boers. A series of setbacks for the British army ensued, climaxed by Black Week in December 1899. The government summoned Lord Roberts and Lord Kitchener, military heroes in earlier colonial wars in India and the Sudan, to win the war and maintain Great Britain's prestige. The war, which ended in May 1902 with a negotiated peace, cost Britain £250,000,000 and the lives of twenty-two thousand soldiers. Moreover, while Britain was so heavily committed militarily in South Africa, its ability to act elsewhere in the world was dramatically limited. This weakness helped to drive Britain out of its traditional diplomatic isolation and into an alliance with Japan in 1902, and to diplomatic agreements with France in 1904 and Russia in 1907.

At the turn of the century, Great Britain faced a crisis of confidence that went far beyond the empire. Even before the Boer War, British confidence was shaken by economic competition from Germany and the United States, as well as by Germany's increasing military and naval power. A series of studies and reforms, touching on many parts of life, was carried out from 1902 to 1914 as critics became obsessed with making the country more efficient.

The British army had been shaped in the nineteenth century to deal with colonial wars. Small army units, headed by an officer who formulated strategy and directed all staff work, sufficed to bring victories over ill-equipped natives. British soldiers, volunteers from the working class who spent much of their careers abroad, were often physically undersized and poorly educated. The navy, on the other hand, was considered to be the first line of home defense and the protector of the empire. On the whole, the navy was well funded. There was almost no systematic cooperation between the two services. Reforms of the army and navy began immediately after the Boer War. Richard Burdon Haldane, the Liberal war secretary, increased the army's efficiency by setting up an intelligence department and a general staff, by organizing larger self-contained army divisions, by streamlining the auxiliary forces, and by setting up officer training corps programs in public schools. The navy, under Lord Fisher, launched the "dreadnought," a large battleship that was designed more to secure the homeland than to protect the colonies. The Committee of Imperial Defence, set up in 1902, was formed to secure closer cooperation between military chiefs and civilian political leaders. Social measures designed to ensure a healthier and more efficient laboring class included minimal medical care and school lunches for poor children, minimum wages for women and children in menial jobs, labor exchanges for the unemployed, and pensions for the elderly.

The most divisive political issue involving the empire was Chamberlain's proposal in 1903 that Great Britain introduce an imperial preference tariff. After a half century of free trade, Chamberlain advocated the imposition of a tariff on all goods entering Britain, while permitting a reduced duty on imperial goods, in the process creating a huge imperial trading union. The revenue gained from the duty would be used to pay for Britain's social programs and defense needs. Chamberlain, like several other political leaders, regarded the development of the empire as the key to maintaining and expanding Britain's political and economic role in the world. He held meetings with the dominions' prime ministers in 1897 and 1902 to explore means of implementing his dream of political, economic, and defense cooperation between Britain and its colonies. In 1904 Chamberlain resigned from the government to devote his time to converting the nation to his concept of tariff reform. While winning converts within conservative circles, his proposal divided the country and failed to gain the support of the prime ministers of the dominions, where the growth of nationalism was leading to looser ties with the mother country.

Queen Victoria came to be closely identified with the empire. For reasons of personal prestige and recognition, the queen wished to be titled "empress of India." To appease the queen and to send a strong message to

Russia and its emperor, Disraeli in 1876 submitted the Royal Titles Bill to Parliament. While many Radicals and Liberals found the term *empress* pretentious and un-English, the bill passed. Although at the time not a particularly popular monarch (Victoria had withdrawn from many of her public activities after the death of her husband, Prince Albert, in 1861), her close identification with the British at home and abroad, as well as with her colonial subjects, increased dramatically over the last quarter of the nineteenth century. Adulation for Queen Victoria and her devotion to the empire peaked in the Diamond Jubilee celebrating the sixtieth year of her reign in 1897. Unlike the Golden Jubilee of 1887, when the heads of European states were present, the Diamond Jubilee featured the leaders of the dominions and dependent colonies. A grand military parade in London, led by Lord Roberts and a captain of the Life Guards, featured over 45,000 British and imperial soldiers. The queen telegraphed to her subjects throughout the empire: "From my heart I thank my beloved people. May God bless them." The imperial theme was incorporated into the inauguration festivities of Edward VII in 1902 and George V in 1911. George V also participated in a huge coronation *durbar*, or formal reception, in Delhi in 1911, as the first reigning British monarch to visit India.

In spite of its extensive involvement in colonial affairs, the British government remained British, not imperial. Parliamentary elections seldom focused on imperial affairs (the 1900 "khaki election," in which the Boer War was a central issue, was an exception). All M.P.'s were residents of the United Kingdom. The imperial autocracy which was so often exercised in the colonies did not alter the government in Great Britain, which became increasingly democratic.

In their daily lives, the British were constantly confronted with evidence of the existence of the empire. It is virtually impossible, however, to measure precisely how this plethora of stimuli from the empire shaped people's social and cultural lives. In the nineteenth century, minds were shaped by the written and spoken word. The reading public grew in numbers following substantial state support of education in 1870 and the transformation of the print industry, which made possible the large-scale, inexpensive production of books, newspapers, and magazines. Lots of printed material was needed for such a readership, and the empire made good, exciting copy, from Captain Frederick Marryat's *The Settlers of Canada* and *Diary of the Continent* (about the invasion of Burma) of the 1830s and 1840s to H. Rider Haggard's novels about Africa and Rudyard Kipling's tales of India toward the end of the century. David Livingstone's *Missionary Travels and Researches in South Africa* (1857) made him an instant folk hero. The Royal Geographic Society sponsored explorers and hosted meetings, whose proceedings were carried in newspapers. Colonial conflicts provided settings for war artists and correspondents; Winston Churchill first gained public notice for his accounts of wars in Sudan and South Africa. Indian words that reshaped the English language during the nineteenth century were *cashmere, karma, khaki, panda, polo, pyjama, sitar, swastika, thug*, and *yoga*. Opposition to imperialism influenced the writings of Olive Schreiner, William Morris, and John Hobson. Theaters presented graphic accounts of the Indian Mutiny, and *Savage South Africa* opened in 1899 to enthusiastic audiences and positive reviews.

Boys' literature on the empire ranged from the pernicious to the wholesome. Many of the novels of G. A. Henty, Robert Louis Stevenson, and H. G. Kingston were set overseas and appealed to juveniles. Publishing companies featured single or collective biographies of colonial heroes. "Penny dreadfuls," on one hand, were graphic stories published in periodicals such as *Sons of Britannia*, replete with the cruelty of schoolboys to one another and occasional travels abroad, during which young men mixed with others of openly "inferior" races. Limbs were lost, lives expended, all with little remorse. Critics, ministers, and public authorities blamed the penny dreadfuls for causing a rise in violence among the youth. On the other hand, *Boys' Own Paper*, sponsored by the Religious Tract Society, ran stories with an acceptable level of violence that aided worthwhile imperial endeavors such as missionary work to the "heathens." For all of its violence, writers of juvenile literature generally embodied British ideals that they believed to be important to the mission of serving the empire. Patrick Dunae contends that the adventure stories "provided boys not only with escapist fiction, but also with a sense of history and an awareness of their imperial heritage" (Dunae, "Boy's Literature," 121).

Many activities for boys were oriented toward the empire and the military. In the public schools, athleticism and the playing fields helped to develop a fierce loyalty to the school, the nation, and the empire. Cadet corps were established in public schools starting in the 1870s and proved to be a useful recruiting tool for the military services. The Boys' Brigade, with a religious and military orientation, had almost seven hundred companies in England and Scotland by 1896. The Boy Scouts, founded in 1908 by Robert Baden-Powell (the defender of Mafeking during the Boer War), was designed to address the social problems and physical shortcomings so graphically exposed by the war and to promote patriotism in the nation and the empire. Baden-Powell, a career army officer with experience throughout the empire, wished to instill obedience, loyalty, courtesy, and thrift in working-class boys.

Music halls, which were phenomenally popular in late nineteenth-century Britain, promoted the glories of empire to all of society, but especially to the working class. The term *jingo* was added to the English language in a music hall song sung by the Great Macdermott in 1877 in the midst of the furor over the Russian advance toward Constantinople. The chorus ran:

> We don't want to fight, but by jingo if we do,
> We've got the ships, we've got the men, we've got the money too.
> We've fought the Bear before, and while we're Britons true,
> The Russians shall not have Constantinople. (Quoted in
>   MacKenzie, *Imperialism and Popular Culture*, 25)

But the patriots did not totally control the music halls. At the other end of the political spectrum was the entertainer Herbert Campbell, who in the nineteenth century sang,

> I don't want to fight, I'll be slaughtered if I do!
> I'll change my gos and sell my kit and pop my rifle too!
> I don't like war, I ain't no Briton true,
> And I'll let the Russians have Constantinople. (Quoted in
>   Senelick, "Politics as Entertainment," 172)

Singers did not attempt to educate or explain; they showed the empire in plain, patriotic terms. The music hall entertainers, however, did not always reflect the views of the working class, who simply enjoyed the entertainment. Some historians argue that fervor for war, as shown in the mindless enthusiasm in England over the relief of the small and inconsequential town of Mafeking during the South African War, was more lower middle class than working class in origin.

Trappings of empire, however, were everywhere in British life by the turn of the century. Photography brought stereoscopes, slides, picture postcards, and motion pictures filled with tropical scenes, wars, and the imperial monarchy to the citizens. Food from the empire was packaged in brightly decorated boxes and tins with idyllic or curious colonial scenes. Plates, mugs, and sheet music commemorated jubilees and other imperial events. The Crystal Palace Exhibition in 1911 was held in three-quarter scale colonial structures connected by a train that chugged through terrain displaying local colonial resources. Many middle- and upper-class organizations, including the Royal Colonial Institute, the Imperial Federation League, the Victoria League, and the League of Empire, engaged in educational or propaganda activities centered on the empire.

Ironically, in a period when Britons were increasingly exposed to the empire and its paraphernalia, there was no appreciable understanding of the nonwhite subjects at home or abroad. The British antislavery movement, which led to the freeing of slaves in the empire in the 1830s and continued thereafter to focus on bondage elsewhere in the world, did little to alter the stereotypical views of the inferiority of Caribbean blacks and Indians. Some blacks in Britain, offspring of freed slaves, worked for improvements in their lives and as a result often felt the wrath of police authorities. Similar attitudes were held in regard to Indians. The Indian Mutiny and the brutal practices of *suttee* (the self-immolation of widows) and *thuggee* (ritual murder and theft), suppressed by the English, caused many British, at home or in India, to look upon the Indians as ungrateful and bestial subjects. Likewise, the popular image of black Africans did not fit the European ideal. The Africans' nakedness was often associated with immorality. Their religions, traditional or Islam, were seen respectively as steeped in ignorance or involved in the slave trade. Armed rebellions by Africans throughout the late nineteenth century, by New Zealand Maoris in the 1860s and by Jamaicans in 1865, reinforced a stereotypical view of inferior and savage subjects unable to appreciate English values and in need of a strong guiding hand. Nineteenth-century Victorian scientists attested to the inferiority of Africans, and this was enhanced by the doctrine of evolution that was currently the rage. Relatively few Britons had any real knowledge of non-European subjects, nor did most know where many of the colonies were or how the empire was administered. By the turn of the century there was a small but growing number of Indians in England, including students studying law for or for the Indian civil service. Those minorities suffered discrimination in housing and were perceived as immoral, sly, and dangerous, particularly after political unrest mounted in India.

The empire offered an alternative life for people in the United Kingdom, and millions moved to the colonies. Public schools and universities taught that students had a moral obligation to help administer the empire, and many middle-class citizens went to white settlement colonies; fewer, to India, Africa, and other nonwhite possessions. In India they served as army officers and government administrators, directing reform movements—especially before the Indian Mutiny—and living on a much higher material scale than they could have in England, because of decent pay and a host of inexpensive servants. The dominions attracted a significant number of single, middle-class men and women who lacked opportunities in Great Britain or simply wished to explore another society. "Gentlemen" appeared on ranches in Canada, and distressed "gentlewomen" adapted quickly in Canada, Australia, and New Zealand to meaningful lives as teachers, governesses, shopkeepers, traders, and servants after 1830. British Protestant missionary societies had sent an estimated ten thousand missionaries abroad by 1899.

The greatest number of emigrants came from the working class. Some were forced to move abroad: from 1788 to 1860, the government shipped 160,000 convicts to penal colonies in Australia where, after serving their time, many became the backbone of a democratic and egalitarian society. Attempting to reduce the cost of poor relief in Great Britain after the end of the Napoleonic wars, the government also dispatched 25,000 paupers to Australia from 1834 to 1860. Retired soldiers took up land in Canada and Cape Colony (South Africa) after 1815. Most workers and members of the lower middle class paid their own fare to the colonies, often as a part of an organized settlement. Edward Gibbon Wakefield was the most well-known advocate of the systematic development of the colonies. He wished to bring together the surplus labor and capital of the United Kingdom and the abundant land of the colonies. While not always successful, his planned settlements in Australia and New Zealand provided for the re-creation of English communities, complete with landlords and laborers, churches and libraries.

British humanitarian societies engaged in the most notorious example of coerced emigration, sending out tens of thousands of children to white settlement colonies, some one hundred thousand to Canada alone from 1870 to 1914. By the middle of the nineteenth century, thousands of children in London had no permanent residence and slept in hovels or under the arches of bridges. Organizations headed by Maria Rye and Annie Macpherson, concerned over the moral corruption of youngsters in the congested cities, arranged for the children's transportation to Canada and New Zealand, where they were placed in homes or institutions. Sponsors also believed that the pauper children would be trained in a skill that would help alleviate the labor shortage in the colonies. The greatest proponent and practitioner of the export of boys was Dr. Thomas Barnardo, who set up an extensive gathering and distribution system starting in 1882. Objections to the high cost of the emigration schemes, the lack of supervision or training, and the hardship on the children were routinely overridden or ignored. While some of the children flourished and became successful businessmen, others fell into a life of crime. Many children fled their new homes, while others later in life attempted to find out the circumstances of their emigration. Subsequent evidence proved that many had not been orphaned but had been placed temporarily in rescue homes in Great Britain when their parents could not provide for them.

The empire's economic impact on Great Britain has proved difficult to measure. Dramatic changes occurred in Britain's economy during the Pax Britannica, as the nation switched from mercantilism, with its extensive regulations and tariffs, to a system of free trade. The period also witnessed the dramatic industrialization of a Britain increasingly dependent on overseas trade for foodstuffs to nourish its growing urban population, and on raw materials to feed its factories. The colonies helped to supply workers with inexpensive sugar, wheat, cocoa, and tea and provided the opportunity for millions of them to better their material life by migrating overseas. Manufacturers acquired cotton, wool, lumber, and jute for their factories, while entrepreneurs such as Cecil Rhodes created companies that extracted mineral wealth—particularly gold and diamonds—from the colonies. Throughout this period, Britain was the leading exporter of capital in the world, and a rather significant portion of it went to the colonies, especially the dominions. Banking and insurance, transportation and communication, and other service industries looked to the empire for business opportunities, especially by the late nineteenth century, as profits shrank because of increasing international competition. Colonies provided British investors with opportunities for secure investments at a reasonable return. The British government played an active role in developing and protecting these markets for British investors and traders. When necessary Britain intervened militarily to protect economic interests, as in Egypt in the early 1880s and South Africa in 1899. Perhaps more important, the British government decided on the course of a colony's economic life, basing such decisions primarily on what was good for the United Kingdom.

Historians have argued inconclusively for the past two centuries over the basic question: Did Great Britain and its people benefit materially from the empire in the long term? Economic historians have been unable to agree on a model to measure the return on investment. It is also difficult to weigh defense costs, since the building of a colonial harbor, for example, helped to protect not only the colony but also Britain's international trade. Certain historians contend that spending on colonial defense helped to bolster the nation's shipbuilding and armaments sectors. Yet Britain's dependence on protected colonial trade made companies less efficient. Goods purchased from the colonies could have been purchased elsewhere at more competitive rates. Hobson, at the turn of the century, argued persuasively that money spent overseas would have been better applied to the home front to the benefit of the working class.

By the beginning of the twentieth century, the daily life of almost everyone in Great Britain was shaped by the empire. The products and trappings of colonial life were evident everywhere. To the privileged classes, empire brought opportunities of wealth, prestige, and power, at home and abroad. Members of the working class had friends and relatives living in the colonies. Regardless of class, most people had a positive outlook on the empire. To many, Britain dutifully spread freedom and Christianity throughout its colonies. Others saw the empire as a logical product of Britain's natural superiority. Nevertheless, for many in the working class, the empire was of secondary importance. Their preoccupations were elsewhere. After the turn of the century, workers began gradually gravitating to the Labour Party, which was mildly critical of the empire, and they engaged in strikes, determined to improve their material lot and to gain more control over the workplace.

World War I brought a symbolic end to the nineteenth century. When Great Britain declared war in August 1914, it did so for herself and all of her colonies. The dominions and the dependent colonies contributed mightily to the war in terms of materials and soldiers. A very moving tribute to the sacrifices made by imperial and British soldiers is found in the 2,500 cemeteries maintained by the Commonwealth War Graves Commission in Belgium and France. The size of the empire grew markedly following the conclusion of the war, as Britain and some of her dominions gained control of former German colonies as well as areas once ruled by the Ottoman Empire.

Ties between Britain and her dominions continued to loosen, however. Dominion participation in the war had encouraged colonial nationalism, and a contingent of Irish Republicans had risen in rebellion in Easter 1916. The Balfour Declaration of 1926 and the Statute of Westminster of 1931 formally defined the dominions as "autonomous Communities within the British Empire." The colonies of the dependent empire gained their independence piecemeal following World War II.

SELECTED BIBLIOGRAPHY

Brantlinger, Patrick. *Rule of Darkness: British Literature and Imperialism, 1830–1914.* Ithaca, NY: Cornell University Press, 1988. On imperial themes in British literature.

Chamberlain, Muriel E. *Pax Britannica: British Foreign Policy, 1789–1914.* New York: Longman, 1988. Incorporates the development of the empire as a determining factor in British foreign policy.

Dunae, Patrick. "Boys' Literature and the Idea of Empire, 1870–1914." *Victorian Studies* 24 (autumn 1980): 105–121; and "Penny Dreadfuls: Late Nineteenth-Century Boys' Literature and Crime." *Victorian Studies*, 22 (winter 1979): 133–150. Empire as subject matter in boys' literature, including critics' response to the penny dreadfuls.

Hammerton, A. J. *Emigrant Gentlewomen: Genteel Poverty and Female Emigration, 1830–1914.* London: Croom Helm, 1979. Opportunities for "gentlewomen" in the empire.

Hobson, John. *Imperialism: A Study.* London: A. Constable, 1905. Classic analysis highly critical of imperialism.

Holt, Christine. *Victorian Attitudes to Race*. London: Routledge, 1971. Examination of British attitudes toward race as seen especially in Victorian Jamaica, Africa, and India.
James, Louis. "Tom Brown's Imperialist Sons." *Victorian Studies*, 17 (September 1973): 89–99. Describes journals publishing penny dreadfuls, including some circulation figures.
Judd, Denis. *Empire: The British Imperial Experience from 1765 to the Present*. London: HarperCollins, 1996. Interesting series of episodes in imperial history, occasionally reflecting on the impact on Great Britain.
Lahiri, Shompa. *Indians in Britain: Anglo-Indian Encounters, Race, and Identity, 1880–1930*. London: Frank Cass, 2000. Study of Indian students in England.
MacKenzie, John M., ed. *Imperialism and Popular Culture*. Manchester: Manchester University Press, 1986. Argues that imperialism was an important theme in British culture.
———. *Propaganda and Empire: The Manipulation of British Public Opinion, 1880–1960*. Manchester: Manchester University Press, 1984. Topics include empire and imperialism, music halls, authors H. Rider Haggard and Rudyard Kipling.
Marshall, P. J., ed. *The Cambridge Illustrated History of the British Empire*. Cambridge: Cambridge University Press, 1996. See especially chapter 12, "Imperial Britain," which briefly discusses the impact of the empire on Parliament, churches, the monarchy, and the economy.
O'Brien, Patrick K. "The Costs and Benefits of British Imperialism, 1846–1914." *Past and Present* 120 (August 1988): 163–200. Excellent summary of arguments over the cost of empire, coming down on the side that defense costs overrode benefits for the taxpayers.
Offer, Avner. "The British Empire, 1870–1914: A Waste of Money?" *Economic History Review* 46 (1993): 215–238. Technical examination of the cost of empire.
Parsons, Timothy H. *The British Imperial Century, 1815–1914: A World History Perspective*. Lanham, MD: Rowman and Littlefield, 1999. Short study of the empire, with a chapter on its impact on Great Britain.
Porter, Andrew. "Religion and Empire: British Expansion in the Long Nineteenth Century, 1780–1914." *Journal of Imperial and Commonwealth History* 20 (1992): 370–390. The impact of empire on missionaries.
Porter, Bernard. *The Lion's Share: A Short History of British Imperialism, 1850–1995*. 3rd ed. New York: Longman, 1996. Argues that the empire was not a source of strength in the late nineteenth century.
Pugh, Martin. *State and Society: A Social and Political History of Britain, 1870–1997*. London: Arnold, 1999. Thoughtful and well-written general survey.
Rao, G. Subba. *Indian Words in English*. Oxford: Oxford University Press, 1954. Includes lists of Indian words, grouped by centuries, that have entered the English language.
Rosenthal, Michael. *The Character Factory: Baden-Powell and the Origins of the Boy Scout Movement*. New York: Pantheon Books, 1986. Describes the scouting movement as a product of the perceived deficiencies of the empire;

includes an interesting chapter on the "deterioration" of the post–Boer War era.

Searle, G. R. *The Quest for National Efficiency: A Study in British Politics and Political Thought, 1899–1914*. Berkeley: University of California Press, 1971. Reaction of some British leaders to the weaknesses in Great Britain and its Empire.

Senelick, Laurence. "Politics as Entertainment: Victorian Music-Hall Songs." *Victorian Studies* 19 (December 1975): 149–180. Includes references to the theme of empire in the music halls.

Springhall, J. O. *Youth, Empire, and Society: British Youth Movements, 1883–1940*. London: Croom Helm, 1977. Youth movements and their ties to the empire.

Thompson, Andrew. *Imperial Britain: The Empire in British Politics, c. 1880–1932*. New York: Longman, 2000. Tariff reform; security, including naval supremacy; and overseas emigration as interests of extraparliamentary organizations.

Wagner, Gillian. *Children of the Empire*. London: Weidenfeld and Nicolson, 1982. Vivid description of child emigration schemes from Great Britain to the dominions.

5

The Reform Act of 1832

INTRODUCTION

By the 1830s, demographic changes in Great Britain had made parliamentary reform necessary. The growth of industrial cities in the north had weakened the influence of agricultural and land-owning interests in national affairs and had created serious disproportions in parliamentary representation. For example, Lancashire had two members of Parliament (M.P.s) representing 1.34 million people, while Cornwall had forty-two M.P.s representing just 300,000. Manchester, Birmingham, Leeds, and Sheffield, all sizeable industrial cities, had no direct parliamentary representation.

The example of the French Revolution had provided some incentive for reform, as did the relative status of the British political parties, the Whigs and the Tories. In the 1820s and 1830s, Whigs were those politicians—many wealthy and aristocratic—who had stood in opposition to the Tory Party governments headed by William Pitt the Younger and Lord Liverpool, and who were generally supportive of reform. These aristocrats felt that the promise of the Glorious Revolution had never been fulfilled. Allied with the upper-class center of Whiggism were reformist intellectuals; less wealthy aristocrats, such as the Earl Grey; and some of Britain's nouveaux riches, such as the Baring family, which had made its fortune in banking.

Lord John Russell (1792–1878) was for many years deeply interested in parliamentary reform, introducing the First Reform Bill in the House of Commons and as opposition leader, supporting the Second Reform Bill in Parliament. Reproduced from the Collections of the Library of Congress.

The Reform Act of 1832

The Tory Party wielded power in Great Britain almost continuously from 1783 until 1830. Socially they were quite diverse, but they were brought together by their loyalty to the crown and their distaste for reform of any sort. Ironically, fewer Tories than Whigs were descendants of the old landed aristocracy and more came from the newer business elite.

Although the Whigs were more inclined toward reform, it should not be assumed that they favored reforms in the political system that would democratize Great Britain. Like the Tories, they believed that an aristocratic elite should manage national affairs, but to prevent revolution they wanted to include some other groups in the political process. Among these other groups were the newly wealthy industrial and business elite. In general, parliamentary reform consisted of two distinct but significant aspects: (1) an increase in the number of individuals (men, at this time) who could vote and (2) a redistribution of parliamentary seats that reflected the demographic changes that had taken place in Britain over the past hundred or more years.

In 1830 the Whigs finally won a general election and the new prime minister, Lord Grey, announced that his government had the king's blessing to introduce a reform bill. Grey and his cabinet wanted to eliminate so-called pocket boroughs—parliamentary districts whose representation was, in a sense, in the pocket of the local wealthy landowner. Perhaps 55 percent of Parliament's seats were controlled in this way, and most of the M.P.s from pocket boroughs were Tories. The Grey government also wanted to reform "rotten" boroughs—districts that because of changing population patterns now had very small numbers of residents. Finally, the Whigs wanted to extend the vote to the entire middle class by standardizing (and lowering) voter qualifications. Tories opposed parliamentary reform because the redistribution of seats would take away "safe" seats and force ministers and M.P.s to be subject to the fickleness of public opinion. Also, the attack on small boroughs was seen as the first step in a campaign to destroy the sanctity of private property, a concept strongly rooted in English tradition. Finally, Tories argued that changes in property ownership, which had not (yet) happened significantly, were more important than changes in population.

It took another general election in 1831, and a titanic political struggle, but in the end the Reform Act of 1832, sometimes referred to as the Great Reform Act, succeeded in obtaining most of the reformers' goals. A total of 143 boroughs, or districts, were eliminated, and a like number of new districts were created in rapidly growing parts of the country. In the redistribution of seats, some sixty-five were given to new population centers including Manchester, Birmingham, Leeds, and Sheffield. In addition, the vote was given to all men in towns or cities who occupied a building with a tax valuation of ten pounds sterling or more and to significantly more men who lived in rural areas, although the process for establishing voter eligibility was more complex there than that employed in towns. Some historians have estimated that the Reform Act increased by 49 percent the number of voters in England and by a much higher percentage in Scotland.

While the Reform Act of 1832 was seen as sweeping in its time (some thought it was the "final settlement" of parliamentary questions), it is clear in retrospect that it did not go that far. Parliamentary seats were still badly distributed, and only 15 percent of adult males had the right to vote. Sporadic attempts to extend reform occurred in the 1840s and 1850s but routinely failed. Although the Chartist movement had voiced strong support for political reform in the 1840s, its collapse in 1848 ushered in an era of public indifference to reform, an indifference brought on partly by the general prosperity of mid-Victorian Great Britain. In addition, foreign affairs, including the Crimean War (1853–1856), were major distractions.

In the 1860s, however, a new interest in reform emerged from the speeches of William Gladstone, who emphasized the morality behind reform; from the National Reform League, a new political action group; and from the enthusiasm for reform engendered by the American Civil War. When the Conservative leader Lord Palmerston died in 1866, a major obstacle to further reform disappeared, and a consensus in Parliament agreed that the reform issue once again merited serious consideration. By this time, too, a realignment in British politics had taken place. Most of those who in the 1830s had been known as Whigs now identified themselves as members of the Liberal Party, while the old Tories were now known as the Conservative Party.

After Lord John Russell's Liberal government failed to pass a Reform Bill in 1866, Russell resigned, and Benjamin Disraeli and Lord Derby were called to lead a minority Conservative government. This government produced the Reform Act of 1867, which was even more radical than the original Liberal Party proposal. Historians have tried to understand how this could have happened. Stephen J. Lee concludes that Disraeli was acting out of political expediency, doing what he needed to do in order to build a Conservative political majority in Parliament. W. D. Rubenstein suggests that Disraeli's actions were somehow connected to his intense rivalry with Liberal Party leader William Gladstone and a calculation that the Conservatives really had little to lose and possibly much to gain from pushing a reform bill. Public opinion also may have been a factor; reform supporters had caused some civil disturbances and some felt that more serious ones would follow, although six months had elapsed between the most serious protests and the passage of the act.

The Reform Act of 1867 gave the vote to most members of the urban working class. It increased the number of voters by lowering property qualifications, requiring little else but a year's residence for urban dwellers and the occupancy or ownership of a small parcel of land for rural residents. All told, the electorate nearly doubled after 1867, although still only one adult male in three could vote in England, Scotland, and Wales. The act also redistributed a number of parliamentary seats, eliminating fifty-two small boroughs and switching their representation to underrepresented urban boroughs and giving graduates of the University of London two seats. Minor redistributing of seats was carried out in the rural areas of the counties as well.

An interesting sidelight to the Reform Act of 1867 is that votes for women was seriously debated for the first time while the act was under consideration. John Stuart Mill, the eminent philosopher and at that time a Liberal M.P., introduced a bill to give women the vote, and 73 M.P.s out of 269 favored it, despite the fact that there were no suffrage organizations yet formed in England nor any popular agitation for woman suffrage.

One electoral problem that the 1867 Reform Act failed to address was the growing problem of corruption and intimidation in parliamentary elections. This was due in large part to the fact that voters had to declare their voting preferences publicly. The Ballot Act of 1872, passed during Gladstone's first ministry, provided for secret ballots and put an end to most instances of voter intimidation. Corruption was addressed in the Corrupt and Illegal Practices Act of 1883, a consequence of a Royal Commission report in 1880 that criticized the large and ethically questionable expenditures of money at each election.

The Reform Act of 1884–1885 followed on the heels of the Corrupt and Illegal Practices Act. Gladstone's Liberal government of 1880–1885 was responsible for this act, in which Parliament approved further lowering of voter qualifications in 1884 and redistribution of parliamentary seats in 1885. The 1884–1885 Reform Act's principal objective was to equalize voting qualifications for urban and rural voters, a distinction that had existed because of a long-standing perception that many agricultural laborers were too poor and ignorant to vote. Essentially, the act extended the qualifications applied to urban voters in 1867 to those living in the countryside. Estimates suggest that this increased the electorate in England and Wales by 67 percent, in Scotland by 163 percent, and in Ireland by 229 percent. This last point was important to Gladstone, since there was a great deal of interest in the issue of Irish home rule at this time, and he knew that increasing the number of Irish voters would be advantageous for those who supported home rule, as he did.

With respect to seats in Parliament, the Reform Act of 1884–1885 redrew the electoral map of Great Britain completely, creating a nation of single-member constituencies. M.P.s from larger cities now had their own geographically defined districts rather than serving as one of two or more M.P.s for the entire city. Thus, each M.P. represented approximately the same number of voters. Only about twenty-five smaller cities retained their multimember representation. Unlike the earlier Reform Acts, the third Reform Act was approved in a spirit of political compromise. The Conservatives, led by Lord Salisbury, supported the Reform Act as a way to gain support among middle-class voters and to compete for the redistributed parliamentary seats that would inevitably result from the act. The 1884 act passed unanimously in the House of Commons, and the 1885 provisions were agreed upon in a series of amicable bipartisan meetings. As for votes for women, that issue would have to wait until 1918.

INTERPRETIVE ESSAY
Thomas C. Mackey

During the night of October 30–31, 1831, the night sky over Bristol flickered red with the burning of public and private buildings. At least one thousand protesters and/or rioters milled about in Queen's Square as the Mansion House, which housed the city government and courthouse, sat sacked and pillaged. On the other side of the square, the Custom House and the Excise Office smoldered after having mysteriously caught fire. Also burned were the Bishop's Palace, several jails, various tollhouses, and many private dwellings. Not surprisingly, the rioters had found supplies of alcohol and had fortified themselves and their courage with this liquid nourishment. Local constables proved inadequate to stop the rioters had they possessed the will to do so, but it was not at all clear that they did. Even members of the local opposition political organization, the Bristol Political Union, felt that they could do nothing to rein in the rioters. This dangerous situation left the local authorities no choice but to ask for assistance from the military. British cavalry troops entered the city on the morning of October 31. With swords and pistols drawn, the cavalry made their way to Queen's Square, where they charged the civilian mobs that, out of fear, drunkenness, and exhaustion following their riotous activities, retreated. Military reinforcements arrived from just outside the city and from Gloucester, and Bristol's domestic disturbance ended with at least four hundred dead.

What was the cause of this dramatic outburst of public protest against authority? Earlier in the month, on October 7, the House of Lords had defeated a bill that would have reformed the political structure of Parliament and moderately modernized the system of political apportionment in Great Britain. When the Lords defeated the bill, thereby defending their position as aristocrats and holding back political reform, spontaneous outbursts of popular protest occurred throughout the country. In Bristol, where resentment against the unreformed Parliament and their own aristocrats ran deep, protest turned to riot, fire, and death. Structural political reforms rarely cause such violent public reactions, but the politics regarding the reform of Parliament were not politics as usual. In June 1832 political reform did occur in Britain, but the road to the Reform Act of 1832 was not an easy one, as the Bristol riots show.

Change often frightens people. Political change can come at a glacial pace in the perception of some, but incremental political change is one of the hallmarks, strengths, and—ironically—weaknesses of the English constitutional system. In Great Britain in the early nineteenth century dramatic change had occurred in economic, urban, and social terms while the political system remained unchanged. As a consequence, the unreformed Parliament had failed to keep pace with the changes in the country. Between 1660 and 1832, Parliament had not significantly reformed its system of electing representatives. Beginning in the 1760s, reformers occasionally called for a reapportionment of the voting districts in the country and for other democratizing reforms such as the secret ballot, but those voices were few and far between. In a Parliament heavily represented by the traditional aristocracies whose power rested on land ownership, the emerging middle class of the nineteenth century, who were overwhelmingly urban and whose wealth was based on commercial enterprise, lacked adequate political representation. Demographic changes within Britain and the democratizing influences of the American and French Revolutions added pressure on the members of Parliament (M.P.s) to reform themselves politically. But political change required talented political leadership and public pressure before reformers could overcome the entrenched opposition and bring political modernization to Parliament.

In order to grasp the problems political reformers faced, it is necessary to understand the unreformed Parliament and the manner of its apportionment. First, the Parliament was large, containing 658 members. This number broke down as follows: England, 489; Wales, 24; Scotland, 45; and Ireland, 100. The key to reform was the distribution of the English seats. Of the 489 English seats, 82 were for representatives of the 40 counties; 403 were for representatives of the 202 boroughs, or local districts within counties; and the remaining 4 were for Oxford and Cambridge University representatives. Borough seats in particular were ripe for reform since many people had moved away from these rural districts to the rapidly growing towns of the north. For example, by 1830 the combined population of Manchester, Birmingham, and Leeds was nearly half a million, almost twice that of 1800. But those areas had no representation in Parliament, while the eleven rural counties between the Wash and Severn Rivers, which had experienced significant population loss, contained more than half of all of the borough seats. Political malapportionment was a significant problem in 1830.

Another area of concern was the manner of voting in the boroughs, which were either "open" or "closed." Open boroughs contained enough voters of independent means to hold actual elections for members of Parliament (although the standards for voting varied from place to place), while closed boroughs were those in which so few people lived—perhaps only one family—that a few individuals simply appointed their representatives to Parliament. Closed boroughs included the infamous "rotten boroughs"—those controlled by one person for one person. Such boroughs occurred because the residents had moved away, but their land, owned and controlled by one person or family, retained the political rights that went along with property ownership. Many of the English boroughs were closed, as were almost all of the Irish and Scottish boroughs, so that at least half of the members of Parliament were not elected but, rather, selected by the landed aristocracy.

Yet political change did not come easily or quickly. Perhaps obviously, the members of the House of Commons—loosely organized in the Tory and Whig parties—whose political power and social status were at stake were not likely to move quickly to undercut their own positions. But more than self-preservation slowed reform. Englishmen feared threats to private property, which they identified as guaranteeing personal liberty; political reapportionment meant denying some property owners their traditional liberties in order to shift political power elsewhere. Property ownership formed a kind of social glue that had held the country together and was vested under English common law. To be fair to the unreformed Parliament, another reason for its extended life was that it did not appear to some to be so badly malapportioned. Since the tradition of virtual representation held that each M.P. represented no one in particular but rather the entire realm, all of the various constituencies were in fact represented in Parliament, even if not directly. This system had been the English political custom from time out of mind, and many influential persons believed that such long established customs should not be overhauled lightly. Another reason political change came slowly to Parliament was the "slippery slope" problem. Opponents argued that if Parliament reformed itself, then what was next? If political reform and reapportionment came to Great Britain, would reform of the Church of England be next? Could the secret ballot mode of voting be far behind? Could those without property be next to demand the vote? Unknowns—the uncertainty about where the slippery slope might lead—held back the cause of political reform.

Perhaps the strongest reason reform did not come quickly to the political system was that the unreformed system worked. From 1660 to 1830, with the notable exception of the loss of the North American colonies, Great Britain had expanded and become wealthy and powerful. Because the unintended consequences of political reform could not be known ahead of time, parliamentary reform might jeopardize the success that Britain had achieved.

Nevertheless, public pressure for political reform came to a head between 1830 and 1832. In addition to the effects of a burgeoning urban population and an expanding industrial economy, the availability of cheaper newspapers led to a greater awareness about the activities of Parliament while providing a forum for political reform. Older restrictions on the press, such as the use of general warrants to search press shops, fell away in the 1770s, and the Libel Act of 1792 made the publication of political news and opinion safer.

Reformers can be grouped into the Whig opposition, as well as those representing the new middle classes and often organized in political interest groups, and radicals, democratically inclined skilled workers, and artisans. None of the politicians and reformers in these loose, shifting categories called for the full democratization of Great Britain. Instead, they pressed for moderate reapportionment of political power from the closed boroughs and landed aristocracy to the respectable middle class. Not surprisingly, the working-class radicals had very little influence in the reform movement while the middle-class reformers and the Whig M.P.s took the lead. Also important were the private political interest groups that had kept political reform alive as an issue from the 1790s to the 1820s. The most important of these interest groups was the Society of Friends of the People. Founded in 1792 and upper middle class in membership, this organization persisted in its pressure for political reform of Parliament and provided the movement with its most important leader, Charles Grey. Grey entered the House of Lords as Earl Grey in 1807 after championing reform in the House of Commons for years, and as prime minister from 1830 to 1834 he shepherded the Reform Bill through the Commons and the Lords. It is important to recall that from 1807 to 1830, the Tories controlled Parliament; their control of Parliament hampered Whig efforts to bring Reform Bills to the floor for debate and deterred the entire issue of political reform.

General political reform had come up before the House of Commons from time to time. As a member of the House of Commons, Grey tried to bring bills to the floor four times between 1792 and 1800 to no avail. By 1830 four more proposals to reform Parliament had come up but failed to garner support. New political interest groups formed to press the members for political reform. The Birmingham Political Union, led by currency reformer Thomas Attwood, and other similar groups understood that general reapportionment of Parliament was a requisite first step to achieving their own goals, such as tax reform and relief.

On June 26, 1830 an important opponent of political reform, King George IV, died after a lingering illness. His brother, William IV, succeeded him. Reformers believed that William IV was more open to reform. While they were incorrect in this impression, his ascension to the throne changed the political situation. William also was more inclined than George IV to accept the policies of his ministers even if he disliked the policies himself. These characteristics of William heartened the reformers.

By statute, new elections for the House of Commons had to be held within six months of the death of the sovereign, and the Tory government of Arthur Wellesley, the Duke of Wellington, wasted no time. He called for elections to occur within a month, which meant that the next Parliament would meet in November 1830. Once the dust had settled from this election Wellington remained as prime minister, but his support and majority in the Commons remained uncertain, in large part because of divisions within his own party.

On November 2, 1830 the new Parliament opened with high expectations that the Wellington government would bring forward political reform. But reapportionment was not even mentioned in the king's speech (though called the "king's speech," this message to Parliament was actually written by the prime minister, outlining his legislative agenda for the session). John Spencer, called Viscount Althrop by courtesy, rose in the Commons and questioned this lack of commitment to reform given the disturbances in the country and abroad, and Lord Grey raised the issue in the Lords. Wellington stated that the government was "totally unprepared with any plan" for reform.

Instead of holding back reform, Wellington's speech advanced its cause. His government fell on November 15, 1830 and King William IV turned to the opposition's most prominent leader, Lord Grey, to form a new government. Grey's conservative cabinet might have been expected to protect the power of the aristocracy, yet it would be the group that began the process of breaking aristocratic power in Great Britain.

On November 22, 1830, in his first speech as prime minister, Grey endorsed the need for political reform and established a committee to draft a reform bill. Grey instructed this committee to craft a minimal plan, one that still based voting on property ownership and maintained existing voting districts as much as possible. However, the plan had to reform the system enough to cool public opinion. Grey sought a prudent and conservative plan that would satisfy the demands for reform but not lead to any further changes.

This committee finished its work by the end of 1830, and in January 1831 Grey brought the bill to his full cabinet, which then debated its provisions. They made only a few changes to the proposal and those cut back some of the more democratizing features of the committee report. As introduced, the bill proposed a new formula for distributing seats to the counties and to the boroughs (in general, those with less population would lose seats and those with more population would gain seats). In the counties, the franchise would remain with the forty-shilling freeholders (men who owned a parcel of land worth forty shillings) but would now include people who paid the ten pounds sterling per year copyhold (a kind of tax) and those who had paid fifty pounds per year leaseholds for at least twenty-one years. In the boroughs, the franchise was broadened to include those who occupied houses taxed at a rate of at least ten pounds per year. One other change between the committee's proposal and the bill as sent to Parliament was that the committee called for Parliament to be reelected at least every five years. But the cabinet reversed the committee's decision and left the period of maximum duration for a Parliament at the then-traditional seven years. Grey's proposed Reform Bill would, if enacted, mean a smaller Parliament through eliminating many closed boroughs but would provide more seats to previously underrepresented parts of the country.

On January 31, 1831 Grey went to William IV to explain his plan for reform. Formally, the king lacked power to veto the proposed policies of the government, but he still wielded great influence and was a difficult person for Grey to handle. Like the Tories, William was suspicious of political change, but Grey persuaded him to support the reform bill to forestall more drastic measures coming forward from more radical proponents of democracy. The king insisted, however, that the Commons and the Lords had to agree, and that the Commons ought not propose a bill that would fail in the Lords.

Thus when the Grey government created a sensation with the introduction of the Reform Bill, the Tory opposition had an opportunity to challenge the bill at first reading and ask for a division of the Commons. But Sir Robert Peel, leader of the Tory opposition, had already decided to wait until the second of the three required readings of the bill to mount a challenge to it. As a result, the Tories missed a parliamentary moment to slow down the political reform that they so feared. Also, Peel may have understood that political reform was inevitable; therefore, his idea may have been only to slow down the pace of change and preserve as much of the old system as possible for as long as possible.

At the end of the second reading, a vote was taken under highly dramatic circumstances. The bill had carried by one vote, with 302 in favor and 301 opposed. Still, the road ahead was fraught with unforeseen problems and obstacles, and one such obstacle cropped up just a few days later when the bill was in committee, the standard practice after the second reading. General Isaac Gascoyne, a conservative Tory, proposed an amendment that the total number of English members in the new Parliament not be decreased. Since one of the central points of the whole reform was to reduce the number of seats in Parliament, an amendment that mandated no diminution of English seats would kill the bill. It was clear to Grey that if the House of Commons adopted the amendment, the whole reform movement might falter. Their worst fears came true on April 19 when the Commons adopted the Gascoyne amendment, 299 to 291. With this amendment attached to the bill and fearing that the Tories were building their support in the Lords to oppose the bill, Grey asked King William to dissolve Parliament and call for new elections. William grudgingly agreed, and with Parliament dissolved, the first Reform Bill died as well. But the principle of reform had passed a second reading.

With the House of Commons committed to reform, the political task became one of electing a new Parliament, pushing a bill through the Commons again, and then taking on the potentially large roadblock of the House of Lords. Whig leadership understood that by seizing the banner of political reform they might maintain their own political position. In this action, as the new elections proved, the Whigs drew increased support from the middle classes in the expanding urban manufacturing areas. Further, because the first Reform Bill would have eliminated some of the rotten boroughs and could be interpreted as an attack on the landed aristocracy, many of the more radical leaders and groups supported the Whig efforts at reform. Whigs also found support from the conservative Tories—or ultra-Tories, as they were sometimes called. Ultras sided with the Whigs on the principle that it was better to reform a little than face disturbances and revolutions in the streets. As a result, when the election results came in, Earl Grey had a majority of more than one hundred seats in the Commons.

The Reform Act of 1832

Grey's government did not waste time. The new Parliament opened on June 21, 1831, and a second Reform Bill (nearly identical to the first bill) was introduced on June 27. Debates on the bill occurred on July 4–6 and the House of Commons passed the second Reform Bill 367 to 231 on second reading, a stunning majority when compared to the one vote victory margin only three months earlier. In late July, while the bill was in committee, the Marquess of Chandos, an ultra-Tory, proposed an amendment to increase the number of people who could vote in the counties. This amendment worried the Grey government because it extended the vote to a greater number of voters than the government's bill had. On July 22 his cabinet decided to resist the amendment in committee but then accept the amendment at third reading. As they expected, Tories, some moderate Whigs, and the radicals carried the Chandos amendment in committee, 232 to 148. In the early hours of September 22, 1831, the Commons passed the Reform Bill, 345 to 236. In part this majority vote for the Reform Bill demonstrated that the Tories had resigned themselves to the passage of the bill in the Commons and had shifted their hopes for stopping political reform to the House of Lords.

Following tradition, the government took the bill to the House of Lords that same day. After a routine first reading, the Lords set October 2–7 for debate. Grey and the Whigs in the Lords made the same arguments that had carried the day in the House of Commons. Yet opponents held a tactical advantage because Grey's government had overestimated its strength in the Lords and failed to win the support of those members on the fence. A spirited debate ensued as to whether political reform was the first step to social revolution and a blow against the long tradition of landed aristocratic control of British government. A majority of the Lords decided that it was and defeated the bill by forty-one votes.

By defeating the Reform Bill, the House of Lords managed to do what the Grey government had not been able to do since March—spark public interest in political reform. Not only were Grey and his fellow Whigs dealt a setback, but the political unions and interest groups in the country supporting reform also felt the sting of defeat. Even people who would not earn the right to vote under the Reform Bill but who still supported the principle of political reform felt outraged that the Lords had stopped the bill. Many people in cities throughout Britain took to the streets to voice their unhappiness with the Lords' decision. Many demonstrations turned to open attacks on symbols of authority. The serious riots in Bristol at the end of October 1831 were just one such occurrence.

Not surprisingly, the political fallout from this defeat was also swift and dramatic. With defeat, the Grey government might have fallen from power and issued a call yet again for new elections. But on October 8, the day after the defeat in the House of Lords, King William asked Grey to continue in office. The House of Commons followed this endorsement of Grey and political reform with a resolution on October 10 supporting political reapportionment and the Grey administration. Grey informed William and the cabinet that his government would stay in office as long as they had the king's support for political reform. William agreed, Parliament continued, and Earl Grey and the Whig leader in the House, Viscount Althrop, informed the Lords and the Commons that they would press on for passage of a reform bill.

On December 6, 1831, Parliament met in regular session with the recent riots foremost in the minds of the members and the government. Eleven days later, a new reform bill, the third bill, received its first reading. Members of the House of Commons began their debate on second reading of the bill on December 15 and the bill easily carried the Commons on December 18, 324 to 162. At the committee stage, not started until after the Christmas recess, the Tories continued their policy of obstruction. As a result, twenty-two meetings were required on the bill before it came out of committee on March 22, 1832, with a vote of 355 to 239. In the Commons, the third Reform Bill passed without a division on March 24.

In spite of the success of the bill in the House of Commons, everyone knew that the political problem in 1832 for the Reform Bill was not the Commons but the House of Lords. Even as the third bill made its way through the Commons, Grey and his cabinet struggled with the issue of how to deal with the obstinate Lords. After considering several options, Grey, with the consent of William IV, decided to have the king ready to appoint enough new peers to the Lords to carry the bill. Although a blunt weapon, packing the Lords with Whig and reform supporters held the most promise because the Whigs would threaten such an option if the Lords did not vote in favor of the Reform Bill on their own.

On January 2, 1832, Grey brought up with the king the issue of packing the House of Lords with reform supporters. Grey apparently sought to educate William on the need for increasing the number of peers in the Lords, but he continually stressed to the king that such a move would be used only as a last resort. William agreed that new peers might be needed but set a limit on the number he would create.

With the possibility of the creation of new peers looming and with the Whig leadership making this possibility known to the Tory opposition, the House of Lords took up the third Reform Bill on March 26, 1832. Debate on second reading began on April 9 with at least three M.P.s who had voted against the bill publicly stating that they had changed their minds and now

The Reform Act of 1832

favored the Reform Bill. When the division of the Lords occurred, the reform bill carried the Lords on second reading by a vote of 184 to 175.

In reaction to this vote, Tory opposition focused on stopping the bill in committee. On May 7, the opposition offered a motion to postpone the sections of the bill that would remove the vote from closed boroughs. Hoping to slow down the process by postponing this crucial part of the legislation, the Tories hoped to scuttle the whole reform effort by postponement and delay. When the motion came to the floor of the committee, it passed 151 to 116. With the bill in danger from this delaying tactic, Grey acted quickly. He met with King William on May 8 and requested that the king either agree to create enough peers to carry the bill in the House of Lords, or allow Grey and his government to resign from office, thereby creating a political crisis of the first order. William agreed to allow Grey to resign, and he did so that afternoon.

With the resignation of Grey and his government, King William asked the Tories to form a government willing to carry on with some form of political reform. To the Tories, however, political reform was anathema. Wellington did offer to establish a government committed to some reform, but Peel and others refused to serve in such a government. On May 15, Wellington reluctantly went to William and told him that the Tories could not form a new government. At that, William turned back to Grey and asked him to continue as prime minister. Grey had gambled successfully that the opposition could not coalesce sufficiently to form a new government. If the Tories could not create a new government, they lacked the collective will to stop political reform as well.

On May 17 the House of Lords met. Earl Grey again asked the king for new peers to ensure the passage of the Reform Bill, and the next day the king gave his consent. On the evening of May 18, Grey and Althrop announced to their houses that they intended to stay in office because they had made arrangements to ensure the passage of the reform bill. With this implied threat to pack the Lords with Whig supporters clear to all, opposition to the bill quickly waned. This "May crisis" passed for Great Britain when the bill easily carried out of the committee stage on the evening of May 18. Many had feared that if a resolution of this conflict in favor of reform did not occur, the much-feared social revolution from below might have begun as it had in France. The Lords passed the bill out of committee, and Britain avoided the excesses of France once again. On June 4, the reform bill came before the Lords for third reading and passed, 106 to 22.

Because the wording of the bill in the House of Lords was slightly different from the bill accepted by the House of Commons, the bill returned to the Commons. On June 5, the Commons accepted the Lords' language. By this time, after all of the political heavy lifting, even the opposition understood the significance of the act. Peel thought that it was the most important measure approved in the past century, and while he continued to oppose the provisions of the act, Peel sensed that the British political landscape was about to change forever. Although Grey had asked the king to come to the Commons and sign the bill himself, William refused. Instead he sent the necessary commission to give the Royal Assent, and on June 7, 1832, the Reform Bill became the Reform Act of 1832.

Historians do not agree on the importance of the Reform Act. Some have argued that all it accomplished was to replace the Tory aristocracy in control of the House of Commons with a Whig aristocracy. Yet this argument is too cynical. This act brought about some much overdue realignment of political boundaries and the enfranchisement of many who had had no political voice prior to it. While redistricting resulted in sixty-two new members of a smaller, reformed Parliament, this change was not an overturning of the membership or a wide open door for anyone to political office-holding. It has been calculated that after reform, slightly fewer than 800,000 men could vote (compared with just over 500,000 prior to reform) out of a population of 13.8 million in England and Wales, 2.3 million in Scotland, and 7.7 million in Ireland. As these figures demonstrate, the Great Reform Act of 1832 can hardly be considered an act of mass democracy. It should also be pointed out that the social and economic status of the voters did not change; they all remained property owners or leaseholders. Grey's Reform Bill nudged the country toward political reform and a new system of apportionment.

Neither the hopes of the radicals for faster democratization of the kingdom nor the fears of the conservative Tories came to pass after the passage of the Great Reform Act. A second Reform Act in 1867 extended the right to vote to still more men and provided more representation to the urban areas of England, but it too was a fairly conservative measure. Political radicals did not see the secret ballot adopted until 1872, and the size of constituencies was not generally equalized until the third Reform Act of 1884–1885. The duration of a Parliament was not shortened to five years until 1911, and full male suffrage did not occur until 1918. Moreover, the fears of the Ultras that any political reform, no matter how minor, would mean the end of the monarchy, the end of the established Church of England, and participation in mass democracy by the worst classes of people were not realized. The monarchy continued after the Reform Act of 1832, and under Queen Victoria may have been more appealing to most Britons. While no longer exercising direct political power, the Church of England continued to minister to the country, and women over the age of thirty did not receive the vote in Great Britain until 1918.

Taken as a whole, what made the Reform Act significant was what it signaled about the future. Grey's Reform Bill made future political reforms possible, and for that reason alone, the 1832 act deserves the label "great." The road to reform had been long, twisting, and uncertain, but the perseverance of talented leaders who seized the moment and pressed forward with their reform agenda succeeded in the end. Great Britain avoided the extended political violence seen on the European continent while maintaining faith with the traditions of the unique British past. The Reform Act of 1832 changed the nature and course of British politics. And credit for these first steps toward political modernization has to be given to Earl Grey and his vision for a more politically open and representative government.

SELECTED BIBLIOGRAPHY

Brock, Michael. *The Great Reform Act*. London: Hutchinson, 1973. Detailed and carefully argued, this book presents the most thorough and persuasive of the modern interpretations of the Great Reform Act. A solid achievement in explaining a complex topic.

Cahill, Gilbert A. "The Popular Movement for Parliamentary Reform, 1829–1832: Some Further Thoughts." *The Historian* 37 (May 1975): 436–52. Emphasizes that pressure from various political unions and radical groups encouraged the elites in Parliament to reform.

Cannon, John Ashton. *Parliamentary Reform, 1640–1832*. Cambridge: Cambridge University Press, 1973. Argues that parliamentary reform must be understood against a background of reform efforts and institutional development from the seventeenth century to the early nineteenth century. One of the standard works in the field.

Gash, Norman. *Politics in the Age of Peel: A Study in the Technique of Parliamentary Representation, 1830–1850*. 1953. Reprint, Atlantic Highlands, NJ: Humanities Press, 1977. Another standard work that argues that the importance of the Great Reform Act has been overrated since the act merely replaced one elite group with another elite group.

Kriegel, Abraham D. "Liberty and Whiggery in Early Nineteenth-Century England." *Journal of Modern History* 52 (June 1980): 253–278. Argues that the concept of "liberty" motivated the Whig elite to reform themselves and the political system.

Lee, Stephen J. *Aspects of British Political History, 1815–1914*. London: Routledge, 1994. A very well-written and useful survey of the major themes of nineteenth-century British political and diplomatic history.

LoPatin, Nancy D. *Political Unions, Popular Politics and the Great Reform Act of 1832*. New York: St. Martin's Press, 1999. A careful and persuasive analysis of the range of political unions in the realm during the era of the Great Reform Act.

Mitchell, L. G. "Foxite Politics and the Great Reform Bill." *English Historical Review* 108 (April 1993): 338–364. Argues that the fear of the threat of excessive executive influence motivated the Whigs to reform the political system in 1832.

Newbould, Ian. *Whiggery and Reform, 1830–41: The Politics of Government.* Stanford, CA: Stanford University Press, 1990. Follows the Whigs in political power from 1830 to 1841 and assesses how they wielded their power in the reformed Parliament.

Phillips, John A., and Charles Wetherell. "The Great Reform Act of 1832 and the Political Modernization of England." *American Historical Review* 100 (April 1995): 411–436. The authors argue that the Great Reform Act was a significant reform moment in British history and truly "great" in its accomplishments.

Rubenstein, W. D. *Britain's Century: A Political and Social History, 1815–1905.* London: Arnold, 1998. A clear survey of British political history in the nineteenth century, with special attention paid to social history.

6

The Great Exhibition of 1851

INTRODUCTION

The Exhibition of the Works of Industry of All Nations, or more commonly, the Crystal Palace Exhibition or the Great Exhibition of 1851, was the single most obvious outward symbol of mid-Victorian progress and prosperity. Held in an industrial-age, prefabricated iron and glass structure 563 meters (1,848 feet) long by 125 meters (410 feet) wide, the exhibition drew more than six million visitors, including Queen Victoria, who admired the fourteen thousand exhibits of machinery, fine arts, industrial products, and raw materials.

The mid-Victorian era is usually chronologically defined as the period from the repeal of the Corn Laws in 1846 and the collapse of Chartism in 1848 to the Reform Act of 1867 and the economic depression of the 1870s. It was a period of considerable economic growth and political stability. National income rose by 80 percent in Great Britain between 1857 and 1871, per capita income was 50 percent greater than that of France, and the economy grew at the healthy rate of about 3 percent annually. What better reason for an international exhibition, so that the rest of the world could admire Britain's success?

While the Crystal Palace Exhibition is acknowledged to be the first modern world's fair (the American term for international exhibitions or exposi-

Six million visitors admired British and worldwide industrial, agricultural, and artistic achievements at the Great Exhibition of 1851 in London. Reproduced from the Collections of the Library of Congress.

tions), its roots are found as far back as medieval fairs held at major European trade centers. These were basically international, at least to the extent to which there were nations. In England, however, these medieval fairs did not have international elements, and the seeds of the Crystal Palace may be said to have begun to sprout with the formation in 1754 of the Royal Society of Arts in London.

In 1761, the society produced a show of its annual prizewinners in "the arts, manufactures, and commerce," which ran very successfully for seven weeks. Later in the eighteenth century, France held the first industrial exhibition, the idea of Marquis d'Avèze, commissioner of three manufacturing outlets that until 1789 had been under the authority of the king of France. After the French Revolution, the marquis found that business was bad, and so in 1797 he arranged an exhibition (really, a bazaar, since items were sold) in Paris to display his tapestries, carpets, and porcelain products as well as products of other trades he invited to the fair. The success of this exhibition was so great that the French government took up the idea and decided to hold an annual national exhibition in three specially constructed buildings. Part of the motivation behind this was to demonstrate to visitors the ability of French industry to compete on favorable terms with that of its main rival, Great Britain, although since the two were at war in 1797, the British did not participate and no comparisons could be made.

French exhibitions continued to be held intermittently, with wars and governmental instability often interfering. In 1849 the eleventh and largest attracted over 4,500 exhibitors and remained open for six months. Nothing was for sale at these exhibitions, but the French adopted the practice of London's Royal Society of Arts and awarded prizes to the best exhibits. In England, no such exhibitions were put on. There was no interest, and the prevailing feeling appears to have been that the French shows were merely efforts to undercut the acknowledged superiority of British manufactured goods. Although there were no national exhibitions in Great Britain, there were industrial shows organized by mechanics' institutes—schools designed to teach scientific principles to working-class people. These institutes began to function in English towns in the 1820s and soon began to hold periodic exhibitions to demonstrate scientific principles and to display mechanical devices, often miniaturized for exhibition purposes.

The idea for the Crystal Palace Exhibition may originally have come from a British entrepreneur, William Fothergill Cooke, in 1845. After two small exhibitions of arts and modern inventions sponsored by the Royal Society of Arts, Cooke suggested to the Society that a national exhibition be held. The society endorsed the idea, although it would be four years before serious planning got underway. Historians have long debated the role of

Prince Albert, Queen Victoria's German-born consort and president of the society from 1843, in originating the Crystal Palace Exhibition. Early versions of the exhibition's history gave the prince more credit than he deserved (or would have wanted to claim); he was smart enough to know that in 1845 the idea of a great national exhibition had no broad public support, nor was he yet popular with the British public.

Albert was drawn into deeper involvement with the exhibition idea through his friendship with Henry Cole, a civil servant with a keen interest in art and design, and a belief that British industrial products needed more in the way of aesthetic allure. Cole, a member of the Royal Society of Arts, helped organize small manufacturing exhibitions in 1847 and 1848. These were popular and helped sustain interest in the idea of a much larger national exhibition. Cole was also interested in the promotion of art education and surmised that he could accomplish that end by collecting the best exhibits and placing them in a national exhibition, housed in a centrally located building, perhaps at Trafalgar Square in London. Successful industrial exhibitions in Paris, as well as those in London, appear to have confirmed the notion that the time was right for a large-scale national exhibition with an international scope. This notion appealed to Prince Albert and drew him deeply into the project. This was exceedingly useful because of his connection with the crown and with political leaders, and it was a way he could make himself even more visibly useful to the British public.

At a planning meeting in June 1849, it was estimated that the exhibition would cost 75,000 pounds sterling (£50,000 for the building, £20,000 for prizes, and £5,000 for administrative expenses), which could be raised from public donations. The Royal Society of Arts and Prince Albert could obtain pledges from wealthy individuals to guarantee that the banks would advance credit. Large prizes were seen as an inducement to manufacturers to raise the quality of their products and to get widespread support of the manufacturing community for the exhibition, which was thought to be essential. The Royal Society decided that it needed £20,000 in seed money to get the project underway, but the government would not provide it and initial attempts at canvassing the London elite did not succeed. Finally a London contracting firm, Messrs. Jas. & Geo. Munday, pledged its support, and the Royal Society was in the exhibition business.

A prestigious royal commission, headed by Albert, was announced on January 1, 1850, and in a year it organized an international exhibition with one hundred thousand exhibits to be displayed in a new building. The commission raised almost £80,000 in private donations, as well as pledges of more than £250,000 for the exhibition, and continued to do all the necessary work to make it a successful event. There was a general feeling that the exhibition would fare better if it were a public and national enterprise; as a consequence, the contract with the Mundays was canceled after public criticism that they would be making a significant profit from a public enterprise.

The commission raised money throughout the country, using local committees as intermediaries. In general, and not surprisingly, northern industrial cities including Manchester and Glasgow supported the exhibition more generously than less-industrialized cities such as Birmingham, Liverpool, and Bath.

In January 1850 the commission appointed a building committee to ask for proposals for a suitable exhibition building. Over the next few months, some 254 proposals were submitted, none was accepted, and the committee started to work on its own plan for a brick, iron, and stone structure with a huge dome larger than that of Saint Paul's cathedral. No one outside the committee liked it. At this point, Joseph Paxton submitted a crude sketch for an iron and glass building that resembled an enormous greenhouse. Paxton was a gardener for the duke of Devonshire and had experience designing greenhouses. When his design for the exhibition building was published in the *Illustrated London News*, the public liked it and the committee accepted it.

Construction started almost immediately since only nine months remained until the opening of the exhibition. The building, with its prefabricated parts, rose quickly and was completed in January 1851. It covered some eighteen acres and was built over several old elm trees that otherwise would have been cut down. The public was fascinated with the idea of a building containing so much glass, and *Punch*, a popular humor magazine, published countless cartoons of the building emphasizing its expanses of glass. Historian John R. Davis credits *Punch* with popularizing the nickname "Crystal Palace" for the building. The Crystal Palace was a remarkable building achievement for its day. Prefabrication was a new technique, and all the iron structural supports—columns, girders, gutters, and sash bars—were interchangeable. Similarly, the thousands of inch-thick glass panes measuring four feet by ten inches were also prefabricated, and at the peak of construction activity, glaziers installed eighteen thousand panes per week. Owen Jones, a London architect and designer, was in charge of interior design, and he followed current practices that dictated the use of primary colors. Blue, red, and yellow paint on the interior columns, railings, and other metalwork provided a vibrant background for the exhibits.

The exhibition opened May 1, 1851 and visitors could see more than a hundred thousand separate exhibits. Half the space was given over to Great Britain and its colonies; half was allocated to foreign countries for their exhibits. After Britain, France and Germany had the most impressive exhibits. The United States had more space than any other foreign country except France but failed to fill it. Still, after some initial criticism, the simple, practical efficiency of manufactured goods from the United States, especially the firearms and agricultural machines and implements, won widespread public approval. But probably the most dramatic single exhibit was the 186-carat Koh-I-Noor diamond from India.

Admission to the Crystal Palace Exhibition was a pricey 5 shillings during the first three weeks and then was lowered substantially, to 1 shilling most days of the week so that "King Mob" could enter. Season tickets were £3 3s. for men and £2 2s. for women. Still, there was a good deal of controversy over whether the fair was affordable (some employers subsidized their workers, which helped). Except for £150,000 the government belatedly provided, the fair was financed through private and voluntary means and taxes were not raised. More than six million visitors attended the Great Exhibition of 1851, and despite the fears of some politicians and the police commissioner, the crowds were pleasant and orderly. By all accounts, the exhibition was marvelously successful. It initiated a long history of international expositions, most recently in Hanover, Germany, where Expo 2000 celebrated the millennium.

A surplus of £186,000 resulting from the Crystal Palace Exhibition was used to buy land in the South Kensington area, the present-day site of the Victoria and Albert Museum, the Royal Albert Hall, and other public buildings. A private corporation purchased the Crystal Palace for £70,000, disassembled it, and rebuilt it in Sydenham, a suburb southwest of London, where it was used for many years as an exhibition hall and conference center until a spectacular fire destroyed it in 1936. A royal commission used other surplus funds from the exhibition to begin a scholarship program in 1891; it still grants scholarships in science and art, fulfilling one of Prince Albert's fondest wishes.

INTERPRETIVE ESSAY
Diana J. Reynolds

The Great Exhibition of 1851 was the defining event of the mid-nineteenth century. It contained both the dreams and the nightmares of the new age of industrial production. The Crystal Palace symbolized the age of science and progress and gave the promise of a better future; its slow decay into an amusement park and its eventual destruction by fire in 1936 paralleled the fate of the world it came to represent. The Great Exhibition celebrated the transformation of the world by the machine and foretold the cataclysmic international consequences this transformation would create.

Inspired by the utopian hopes of its organizers, the Great Exhibition gained the confidence of the nation and eventually defined the emerging values of mid-Victorian England: work, commerce, self-discipline, and consumption. Outside of England, the Great Exhibition of 1851 inaugurated a century of display, self-congratulation, self-promotion, and competition among the industrialized nations of the world; it began a new epoch of international exhibitions that continued well into the twentieth century. [As the largest public events to date, these world's fairs helped create many of the social structures of modern industrial society: mass tourism, new forms of leisure, consumerism, new standards of public behavior, and the integration of various social classes into the same public place. The Great Exhibition inaugurated a new form of state involvement in public exhibition and display that combined education and entertainment with government support. This new combination of exhibitionary techniques and public appeal gave rise to the modern museum.]

The Great Exhibition reflected the new relationships between people and products in the nineteenth century. This new relationship was most clearly seen in the overwhelming grandeur of the Crystal Palace itself. For the six million visitors to the Great Exhibition, the Crystal Palace was both an architectural wonder and a fairyland of industrial products assembled in one place—the precursor of the modern department store or shopping mall. Visitors to the Great Exhibition were not only overwhelmed by the vast amounts of goods, they were also seduced by the promise of increased access to these new things. In Victorian England and elsewhere in industrializing Europe, the Industrial Revolution meant that untold amounts of products were now available in the marketplace. With this began a change in relationships among people, products, and patterns of consumption; it helped to create today's world of restless fashion and consumerism.

The Great Exhibition also began a debate on problems of architecture and industrial design that culminated in the modernist aesthetic of the early twentieth century. The Crystal Palace was the harbinger of the modern steel and glass skyscraper; its ingenious modular construction from prefabricated cast iron represented a new use of industrial materials in public architecture and gave rise to a new form of "engineering architecture." The modern city of steel and glass begins with the Crystal Palace. Finally, the displays of raw materials from the far corners of the globe at the Great Exhibition introduced British visitors to the wealth and exoticism of British possessions overseas. Although the British Empire would double in size over the next fifty years, it was the Great Exhibition that began the process of imperial display that would become an important feature of subsequent world's fairs. In the Crystal Palace, we see dreams of the nineteenth century and the nightmares of the twentieth.

SOCIAL TRANSFORMATIONS

The Great Exhibition was conceived, first and foremost, to educate the British public about the processes of industrialization. In 1851 England was still only partially industrialized, but the first phase of the mechanization of production that began with the steam engine around 1800 was complete; increased industrialization and mechanization was a foregone conclusion. At midcentury the exhibition's organizers were particularly concerned with educating the public about the future and soothing the emerging social tensions created by the new industrializing economy. The 1840s had been a decade of civil strife in England. Political tensions in England were framed by the demands of both the increasingly discontented industrial workers and the radicals of the Chartist movement. A wave of revolutions on the Continent in 1848 was further evidence of the social instability of the industrializing nations. To upper- and middle-class observers, evidence of social unrest was everywhere. In England, the rapid increase in urban populations due to industrialization had created a paradox: traditional social theory held that urban crowds were potentially revolutionary and dangerous to the security of the state, but the new industrial cities created precisely these crowds, whose individual members were slowly becoming conscious of their economic plight and their political potential. The young German manufacturer Friedrich Engels had described the awful plight of these urban workers in *The Condition of the Working Class in England*, published in 1844. Finally, Karl Marx had published his *Communist Manifesto* in 1848, in which he encouraged industrial workers to unite in a struggle against the new industrial capitalism. The upper classes, factory owners, and the new middle classes believed they had much to fear from these social transformations.

The Great Exhibition was designed to address these fears. In the words of Prince Albert, the exhibition was to be "a great school of science, of art, of industry, and of universal brotherhood." The organizers of the exhibition held fast to the goal of educating the public about the benefits of industry and new mechanical processes. Education and brotherhood meant including as much of the public as possible, and the organizers created an admissions pricing structure that was remarkably inclusive for its time. Out of 144 open days, 80 days were designated "one shilling days," when a reduced admission price allowed the working classes to visit. While this price still excluded the indigent and the poorest classes, it was nevertheless an innovative step in creating a public event that was accessible to more people than ever before. While critics were fearful of the potential unruly behavior of the crowds, the final results confirmed the hopes of the exhibition's organizers: of six million paid admissions, over four million of those were on the one-shilling days. Altogether, the figure of six million was approximately one-fifth the population of Britain. The Great Exhibition was a public event in a new sense.

Thus the Great Exhibition transformed the way millions of ordinary people viewed travel and inaugurated the era of mass tourism. Many working-class visitors to the Exhibition ("day trippers") took advantage of rail tours such as those organized by the enterprising Thomas Cook, and traveled to London—sometimes traveling home by night to be back at work in the morning—to visit the Crystal Palace. After 1851 international exhibitions became the travel destination of millions of Europeans and created new forms of leisure travel: five million visitors attended the Paris exposition in 1855; another six million came to London again in 1862. These attendance figures grew steadily for the remainder of the century: the Paris exposition of 1867 drew nine million visitors; Vienna's *Weltausstelling* of 1873 attracted five million guests; the 1889 Centennial Exposition in Paris attracted twenty-seven million visitors; and the Paris exposition of 1900 was the greatest mass event of all time with fifty million attendees. The millions of people drawn to these events were unprecedented; the expositions merged a public hunger for travel with railroad technology and created a new tourist industry.

The huge numbers of visitors to the Great Exhibition created new standards of public behavior in the public space. A population that was still mostly rural and untraveled in 1851 needed to be educated in forms of behavior appropriate to the city. Traveler's guides, such as Richard Askrill's *Yorkshire Visitors' Guide to the Great Exhibition*, instructed visitors on how to behave in the city: avoid spitting and be careful to bathe and wear clean clothes. Another instructed visitors to avoid pushing and to move in a clockwise direction through the building. Still another guidebook instructed first-time visitors to gather around members of their group who had been to the exhibition before—allowing themselves to be guided and instructed peacefully by more experienced colleagues. An important aspect of this new public behavior was the element of self-regulation. While police surveillance was heightened on the shilling days, a feature of the Crystal Palace was the way in which its construction allowed the visitors to scrutinize one another. The second-story galleries afforded a view of the crowd as well as of the objects on display. The effect of these efforts to instill habits of self-regulation and mutual observation can be seen in a guidebook for visitors to the Pan-American Exposition of 1901: "Please remember when you get inside the gates you are part of the show." The Great Exhibition of 1851 began this process of educating the masses in the models of behavior appropriate for the public spaces of the new industrial society—the orderly, self-regulated behavior we mostly take for granted in shopping malls and airports today.

The Great Exhibition soothed middle-class and aristocratic concerns about the behavior of large masses and became, for a short time, a location of contact and cooperation—or brotherhood—between the upper class and the working class. In the highly regulated class structure of Victorian England, the Crystal Palace was the first location where the classes came face to face in large numbers in an undifferentiated public space. The upper and middle classes tended to congregate in the huge nave of the Crystal Palace, but on shilling days these classes shared this space with the working class. The meeting of the "pound and the shilling" (upper- and middle-class visitors paid higher admission prices) was commented upon regularly in the popular press. As a result of this mixing, middle-class visitors to the exhibition were surprised to find not the "filthy, foul mouthed, drunken brutes" they had expected, but "clean, orderly [working] men" and their families. Reconciling class tension was fundamental to the spirit of the Great Exhibition.

An unprecedented form of cooperation between management and labor was also part of the rhetoric of brotherhood at the Great Exhibition. Factory owners often paid for employees to attend the exhibition; working men's societies also created savings plans through which a factory hand could donate a small portion of the weekly wage toward a journey. This created another paradox: factory owners hoped to educate factory hands about the potential of industrial production, while working men's delegations to exhibitions gradually became aware of their plight in an international sense; the communist International Working Men's Association formed as a result of the London exhibition of 1862. In this way, the epoch of world's fairs that began after 1851 formed a space where a new class consciousness on the part of workers could emerge.

The huge popular success of the Great Exhibition exceeded the wildest dreams of its organizers and created a change in the attitude of the state toward matters of exhibition, display, and public education. Thus the most significant educational legacy of the Great Exhibition in England was the formation of the South Kensington Museum in 1857 in order to continue the process of education about industrial processes that had begun in 1851. Like the Great Exhibition, this new museum created an undifferentiated public space that encouraged the mixing of social classes; it inaugurated a new era in which the museum became a place of public access and education. The South Kensington Museum was not the first museum in England (several important museums, such as the British Museum, existed long before 1857), but it was public in a new way. Visitors to the British Museum in the 1850s were required to write for admission in advance; this requirement effectively blocked widespread public attendance at the museum. In addition, the British Museum's hours were limited; its directors resisted installing gas lighting to extend opening hours. In contrast, the new South Kensington Museum included such friendly innovations as a public restaurant on the premises and evening hours (made possible by gas lighting) for working-class visitors. This innovative combination of public access, education, and display after 1851 has been described as the emergence of an "exhibitionary complex." The historian Tony Bennett defines this exhibitionary complex as the emergence of new disciplinary mechanisms of the state designed to regulate and control the public. In the same era that forms of punishment became less public (the modern prison system removes the offender from public view), the exhibitionary complex became a softer form of discipline and control—not a display of state force, but an effort to "win the hearts and minds" of the public through the display of knowledge.

After the Great Exhibition, museums proliferated in England and its colonies, in central Europe, and in the United States. New applied arts museums, such as the Museum for Art and Industry in Vienna (1863) and the Applied Arts Museum in Berlin (1875), were modeled on the South Kensington Museum. In other cases, princely or aristocratic collections were gradually transformed into places of public access; this was the case in the formation of the Imperial Art History Museum in Vienna and many others like it across Europe. The common feature of this museum-building craze was the role of the state in creating spaces for public display and the production of knowledge. Dozens of new museums and new academic disciplines (such as art history and anthropology) emerged after the Great Exhibition, as the public hunger for objects on display merged with a new state role as a regulator and organizer of knowledge. The museum was a way to tame the world and bring it home; the power of the state was exhibited in its ability to educate its citizens about that world. The exhibitionary complex organized emerging forms of knowledge for public education.

While promoting education and brotherhood, the Great Exhibition of 1851 also extended the promise of future comfort and prosperity to the laboring poor. The Great Exhibition began the process by which rural and urban working classes were introduced to new patterns of consumption. The educational goals of the exhibition were clearly meant to inculcate the working classes with the values of an emerging Victorian industrial society: work, self-discipline, imperialism, and consumerism. The organization and classification of objects at the exhibition—raw materials, machines, and manufactured items—introduced the public to the power and potential of industrial manufacturing, but the overwhelming display of "manufactures" also held out the promise of increased access to consumer goods. Every visitor to the Crystal Palace was awestruck by the unprecedented display of goods. Even Queen Victoria described the Crystal Palace as a "fairyland" of things. Never before in the history of the world had so many things been put on public display. From machines for manufacturing to mass-produced shoes and shawls, the Crystal Palace was a fantasyland of industrial products. To a public that was still largely rural this display of goods was overwhelming. While the objects on display were shown without prices (price tags were first permitted in 1855), consumption was at the heart of the Great Exhibition. In this sense, the Crystal Palace was the precursor of the modern department store or shopping mall: unlimited objects of desire in one public space. This display was a great equalizer, for all classes met there; at the same time it held out the promise of future benefits to the working classes. The Great Exhibition created an industrial and consumer identity that all men and women could share.

The "fairyland" of objects on display at the Crystal Palace produced a phenomenon of consumption that Karl Marx described as "commodity fetishism." According to Marx, one of the indicators of the new economic and social order arising from the industrial system is the creation of the commodity—an item that was the product of an impersonal factory process and sold in an impersonal marketplace. When an object (a pair of shoes, for example) enters the marketplace, it takes on a life of its own. The consumer buys the object without thinking of the industrial processes or impersonal production that made it; the shoes are now a commodity. But the commodity has significance far beyond its usefulness; in some instances, the commodity has symbolic value. For Marx, the "fetish" is an object that is invested with some symbolic meaning. In the world created by industrial processes, a new psychological condition of commodity fetishism emerges in which the purchaser is so enthralled by the object that he or she is blinded to the often dehumanizing industrial work that made it possible to buy it. We rarely think about the shoe factory in some far-off country, and we often purchase for reasons that go beyond simple need. (Hence the fascination with status symbols, brand names, or logos.)

At the Crystal Palace, the worker did not notice that his labor had been transformed by the machine into a consumer item. Instead, the thrall of the fairyland disguised the injustices suffered by industrial workers. The Crystal Palace was a "glittering temple in which both the devotees and the slaves of progress could join in worship" (Bird, 3). Soothed by the promise of better conditions and a share in these material benefits, the workers in England who visited the exhibition found their revolutionary potential blunted. Subsequent exhibitions became places of pilgrimage to consumerism; the powerful feelings of gratification through consumption became established in modern industrial societies in the twentieth century.

DESIGN THEORIES

The Great Exhibition of 1851 demonstrated how middle-class values of consumption could be grafted onto the emerging working class. Part of the lure of consumption was the concept of upward mobility that became associated with the cultivation of good taste. Thus another educational thrust of the Great Exhibition was the improvement of public taste. Prince Albert described the task of educating the public in matters of taste as the "marriage of Art and Industry." This reflected the merging of aristocratic definitions of taste (art) with new industrial processes (industry). For Prince Albert, the problem of taste was the most pressing matter now facing industrial producers and consumers. The question was one of quality versus quantity, artistic merit versus industrial practicality.

Contemporary critics argued that while England led the world in industrial productivity, its manufactured goods were not always beautiful. It was now necessary to merge English technical skill with an aesthetic sensibility, much as the French had succeeded in doing. The problem of taste meant the application of proper ornamentation to industrial products, while at the same time not undoing their practicality.

This debate on taste was one of the most enduring legacies of the Great Exhibition. From this debate emerged two of the most significant, although contradictory, currents of late nineteenth-century design theory: the arts and crafts reform movement and the development of the modernist aesthetic. The first, by critiquing industrial processes and the reduction of workers to automatons, emphasized the plight of the industrial worker and advocated an aesthetic of simplicity and a politics that culminated in the socialist thought of William Morris. The second, by embracing the machine and its possibilities, pushed design into the modernist aesthetic of functionality.

The arts and crafts reform movement began when the young William Morris visited the Crystal Palace and described the articles he found inside as "wonderfully ugly." In the late 1840s Morris and a group of friends at

Oxford University had formed the "Pre-Raphaelite Brotherhood" of artists and poets who were concerned with the moral and social function of art in the rapidly changing industrial society. For Morris, the products displayed at the exhibition illustrated the excesses and moral dangers of mechanized production: manufacturers could produce whatever they wanted (or the public wanted) in unlimited quantities but gave little thought to the beauty of the objects they created. For some critics, poorly designed objects would result in poor sales; for Morris, poorly designed objects reflected social injustices. To Morris, the moral dilemma of modern industrial society found expression in the ugliness and uselessness of the objects displayed in the Crystal Palace. The art critic John Ruskin also developed a critique of English industrial society from the Great Exhibition. Ruskin agreed with Morris that modern industrial processes disrupted the worker's traditional relationship to his work; his skill was lost to the machine. The artisan became a mere factory hand and the worker's relationship to the product was no longer personal. The "alienation" (a term coined by Marx) of the worker from the product was the social outcome; the plight of the working classes was therefore directly related to this problem of decoration, industrial manufactures, and consumption. For Morris and Ruskin, the Crystal Palace was the site of false desires and the creation of false needs. Morris and Ruskin agreed that something was fundamentally wrong with a society that could produce and consume so much ugliness.

In his attempts to reintroduce handcrafted production, Morris made several attempts to create workers' communities and to rehabilitate craft production. In the years that followed the Great Exhibition, Morris became a successful designer. The wallpapers, textiles, and furnishings produced by Morris & Company expressed his belief that people should own nothing that is "not either useful or beautiful." Ironically, Morris's products, exquisitely designed and handmade, could only be purchased by the well-to-do. Morris was never able to reconcile his critique of factory production with his dependence upon wealthy consumers. But the arts and crafts reform movement associated with his theories was an important critique of the overly ornamented and poorly crafted products displayed in the Crystal Palace. Theorists involved in arts and crafts reform created an aesthetic of simplicity, restrained ornamentation, and handcrafted products that was to have enormous influence: Movements like the "Vienna Workshops" in Austria and Gustav Stickley's "Craftsman" designs in the United States shaped design theory well into the twentieth century.

Another set of theories that emerged from the Great Exhibition embraced industrial processes, emphasized function over ornamentation, and evolved into modernism in design. This school of thought had its origins in the obvious gulf between the heavily ornamented "manufactured products" of the exhibition and the machinery located inside the Hall of Machines. This was articulated most clearly by observers who contrasted unnecessary ornament to the functional designs of the machines; the steam locomotive, for example, possessed an "external form [that was] dictated by intrinsic necessities." The "power, eloquence . . . fitness, . . . harmonious combinations and simple outlines" of the machines were a contrast to the "incongruous ornament" of consumer items: even while the exhibition was going on, critics were clear about the difference in ornamentation between manufactured goods and the machines that made them. The German theorist Gottfried Semper articulated a theory of functionalism in design most clearly: "Only in products in which the seriousness of their use does not allow anything unnecessary, . . . (coaches, weapons, medical instruments) . . . can one occasionally see a sounder way of . . . improving form" (quoted in Briggs, *Victorian Things*, 78). For Semper, the decoration of the object should remain secondary to its function. This principle was self-evident in machinery but needed to be applied to manufactured things. This idea would culminate in the modernist aesthetic of functionality—form follows function—of early twentieth-century design.

The emblem of this debate between ornamentation and functionality was the Crystal Palace itself. While critics might have disagreed about its contents, the structure was a triumph of engineering. Its architect, Joseph Paxton, bypassed the architectural materials (such as carved stone) that were traditionally associated with grand design and created a new form of architecture. It was the largest building constructed to date; 1,848 feet long and covering eighteen acres, the Crystal Palace was an epic demonstration of the new potential of iron and glass construction. The building was constructed in less than four months using prefabricated pieces. Load-bearing walls made of cast iron columns, second- and third-story galleries supported by iron girders; this was an entirely new form of engineering architecture. The extensive use of glass supported by thin columns of iron created an entirely new interior space and aesthetic experience. Nothing like this had ever been built to this scale before; it was a visual encounter entirely new to everyone who saw it. This principle of iron and glass architecture would find increased use at subsequent exhibitions and in railroad stations, eventually culminating in the steel and glass construction of the twentieth century. Once the principle of a load-bearing shell of metal became linked to the invention of the elevator in the 1870s, there was no limit to the height that a steel and glass structure could be built. The Great Exhibition was prophetic in this way, too: A. W. Otis displayed his new device called a "lift" at the Crystal Palace. When the lift became linked to electrical power in the 1880s, the skyscraper was born.

The Crystal Palace contributed to the debate surrounding ornamentation and functionality in design, while the transparency of its glass walls served as a metaphor for the success of industry and the social and political stability of England. The design of the building was innovative in the ways in which it shaped the formation of the well-ordered public. With its areas of movement and rest, second-story galleries for observation, and such prosaic considerations as the first construction of public restrooms, Paxton created a total environment of spectacle and display that captured the imagination of everyone who saw it.

The problem of ornamentation created a national debate concerning taste, national identity, and industrial design that was one of the most enduring legacies of the Great Exhibition. But this debate quickly became linked to international competition and emerging nationalism in Europe. After 1851 manufacturers and political economists maintained that artistic quality was linked not only to domestic progress but also to an international struggle for market share. Good design meant higher sales. After 1851 the competition among industrializing nations centered on gaining control of markets; all subsequent exhibitions brought questions of design to the forefront and linked them to questions of national identity and economic strength. In the case of England, the aesthetic of good taste merged new consumer desires into an aristocratic canon of beauty. In less-developed or -colonized regions of Europe, such as Ireland or Poland, the question of design became linked to national identity. For example, when an Irish manufacturer sent a replica of the Tara Brooch (a recent archaeological find) to the exhibition, its Celtic design vocabulary was immediately linked to Irish nationalism. The search for a national style became part of the rhetoric of world's fairs after 1851; design questions became linked to nationalism. As fairs became more nationalistic later in the century, the question of national style became even more pronounced. Excellence in manufactured goods and tasteful ornamentation were not only the key to market share but also signs of cultural superiority. And nothing less than survival in the international marketplace was at stake. The linkage of industrial productivity to national interests created an increasingly intense rivalry among Europe's industrialized nations after 1851.

Nowhere was this rivalry more pronounced than in the display of colonies and empire at international exhibitions. In the final decades of the nineteenth century, European nations began to devote increasingly larger amounts of space and money to colonial displays. This pattern, too, was first shaped in 1851. At the Great Exhibition, the significance of the colonies to manufacturing greatness was only slightly understood. Nevertheless, the East India Company section of the Crystal Palace was hugely popular. Articles sent to the Crystal Palace by the company featured exotic animals (such as a stuffed elephant), raw materials that were useful for manufacturing processes, and the decorative arts of India (such as cashmere shawls) that inspired consumers and manufacturers. In one section of the exhibit, Bengali artisans fashioned ivory trinkets for the enjoyment of the audience. The process of exotic display begun in 1851 linked the idea of empire with progress and national well-being. More importantly, it accustomed the British to the idea of imperial conquest. Long before the dramatic expansion of the empire that would occur in the next few decades, the Great Exhibition served to inculcate the *idea* of an empire in the British consciousness. Visitors to the exhibition learned what their empire had to offer. Putting products of the empire on display forged links between commercial success and political control of distant colonies. In the years to come, the display of empire would become highly important to participants in world's fairs, culminating in the construction of native villages where Europeans (and, later, Americans) could view their colonized peoples in natural settings. The pseudoscientific, educational goals of these human zoos meshed with a carnival atmosphere of voyeurism (here it was possible to view the uncovered breasts of African women) and spectacle (villagers performed ritual dances on a predetermined schedule). These imperial displays taught Europeans about their rights and their duty to rule the globe and to share the advantages of civilization, commerce, and industry with the lesser races.

The Great Exhibition of 1851 shaped the values of mid-Victorian England and demonstrated English industrial power and political stability to the world. Never again would public confidence in unlimited progress and the power of science and technology be so great. The Great Exhibition acted as a catalyst for many of the social structures of modern industrial society: mass tourism, new forms of leisure, consumerism, new standards of public behavior, and the integration of various social classes in public space. These social transformations created a new form of urban public behavior of self-regulation and a new form of state involvement in public education through the museum. The exhibition began a half-century of debate about good taste and arts and crafts reform that culminated in the modernist aesthetic of the early twentieth century. The temple of the workshop of the world, the Crystal Palace displayed the tremendous productive power of new industrial technologies; the fairytale utopia of consumer goods, it stood as a beacon of hope to potential consumers; the place of stupefaction, it disguised the often unjust factory systems that created these new products. Thus the Crystal Palace embodied the promises and paradoxes of the industrializing world. The shining hopes of the nineteenth century shimmered in the glass construction, but the destructive tendencies of the future were contained within it as well. Here the Krupps steel cannon was exhibited for the first time—here the colony was displayed as a source of raw materials and wealth for the British public—here the alienation of the factory worker was transformed into a glittering commodity. The Crystal Palace was a world-class icon of progress, industry, and empire, and when it was destroyed by fire in 1936 the world it had come to represent was about to be engulfed in the flames of World War II. From glowing beginning to fiery collapse, the Crystal Palace was the emblem of the nineteenth-century world.

SELECTED BIBLIOGRAPHY

Allwood, John. *The Great Exhibitions*. London: Cassell, 1977. An excellent general introduction to world's fairs.

Anderson, Benedict. *Imagined Communities*. Rev. ed. London: Verso, 1991. The rise of nationalism and the significance of public spectacles to the formation of a national consciousness.

Auerbach, Jeffrey. *The Great Exhibition of 1851: A Nation on Display*. New Haven: Yale University Press, 1999. An excellent and well-illustrated discussion of the exhibition and its significance for forming a British national identity.

Baker, Malcom, and Brenda Richardson, eds. *A Grand Design: The Art of the Victoria and Albert Museum. (Exhibition Catalog.)* New York: Harry N. Abrams, 1999. Contains several essays about the Great Exhibition of 1851, the formation of the South Kensington Museum, and the significance of the industrial arts ideal in Victorian England.

Beaver, Patrick. *The Crystal Palace, 1851–1936*. London: Hugh Evelyn, 1970. A well-illustrated overview of the Crystal Palace, its architecture, and its history until 1936.

Bennett, Tony. *The Birth of the Museum: History, Theory, Politics*. London: Routledge, 1995. The origins of the museum in England, with a chapter on the exhibitionary complex.

Bird, Anthony. *Paxton's Palace*. London: Cassell, 1976. The construction and history of the Crystal Palace.

Black, Barbara. *On Exhibit: Victorians and Their Museums*. Charlottesville: University Press of Virginia, 1984. The development and the decline of museum culture in Victorian England.

Briggs, Asa. *Victorian Things*. London: B. T. Batsford, 1988. Excellent introduction to the material culture of mid-Victorian England.

Davis, John R. *The Great Exhibition*. Thrupp-Stroud, England: Sutton, 1999. The most recent thorough general history of the exhibition, with a careful discussion of Prince Albert's role.

Findling, John E., ed. *Historical Dictionary of World's Fairs and Expositions, 1851–1988*. Westport, CT: Greenwood Press, 1990. Best single source for finding the facts, figures, and sources on the most significant expositions between the dates given. Useful appendixes on fair statistics.

Greenhalgh, Paul. *Ephemeral Vistas: The Expositions Universelles, Exhibitions, and World's Fairs, 1851–1939*. Manchester: Manchester University Press, 1988. Excellent overview of expositions arranged thematically, with an especially good chapter on colonialism at expositions.

Rydell, Robert W. *All the World's A Fair: Visions of Empire at American International Expositions, 1876–1916*. Chicago: University of Chicago Press, 1984. Discusses imperialism and colonialism at world's fairs held in the United States.

———. *Books of the Fairs*. Washington, D.C.: Smithsonian Institution Press, 1990. Comprehensive introduction to the evolution of world's fairs. Includes an excellent bibliography.

Schivelbusch, Wolfgang. *The Railway Journey: The Industrialization of Time and Space in the Nineteenth Century*. Berkeley: University of California Press, 1986. The significance of rail travel to social change in the nineteenth century.

Swinglehurst, Edmund. *Cook's Tours: The Story of Popular Travel*. Poole, England: Blandford Press, 1982. Brief, noncritical introduction to Thomas Cook and the development of the tourist industry in England.

Verlinden, O. "Markets and Fairs." In *Cambridge Economic History of Europe*, Vol. 3. Cambridge: Cambridge University Press, 1963. The origins of trade and industrial fairs.

The confrontational strategy of many British suffragettes campaigning for the right to vote often placed them in physically demanding situations. This photograph shows Emmeline Pankhurst collapsing after her re-arrest in May 1913. Reproduced from the Collections of the Library of Congress.

7

Sinn Fein and the Suffragettes: The Movements for Irish Independence and Women's Suffrage, c. 1880–1921

INTRODUCTION

British political and social history of the late nineteenth and early twentieth centuries was characterized by an accelerating drive for social reform that involved a good deal of grassroots agitation and would forever change the British political landscape. In 1935 the eminent British historian George Dangerfield published *The Strange Death of Liberal England, 1910–1914*, which for the first time focused attention on this era by chronicling the climax of these reformist campaigns and the changes they brought to Great Britain. Of the various reform movements, those for Irish independence and for women's suffrage stand out as the most prominent.

IRISH INDEPENDENCE

In 1801 Ireland was joined with England in the Act of Union, which dissolved the Irish Parliament and provided for one hundred Irish members of Parliament (M.P.s) in the House of Commons and twenty-eight Irish peers and four bishops in the House of Lords. Colonial administrators, appointed in London, ran Irish affairs from offices in Dublin.

Irish unhappiness with the Act of Union was exacerbated by the exclusion of Catholics from Parliament and from appointive offices. This issue propelled an Irish nationalist named Daniel O'Connell to the forefront of Irish political affairs, and his election to Parliament as a Catholic in 1828 threatened revolution unless Parliament approved the Catholic Emancipation Bill then before it. Supported by both Tories and Whigs fearful of revolution, the act passed in 1829 and helped lead to the election of a Whig government in 1830 and further political reform.

As an M.P., O'Connell pressed for other reforms and, ultimately, for the repeal of the Act of Union. But continuing resistance from the Tories prevented this, and O'Connell's influence had waned by his death in 1851. Part of the reason for O'Connell's diminished influence was the great famine of the 1840s, which reduced the population of Ireland by about one-third and raised the level of Irish distrust of Parliament to new heights. Although the Tory government of Sir Robert Peel tried to mitigate the worst effects of the famine, traditional *laissez-faire* attitudes prevented much direct relief for hungry people and allowed the profitable export of food from Ireland to continue.

One of the consequences of the famine was the creation in 1858 of the extremist Fenian movement. Known as the Irish Republican Brotherhood (IRB) after 1865, it was fundamentally a no-compromise independence movement. The IRB instigated a rebellion in 1867 that failed miserably, and most of its leaders were jailed or fled to America. Its legacy a generation or so later was the Sinn Fein and the Irish Republican Army, critical elements in the troubled times between 1916 and 1921. In the 1874 general election, which Benjamin Disraeli and the Conservatives won, a new Irish party, the Home Rule Party, captured fifty-eight seats in Parliament. Dedicated to securing a separate government for Ireland, this party was originally led by the moderate Isaac Butt, a former Conservative. In 1878, however, the mercurial nationalist Charles Stewart Parnell took over and championed the Irish cause until his death in 1891.

Irish Home Rule was the most important political question facing Britain in the 1880s. Poverty and political discrimination generated increasing Irish hostility toward London, and Parnell and the Home Rule M.P.s used clever parliamentary tactics to tie up the nation's political business. Meanwhile, the dominant Liberal government of William Gladstone attempted to coopt Parnell, even as Irish terrorists assassinated two high-ranking London officials in Dublin, an act that horrified the Conservative opposition. Although the violence eased within a year, the issue remained very much in the forefront of political affairs. In the general election of 1885, Home Rule was the central issue, and when it was leaked to the press that Gladstone now favored Home Rule for Ireland, Parnell voiced his support for the Liberals.

Safely reelected, Gladstone and the Liberal majority in Parliament crafted a Home Rule Bill that established an Irish parliament to meet in Dublin. A related bill contained a plan to buy out absentee Irish landlords at a total cost of £120 million. The introduction of the Home Rule Bill brought about the resignation of two key members of the cabinet, provoked a great sensation among the public, and led to a lengthy debate in the House of Commons. After two months, the bill was defeated 343–313, with a number of Liberal M.P.s defecting (some later changed parties and became Conservatives). Parnell's influence declined after the defeat of Home Rule. He was involved in a messy dispute with the *Times* over ultranationalistic letters he had allegedly written; he was also a party in a nasty divorce case in which the husband of his mistress named him as a corespondent. When Parnell died of a heart attack in 1891, his political career was in ruins.

Meanwhile, not everyone in Ireland was happy about Home Rule. The Unionist movement against Home Rule began in 1886 with the creation of the Ulster Loyalist Anti-Repeal Union. Protestants living in Ulster (part of present-day Northern Ireland) feared Home Rule because they feared living under a Catholic majority and because Ulster, as the most industrialized part of Ireland, had close economic ties with England that an Irish parliament might threaten with tariffs or other barriers to trade. Ulster Unionists forged close ties with the Conservative Party, and for a while it was a fruitful alliance.

By 1914 the political situation had changed. The general election of 1910 and the passage of the Parliament Act of 1911 enhanced Irish nationalists' hopes for Home Rule. The election made the ruling Liberals dependent on eighty-two Irish M.P.s to maintain their majority, and the Parliament Act had removed the threat of a House of Lords veto. In April 1912 the third Home Rule bill was introduced in the House of Commons and it passed its third reading in May 1914. During the two years of its travel through Parliament, opponents emphasized the dangers that would accompany Home Rule: it would oppress the Protestant minority, endanger the economic advantages of Irish-British free trade, and might even imperil British national security. Unionists, still the dominant faction in Ulster, were privately concerned about losing their political power and social status. They decided to protect themselves by creating the ninety-thousand–man Ulster Volunteer force and making it clear that Home Rule would be met with armed resistance.

Meanwhile, the government in London, certain that a majority of Irish people favored Home Rule, downplayed the Ulster opposition as well as that of the Conservative Party in Parliament. But the Curragh Mutiny of March 1914 underscored the seriousness of the situation. Encouraged by senior army officers in London, fifty-seven British army officers stationed in Dublin offered to resign their commissions rather than enforce Home Rule. That the Herbert Asquith government did not court-martial the senior officers demonstrates how shaky its position had become. In August, however, world war broke out and the Irish question was held in suspension as most Irish nationalists remained loyal to Great Britain.

Meanwhile, radical nationalists in Ireland, frustrated by the failure of London to implement Home Rule, brought about the Easter Rising of 1916 (discussed in the following essay), and by 1918 their organization, Sinn Fein, had seized political power from the more moderate nationalists. Under the leadership of Eamon de Valera, the radicals created an Irish parliament (*Dail*) and undertook a terrorist campaign against the Ulster unionists. David Lloyd George, the prime minister, responded by sending over the "Black and Tans," a kind of mercenary force, to assist the Ulster forces, and a bloody conflict ensued. By 1921 Lloyd George concluded that his government was not going to win by force, and at the very real risk of destroying his own ruling coalition he agreed in December 1921 to create the Irish Free State as a dominion within the British Commonwealth. By March 1922 all of Ireland—except the six counties constituting Ulster—was an independent nation. It remained a part of the British Commonwealth until 1949.

WOMAN SUFFRAGE

Not long after John Stuart Mill's introduction of a bill in 1867 giving women the vote, some towns in England began granting women the right to vote in local elections, but further efforts to make votes for women national routinely failed in Parliament. In 1897 the National Union of Women's Suffrage Societies (NUWSS) was created; six years later the even more significant Women's Social and Political Union (WSPU) came into being. While the right to vote was in itself very important, many women also saw votes for women as a way by which other legal and social inequalities could be corrected. In 1903 Emmeline Pankhurst and her daughters, Christabel and Sylvia, brought new energy into the suffrage movement through their leadership of the WSPU. At first they quietly publicized their cause among working-class women, but in 1905, at the same time Parliament began to consider another suffrage bill, the WSPU escalated the contentiousness of the debate by holding a noisy street demonstration outside a Liberal political meeting in Manchester. It was the first of many times WSPU leaders would be arrested.

The Pankhursts and their WSPU colleagues understood very well the value of publicity, and they knew that newspaper accounts and pictures of women being literally dragged off to jail would evoke considerable sympathy for their cause. Between 1905 and the outbreak of World War I in 1914, the suffragettes (as they came to be known) provoked authorities to arrest them following demonstrations or incidents of property damage, such as setting fires in mailboxes or pouring acid on golf course greens. Apparently eager to go to jail, these women went on hunger strikes once imprisoned, forcing authorities to release them lest they died in a government prison. In 1913 Parliament passed the "Cat and Mouse Act," which allowed hunger-striking women to be released and then rearrested when it appeared they had regained their strength. Not all suffragettes went along with the Pankhursts; the members of the NUWSS employed a more patient, less confrontational strategy.

As early as 1906 a majority of M.P.s in both major parties probably favored votes for women in some form, but there was no general agreement as to what form suffrage should take; that is, which women should be allowed to vote. Still, the movement did win some victories along the way. In 1907 women were allowed to serve on town and county councils, a major gain for women since these councils had considerable financial responsibility. Moreover, it made far less valid the arguments against women voting on the national level. In 1908 the Liberal government of Herbert Henry Asquith spent much time debating voting reform in general, and Asquith, who did not support women's suffrage, even conceded that the House of Commons could insert a suffrage amendment into a franchise Reform Bill if it so chose. Nothing along these lines happened until 1912, however, partly because the Liberal Party was split over the issue and partly because the aggressive tactics of the WSPU alienated some would-be supporters. An attempt to bring about very limited women's suffrage was seen in the 1910 Conciliation Bill, which would have given the vote to women who owned property independently from their husbands or other male members of their family. Despite the fact that the bill would have given the vote to only about 8 percent of women, both of the major suffrage organizations supported it. Unfortunately, after giving the bill a favorable second reading, Parliament then voted to send it to a committee, which killed it. A similar fate met two subsequent Conciliation Bills.

When World War I broke out in 1914, the militant suffragettes abruptly changed their strategy from confrontation to cooperation. Adopting a stance of enthusiastic patriotism, the Pankhursts and others urged Britons to rally 'round the flag, and many women went to work in war-related industries or in auxiliary military service organizations. Their outstanding war work contributed to the passage in 1918 of the Representation of the People Act, granting the vote to women over the age of thirty and to all men over the age of twenty-one. Eleven years later the voting age for women was lowered to twenty-one, the same as that for men.

INTERPRETIVE ESSAY
Kenneth L. Campbell

The causes of women's suffrage and Irish independence were first linked in 1935 in George Dangerfield's important and provocative book *The Strange Death of Liberal England, 1910–1914*. Dangerfield believed that these two movements combined with growing worker unrest to create a constitutional crisis in pre–World War I England that had the potential to cause the collapse of the British government. Dangerfield wrote eloquently and persuasively, but his main thesis has undergone criticism and revision at the hands of subsequent historians. David Brooks (*The Age of Upheaval*), for example, found a series of disturbances that demonstrated a degree of disorder but nothing approaching a revolutionary crisis. We will never know what would have happened in Great Britain had World War I not intervened, but in the years preceding 1914 disputes with no easy solutions were pursued in increasingly fanatical and violent ways. It is legitimate to raise the question of whether the movements for Irish independence and women's suffrage have any inherent connections or if they merely happened to coincide chronologically.

Perhaps most obviously, these two movements shared a concern for social and economic justice. The movement for Irish independence was inextricably linked with social and economic concerns about the general welfare of the Irish people. Irish nationalism arose in the second half of the nineteenth century against a backdrop of famine, economic decline, agricultural depression, and large-scale emigration from the island. More than four million people emigrated between the famine of the 1840s and the establishment of the Irish Free State in 1922, but population pressures still weighed heavily on the island, especially in times of economic difficulty. In fact, a land-reform campaign preceded the movement for Irish independence and for some time confusion existed about the priorities of the Irish movement. A "Land War" from 1879 to 1882 perpetuated violence against landowners seeking to evict their tenants during a time of economic depression. It is no coincidence that violence erupted in periods of depression, first in the Land War, later in the Easter Rising of 1916. The emphasis upon these events by nationalist historians ignores the relative prosperity that the reduced popu-

Sinn Fein and the Suffragettes

lation enjoyed at other times, but these times of economic hardship proved critical to the political movement for independence.

While the Land War served as a prelude for the demands and eventual realization of Irish independence, demands for increased opportunities for women outside of the home coincided with demands for women's right to vote. Women's emancipation related closely to social and economic issues as well. Women—and an increasing number of men, including the playwright George Bernard Shaw—recognized that they had much more to offer society than their traditional and accepted roles of obedient wife and dutiful mother. Women's access to education provided a pressing issue for a rapidly growing number of women who regarded this as critical for political participation and progress toward greater equality between the sexes. (London, Oxford, and Cambridge each established colleges for women in the late nineteenth century.) The vote was generally taken to represent more than just the vote; it became symbolic of the whole issue of women's opportunities and freedom. Women who supported the suffragist movement generally supported women's rights in other areas and vice versa, just as Irish nationalists tended to support both political independence and land reform.

In 1882 Charles Stewart Parnell founded the Irish National League as a replacement for the defunct Land League, which he converted into an association committed to Home Rule for Ireland, even ahead of the popular issue of land reform. Peaceful initiatives in Parliament represented the means employed by the new league, in contrast to the violence and radical activity sometimes associated with the Land League. The platform for the Irish National League still included land reform, local self-government, extension of voting rights, and support for labor and industry, but Home Rule with a freely elected Irish parliament clearly represented Parnell's primary objective. While Parnell made it clear that he sought this redress for what he regarded as England's usurpation of Ireland's independence through legal, constitutional means, he implied that England would not be wise to oppose it. He gave a speech on January 22, 1885 in which he declared, to great cheers, that "no man has the right to fix the boundary of a nation."

Politically, the movements for women's suffrage and Irish independence are linked by the role that each played in the history of the Liberal Party in the late nineteenth and early twentieth centuries, including its eventual downfall. In 1885 Parnell had to compromise with the leader of the Liberal Party, William Ewart Gladstone, in order to have a chance to achieve his objective of Home Rule. Some nationalists, such as Michael Davitt, the former leader of the Land League, remained skeptical of Parnell's motives; Davitt remarked that "Parnellism" had replaced nationalism. But

Parnell knew that Gladstone, despite his conversion to the cause of Home Rule, would not be able to achieve complete independence for Ireland. Gladstone had to allay the fear of his constituents in the 1885 campaign by promising not to do anything that would diminish "the supremacy of the Crown, the unity of the Empire and all the authority of Parliament necessary for the conservation of that unity." Parnell and the Irish Party had clout, however, because of the relatively equal strength of the Liberal and Conservative Parties. In late 1885 he temporarily swung the support of his party to the Conservatives in an effort to gain their support and put pressure on the Liberals to honor their commitment to Home Rule. He knew that he could use his seventy followers in the House of Commons to obstruct other business unless whichever party held power introduced the Home Rule bill he sought.

When Gladstone originally decided to commit to the cause of Irish Home Rule, he displayed a pronounced concern for international opinion about English policy and actions in Ireland. At one point he expressed doubt that a single newspaper article could be found outside of England that did not treat English conduct toward Ireland "except with profound and bitter condemnation." This did not seriously alter British international relations, but Gladstone did recognize that it represented a serious moral blot on the British record that might make it hard for Great Britain to claim the position of political leadership in the world to which it otherwise might have been entitled. Given the importance of claims of moral prestige in the diplomatic and military conflicts of the twentieth century, most notably during World War II, Gladstone's concerns appear more legitimate in retrospect than they might have seemed, in practical terms, at the time.

Some leaders of the Conservative Party, such as Lord Carnarvon, actually considered taking the initiative on Home Rule, on the grounds that it had been working well in Canada for about twelve years, and entered into negotiations with Parnell. However, the membership of the Conservative Party would have been bitterly divided over this issue and the risk of splitting the party was deemed too great. The Conservative Party had already split once in the nineteenth century, over the repeal of the Corn Laws in the 1840s, and its leaders were leery of repeating the same mistake. Conservatives also believed that the major grievance in Ireland was not political but, rather, social and economic. Thus they believed that the Irish problem could be resolved through land reform, and they later passed important land legislation. Parnell may have preferred to work with the Conservatives because of their control of the House of Lords, but when it became apparent that he was being used without any real prospect of success he helped to orchestrate the fall of the Conservative government. Thus Home

Rule fell to Gladstone and the Liberals, who did introduce a bill, even though they ran the same risk of splitting ranks as the Conservatives.

At this time ominous noises began to emanate from Belfast in the form of riots there in demonstration against the Home Rule Bill. The Protestant majority of the northern counties made clear their unwillingness to accept even the moderate measure opposed by Gladstone. Parnell rejected the proposal for a separate parliament for Ulster in the north. Division would not benefit the Protestants in the south or the Catholics in the north, a point that Parnell, a Protestant Irish nationalist, was particularly qualified to make. Still, the opposition in the north, defections within Gladstone's party, the shift of the Conservatives to a policy of determined resistance, and the improbability of support from the Lords should Gladstone successfully maneuver the bill through the House of Commons provided major obstacles to Home Rule at that time.

About ninety Liberal members of Parliament (M.P.s) voted against Gladstone and the Home Rule Bill, which was defeated by a vote of 341 to 311. The vote on Home Rule not only caused a division within the ranks of the Liberal Party; it seemed to doom the cause of Parnell and Home Rule. Joseph Chamberlain, Gladstone's chief opponent in the party, defected and formed the Liberal Unionist Party, while the Conservatives became the dominant party for most of the next twenty years. Parnell remained unbowed and helped to keep the cause alive by declaring calmly, "We are going to have a Home Rule Bill." One of his followers, William O'Brien, later recalled:

> The youth of a more fortunate time will never understand the flow of incredulous rapture the words sent through every fiber of one like myself who had entered upon the *via dolorosa* of the nationalist struggle with an all but fatalist persuasion that it was bound to end in failure, desperation, penal servitude, or the gallows.... (William O'Brien, *The Parnell of Real Life*, London: T. F. Unwim, 1926, 106–7)

By 1890, however, Parnell had been discredited by his involvement in a nasty divorce scandal, and he died in October of the following year. Although a core of supporters retained their allegiance to the ideals of their fallen leader, the political movement for Irish independence fell, divided, into a decade of ineffectiveness. Gladstone managed to steer a Home Rule Bill through the House of Commons in 1893, but the House of Lords rejected it, leaving no prospect at the time for further recourse.

The division in British politics over Irish Home Rule represented just one aspect of the significantly altered political landscape that had emerged by the last decade of the nineteenth century. In the first half of the nineteenth century, women began to play a role in politics through their participation in such political organizations as the Anti-Corn Law League and the Chartist movement, where they first pushed the idea of women's suffrage. In the 1860s women's rights groups formed in London and Manchester.

The cause of women's suffrage in the nineteenth century attracted a number of Liberal supporters, including the famous political philosopher John Stuart Mill, who unsuccessfully advocated that votes for women be provided for in the Reform Bill of 1867. Reform Acts in 1867 and 1884–1885 had expanded the electorate, so that the interests and concerns of the lower middle class and some segments of the working classes now had a place on the political agenda. Women's suffrage bills had been introduced in the 1870s, but an amendment to the 1884 bill to allow women property owners to vote was defeated by a 2–1 margin. No women could as yet vote, and this glaring neglect of at least 50 percent of the population became a growing issue by the end of the century.

In the later decades of the nineteenth century, women gained the right to vote in local elections and to hold office at the local level. Once they received the right to vote in local elections, women frequently helped to elect women candidates to local positions. Even in local elections, women generally received support for positions that fell within "women's" domain, such as those on boards overseeing education and poor relief. These accorded with the traditional notions of women as caretakers. It remained difficult for women candidates to get elected to sit on town councils, mostly because the major parties did not support their nomination to these positions. Furthermore, women had failed to gain any commitment from either the Liberal or the Conservative Party to support votes for women on a national level. Both parties remained even more divided on this issue than on Home Rule, and no male politician of the status of William Gladstone, who supported Home rule, announced his conversion to the women's cause. In fact, Gladstone himself opposed women's suffrage because he thought that it would detract from women's main role in society (which he believed was at home with the family) and that women as a group did not possess the maturity to exercise the duties of citizenship, though individual women might.

For women, the right to dress as they pleased, to dine where and with whomever they pleased, to engage in sports, and to enter the male-dominated workforce all intermingled with the cause of women's suffrage. Women made some professional advances by 1900, though mainly in traditional female occupations such as nursing. For some women these other issues—especially the economic issue of jobs and pay—took precedence over suffrage; for others, like the Pankhursts, suffrage was paramount. Success in one area did not necessarily mean success in the others, but all of these issues were inextricably linked nonetheless.

The movement for women's suffrage implied something of a social revolution by its very nature. It challenged contemporary ideas of male patriarchy and dominance and led men to speculate on what the world was coming to. If the traditional relationship between the male and female sexes dissolved, what else could provide the kind of stability to which Englishmen raised in the nineteenth century had become accustomed? The working classes had gradually achieved inclusion in the political system; to give more of them the vote did not represent a totally new change. To give any women the vote did. Even some women opposed women's suffrage, because they saw it as undermining the traditional role that women played in society, not because they viewed women as inherently inferior.

The lack of support from any prominent male politician did not prevent women's suffrage on the national level from becoming a major political issue. However, it required an increasingly radical approach to make it so. Mrs. Emmeline Pankhurst and her daughters, Sylvia and Christabel, supplied this and emerged as the leaders of the "suffragette" movement. In 1903 Emmeline founded the Women's Social and Political Union (WSPU), an organization devoted to accelerating activity intended to call attention to the cause of women's suffrage. It built on the growing support for women's suffrage within the Liberal Party that had been achieved by the National Union of Women's Suffrage Societies (NUWSS), headed by Millicent Fawcett, which operated more in the mainstream liberal political tradition. Fawcett continued to expand the membership and revenues for the NUWSS, while supporting the role of the militant WSPU in calling attention to the cause.

The Irish independence movement had shifted its emphasis in the 1890s, giving the movement more of a cultural significance and allowing it to transcend its political and economic aspirations. The Irish Literary Society in London and the National Literary Society in Dublin both originated under the leadership of William Butler Yeats, a major Irish poet and literary leader, in the early 1890s. These associations reflected a shift in the Irish nationalist movement after the death of Parnell toward cultural nationalism as they sought to promote interest in Ireland's history, literature, popular culture, and the Gaelic language. As the Irish nationalist Desmond Fitzgerald wrote in his memoirs of the years preceding the Easter Rising of 1916,

> We were subconsciously aware that the continued decay of the Irish language was bringing ominously near a further great break with our past. . . . Irishmen volunteering to train for the defense of their rights would gradually become conscious that

they possessed natural rights, rights that had their roots in our racial past. (Desmond Fitzgerald, London: Routledge, 1968, *Memoirs* . . . , 73)

In his poem "The Rebel," Padraic Pearse, a leading proponent of the Gaelic revival, wrote:

I am come of the seed of the people, the people that sorrow,
That have no treasure but hope,
No riches laid up but a memory
Of an ancient glory. (Padraic Pearse, *Literary Writings*, Dublin: Mercier Press, 1979, 25)

The cultural element of the independence movement has colored the ways in which Irish nationalism has been seen ever since. It gave the movement what almost might be considered a spiritual dimension as independence became linked with the preservation of Ireland's precious cultural heritage and the values that it represented as opposed to those of the dominant culture of England. This is reflected even in recent works such as Thomas Cahill's best-selling and provocative book *How the Irish Saved Civilization* (New York: Doubleday, 1995). The Easter Rising, for example, became for the proponents of this cultural nationalism more than just a political act designed to further the creation of the Irish Republic. It became a poetic statement in which the failure of the rebellion would create martyrs whose blood would redeem the Irish people in the same way that Jesus' death had been necessary to redeem a fallen humanity. Pearse's poems from the period of the rebellion are full of religious allusions that compare the cause and experience of the Irish rebels to that of Christ.

Thus religion became an important factor in addition to the cultural elements of the Irish nationalist movement such as the preservation of Gaelic literature and language. Catholicism and nationalism became intertwined in this period to a degree that had not appeared before and that was not necessarily inherent in a movement for home rule. Canada and Australia, for example, had both achieved home rule status without any pressing religious issues. Prior to this period plenty of southern Protestants had supported Irish independence. These "Southern Unionists" increasingly found themselves ostracized from the main movement as its religious overtones grew heavier. In the years after the Easter Rebellion Catholic leaders in Ireland and Rome spoke out in condemnation of the injustices and harsh brutality of British rule in Ireland.

The cause of women's suffrage evoked certain cultural issues as well, especially the contributions that women had to bring to the social culture at large. The late Victorians placed a strong emphasis on women's role as mothers, something hardly unique to them. But when this emphasis became intertwined with increased concerns about women's exclusion from the realm of politics, it resulted in a more serious consideration of what women as mothers had to offer beyond the act of giving birth and the rearing of children. Women's rights advocates such as Josephine Butler and Millicent Fawcett believed that women's perspectives as mothers and women needed to be represented in government, which, they suggested, would be more likely to ameliorate the problems faced by society if infused with feminine wisdom and spirituality. Women showed a higher level of concern about children's rights and health care issues, perhaps reinforcing cultural stereotypes of women as caretakers but still providing a strong case for women's increased participation in the political system.

To understand the resistance to something as seemingly innocuous as women's suffrage, it has to be seen in the context of other women's issues, including divorce, legal and property rights, women's full participation in the workforce, and even prostitution. When a sadomasochist sex scandal occurred among British politicians in 1913, Christabel Pankhurst used the opportunity to write a number of articles linking men with sexual exploitation of women. She blamed men for causing the prevalence of venereal disease among women and then using that as an excuse to oppose women's suffrage. She estimated that approximately four out of every five men had venereal disease and suggested that most men opposed women's suffrage because it would no longer allow them to sexually abuse women and because it could bring about the end of prostitution. For Christabel, women's suffrage stood for women's full equality and an end to sexual exploitation and disrespect. "Upon men the effect of women's enfranchisement will be to teach them that women are their human equals, and not the sub-human species that so many men now think them; not slaves to be bought and soiled and degraded and then cast away," she wrote (quoted in Bell and Offen, *Women, the Family, and Freedom*, 219).

Not all suffragettes, including her sister Sylvia, agreed with Christabel's approach, but she was right about one thing. Change in women's political status allowing them the right to support candidates who favored women's rights in other areas did threaten the male-dominated social and economic order, as well as their monopoly on politics. Individuals, groups, and genders do not generally give up power willingly. Women's vote became an acceptable alteration to the political system only after World War I had destroyed the illusions that many held about the stability of English society. It is hard to imagine that women's suffrage could have been postponed much longer even without the war, but one never knows.

The movements for both women's suffrage and Irish Home Rule had received a boost in 1906 when the Liberal Party returned to power and formed a government that ostensibly would be more supportive to these causes than the Conservatives. After 1906 the newly revived Liberal Party, led first by Henry Campbell-Bannerman and then by H. H. Asquith, renewed its commitment to a new Home Rule Bill but refused to consider women's suffrage legislation. By 1912 the leadership of the Liberal Party had proved not only disappointing on the issue of women's suffrage but also had become implacably opposed to the suffragettes' increasingly radical tactics.

The Liberal Party had a great opportunity to make progress on both issues after the Parliament Act of 1911 restricted the veto power of the House of Lords to the ability to delay, but not prevent, legislation. This meant that a bill passed by the House of Commons in three successive years could become law, and it opened the door for the introduction of an Electoral Reform Bill and a new Home Rule Bill. The Liberals introduced both in 1912. The first failed to receive a hearing when the speaker ruled against an amendment to include women's suffrage, but home rule was anticipated to become law in 1914.

Opposition from defiant members of the Conservative Party and even more truculent Ulstermen made this prospect fraught with danger and necessitated a compromise in order to preserve the appearance of parliamentary sovereignty and prevent a possible civil war in Ireland. In 1910 Sir Edward Carson, an M.P. from southern Ireland, emerged as the determined leader of the Ulster movement and voiced fierce resistance to the prospect of Home Rule becoming law in 1914, as did the British Conservative leader Andrew Bonar Law, who stated emphatically in 1912 that "Ireland is not a nation; it is two nations." Asquith essentially ignored the threat rather than stand up to it and never revealed how he proposed to deal with this prospective constitutional crisis, much less the very real prospect of armed resistance. There was some discussion of partition at this time, but it lacked support from either side.

Meanwhile, the supporters of women's suffrage—women and men alike—had been conducting their own increasingly militant campaign. They demonstrated at public meetings and at the houses of Parliament to call attention to their cause. They sent representatives to meet with the prime minister to discuss their goals. They even tried chaining themselves to the railing of the gallery at the House of Commons. They increasingly employed violence in their protest efforts, especially after 1908, but directed most of their destructive tendencies against property rather than people. Among other things they broke windows; destroyed artworks;

vandalized golf courses; and included arson, even of churches, in their repertoire. When they did inflict bodily harm, it was mostly to themselves. The most sensational example of this occurred in 1913 when a young suffragette named Emily Wilding Davison ran onto the Epsom Downs racetrack during a Derby, the most important race of the year, and was trampled to death by the king's horse. Suffragettes who found themselves arrested engaged in hunger strikes, to which the authorities responded with forced feedings of a particularly violent and unpleasant nature. The government enacted legislation, the infamous "Cat and Mouse Act," which allowed women hunger strikers to go free only to be recaptured as soon as their health recovered. Emmeline Pankhurst herself endured four periods of internment, each accompanied by a hunger strike.

An additional comparison of the significance of the two movements involves the violent tactics used by both in their efforts to achieve their goals. World War I intervened in 1914 just as the Liberal government finally gave its assurance to bring forth a bill to introduce women's suffrage and as Irish Home Rule was scheduled to go into effect. The women responded to the war by postponing their own demands and throwing their support behind the government and the war effort. Clearly, the women did not achieve their goals through increasingly radical and violent tactics. To the extent that they called attention to their cause through hunger strikes, arson, property destruction by other means, and physical attacks on politicians, they did not seem to gain additional sympathy. Nor did the radical feminist articles of Christabel Pankhurst awaken the political leaders responsible for granting women the vote to the inherent injustices against women that resulted from their political inequality. Women over the age of thirty achieved the vote peacefully and with little controversy after the war, a period during which even the suffragettes supported the government.

But when the war accomplished what the House of Lords no longer could (a further postponement of Home Rule), a militant, armed Irish movement formed once again. Using the name *Sinn Fein* (We Ourselves), a movement for Irish independence to rival those of John Redmond and the heirs of Parnell had emerged. Unlike Redmond's Irish Nationalist Party, Sinn Fein opposed Irish support for the British war effort and discouraged Irishmen from joining the British army.

While many Irishmen were dying in the British armies, a minority of intellectual revolutionaries led by Padraic Pearse and James Connolly determined that they would not wait for Redmond and the parliamentary party to negotiate. Given the defiance of the Conservatives in Britain, and of the Ulster Unionists in northern Ireland led by Sir Edward Carson, Irish nationalists could scarcely be sure that Parliament would be able to grant

Home Rule, even if they so desired. To prevent the cause for Irish independence from disappearing altogether, they staged a rebellion known as the Easter Rising in April 1916 that involved seizure of the general post office in Dublin. The rebels herded most of the people who happened to be in the building outside before Pearse read a declaration from the steps. Pearse and a flag that had been hoisted above the general post office both proclaimed the birth of the Irish Republic. Pearse announced the creation of a provisional government that would rule until the creation of a permanent government, "representative of the whole people of Ireland and elected by the suffrages of all her men and women" (thus uniting the two movements under consideration in this essay).

Unlike the suffragettes, the Irish Republican Army (IRA) gained in sympathy from their uncompromising stand against British authority. The cause of Irish home rule arguably was achieved in 1922 only through escalating violence that began with the Easter Rebellion of 1916. True, Sinn Fein and the IRA were aided by the harsh repressive measures that the British adopted in response to them. The arrest and imprisonment of those suspected of supporting Sinn Fein provoked widespread sympathy for those killed, imprisoned, or executed in the aftermath of the uprising. The execution of the Easter Rising leaders created martyrs who became powerful symbols for the cause of Irish independence. The Irish continued to fight back through the period of martial law that followed the rebellion. Their resort to violence and the destruction of British property attracted much additional support.

But what of the women brutalized through forced feedings? The violent tactics of the suffragettes even received criticism from other women advocates of the suffrage movement abroad, such as Helene Lange in Germany, who believed that "militant methods have spoiled the mood for woman's suffrage instead of enhancing it" (quoted in Bell and Offen, *Women, the Family, and Freedom* [1983] 243). Perhaps people psychologically accept violence more readily when it is carried out by men rather than by women, in the same way that aggressive men are often rewarded and valued by society, whereas aggressive women tend to be ostracized and treated with scorn. Perhaps it is more acceptable to engage in violence and terrorism on behalf of a suppressed nation than to do so in the political interests of an oppressed gender. These are, admittedly, oversimplifications of two complex movements whose ultimate success hinged on a variety of factors. But they are worth considering, especially since the idealization of the Irish revolutionaries of the period from 1918–1922, such as Michael Collins, created a legitimization of violence in the minds of some people in Ireland that fueled the IRA in Northern Ireland for many years.

As for the Liberal Party, other factors besides the movements for Irish independence and women's suffrage played a role in its decline, including the formation of a Labour Party that specifically represented workers and drained away some of the Liberals' working-class support. The Liberals had begun to appeal to workers through social reforms that the government enacted after 1906. Furthermore, how serious could the Liberal Party split over Irish Home Rule in 1886 have been, given the resurgence of that party in the early twentieth century and the existence of other factors that played into its decline? For example, the Conservatives benefited from the popularity of imperialism in the last quarter of the nineteenth century, though some imperialists remained committed to liberalism.

Yet the Home Rule issue significantly affected the fortunes of the Liberal Party for twenty years, not an insignificant stretch of time in politics. Furthermore, when the Liberal Party did reemerge as the dominant party in Parliament after 1906, it depended to a large extent on the support from the Irish Party and thus had to renew its commitment to Home Rule. This time, Home Rule did not split the party but it almost split the country. Only the outbreak of World War I in 1914 prevents us from knowing how divisive this split would have been or the seriousness of its repercussions. David Lloyd George's repressive policy in Ireland after the war finally destroyed the Liberal Party's claim to rule, even though most liberals opposed his tactics.

As for the effect of the demands for women's suffrage on the Liberal Party, these helped to expose the limitations of the party and just how nonliberal it was on certain issues. The failure of the Liberal government to make any serious strides toward women's suffrage infuriated some and frustrated others and seemed to symbolize its inability to address or cope with the important social issues that emerged in the years prior to World War I. If the Liberal party could not meet the demands of potential supporters such as the working classes, the Irish nationalists, or women, how could it continue to build support and grow a strong base from which to draw?

Women may not have achieved full equality in every sense of the word, but enormous changes in politics and society in their favor have followed the inception of women's suffrage in 1918, when women over thirty received the right to vote. The suffrage movement, however, continues to inspire interest, controversy, and discussion related to the relationship between the sexes and cultural constructions of femininity and masculinity. An organization of men in support of women's suffrage and one of women in opposition in the first decade of the twentieth century demonstrate the blurring of gender divisions on gender issues. Society continues to struggle with concepts of masculinity and femininity in ways that defy simple opposition between the sexes.

Northern Ireland remains a thorny problem for the government of the United Kingdom, even though its leaders have made numerous attempts to reach a resolution to the "troubles" that have plagued that region since the late 1960s. In retrospect, the opposition of Ulster to Irish Home Rule since the 1880s has had great significance not only for Ireland, but for any politician who has either made Ireland an issue or tried to resolve the problems in Northern Ireland ever since.

SELECTED BIBLIOGRAPHY

Bell, Susan Groag, and Karen M. Offen, eds. *Women, the Family, and Freedom: The Debate in Documents*, Vol. 2, *1880–1950*. Stanford, CA: Stanford University Press, 1983. Although this collection of primary source documents covers a much wider chronological and geographical range than this essay, it is recommended both for the superb primary source selections on the British movement for women's suffrage, the outstanding introductions to those sources, and the larger international context it provides.

Bew, Paul. *Conflict and Conciliation in Ireland, 1890–1910: Parnellites and Radical Agrarians*. Oxford: Clarendon Press, 1987. An excellent study of the two decades following the fall of Charles Stewart Parnell, providing a good account of the split in the Irish nationalist movement that occurred at that time and a good understanding of Parnell's successor, John Redmond.

Bradshaw, Brendan. "Nationalism and Historical Scholarship in Modern Ireland," *Irish Historical Studies* 26, no. 104 (1989): 329–51. Bradshaw was one of the first writers to criticize the revisionist movement in Irish historiography that had questioned the nationalist slant of much writing of Irish history; he offers something of a defense of the nationalist interpretation.

Brooks, David. *The Age of Upheaval: Edwardian Politics, 1899–1914*. Manchester: Manchester University Press, 1995. Brooks challenges George Dangerfield's interpretation, arguing that the suffragettes engaged in self-defeating tactics and that a solution to the Irish problem might have emerged had war not intervened; hence, disorder but no crisis.

Coogan, Tim Pat. *The Man Who Made Ireland: The Life and Death of Michael Collins*. Niwot, CO: Roberts Rhinehart, 1992. Coogan has written more than just an excellent biography of Collins; he gives the reader a good understanding of the social and political context of Collins's life and the movement for Irish independence.

Dangerfield, George. *The Strange Death of Liberal England 1910–1914*. 1935. Reprint, New York: Perigree Books, 1980. In this important but highly impressionistic treatment of prewar England, Dangerfield argues that the increased militancy of the working classes, the suffragettes, and opponents of Irish Home Rule led to a crisis that meant the end of "liberal" England prior to the outbreak of World War I.

Dwyer, T. Ryle. *Big Fellow, Long Fellow: A Joint Biography of Collins and de Valera*. New York: St. Martin's Press, 1998. Dwyer has written a readable and comparative account of the lives of and relationship between these two important leaders in the movement for Irish independence, arguing that personal differences largely contributed to the division between them on the eve of the realization of Irish Home Rule.

Hennessey, Thomas. *Dividing Ireland: World War I and Partition.* London: Routledge, 1998. Hennessey deals with the Easter Rebellion and its aftermath and shows in detail how the British, against sound advice from within their ranks, went about completely alienating many in Ireland who otherwise might have had little sympathy for the rebels or the IRA.

Holton, Sandra Stanley. *Feminism and Democracy: Women's Suffrage and Reform Politics in Britain, 1900–1918.* New York: Cambridge University Press, 1986. This important book focuses on the relationship between class and the women's suffrage movement and argues that the gender concerns of the suffrage movement united women of all social classes and different economic backgrounds.

Hume, Leslie Parker. *The National Union of Women's Suffrage Societies, 1897–1914.* New York: Garland, 1982. Hume concentrates on the importance of the National Union and gives them credit for preparing the way for women's suffrage, providing a counterbalance to the attention that the more militant Women's Social and Political Union has received.

John, Angela, and Claire Eustance, eds. *The Men's Share: Masculinities, Male Support, and Women's Suffrage in Britain, 1890–1920.* London: Routledge, 1997. The essays in this volume explore different dimensions of the role that men played in the suffrage movement and the ways that their support led to different ideas about gender and what it meant to be a man; especially recommended are the chapters by Angela John and Sandra Stanley Holton.

Kee, Robert. *The Laurel and the Ivy: The Story of Charles Stewart Parnell and Irish Nationalism.* London: Harris and Hamilton, 1993. Along with F.S.L. Lyons, Kee provides a readable, interesting account of the life of Parnell and his importance for the nationalist movement in Ireland.

Lyons, F.S.L. *Charles Stewart Parnell.* New York: Oxford University Press, 1977. Lyons, who has written a number of outstanding books on Irish history, has also written the standard biography of Parnell, which is recommended as the place to start for readers interested in his life.

Morley, Ann, with Liz Stanley. *The Life and Death of Emily Wilding Davison, with Gertrude Colmore's "The Life of Emily Davison."* London: Women's Press, 1988. Morley and Stanley offer a revision of the life of Emily Wilding Davison, the suffragette who was trampled to death by the king's horse, arguing that her life and death have been distorted for political purposes.

O'Connor, Ulick. *Michael Collins and the Troubles: The Struggle for Irish Freedom, 1912–1922.* New York: W. W. Norton, 1996. O'Connor's treatment is not quite as scholarly as Coogan's biography of Collins, but it is quite worthwhile as an overview of the decade preceding Irish home rule and provides a good understanding of Collins's role in the movement for Irish independence.

Powell, David. *The Edwardian Crisis: Britain 1901–14.* London: Macmillan, 1996. Powell addresses George Dangerfield's thesis by considering the fourteen years prior to World War I; this good, up-to-date treatment of the period should be read as a supplement to Dangerfield.

Pugh, Martin. *The March of Women: A Revisionist Analysis of the Campaign for Women's Suffrage, 1866–1914*. Oxford: Oxford University Press, 2000. Pugh combines social and political analysis of the women's suffrage movement and attempts to place the movement within the context of its times rather than examining it from a current feminist perspective.

Rubinstein, David. *A Different World for Women: The Life of Millicent Garrett Fawcett*. Columbus: Ohio State University Press, 1991. In this sympathetic account of the life of the leader of the National Union of Women's Suffrage Societies, Rubinstein acknowledges Fawcett's willingness to risk alienating her own supporters by endorsing the militant tactics of the suffragettes in order to achieve the larger goal of women's suffrage.

Smith, Harold L. *The British Women's Suffrage Campaign, 1866–1928*. London: Longman, 1998. This book provides a good factual overview of the suffrage campaign, scholarly and historiographical analysis, and primary source documents, making it an excellent place to start for a consideration of the topic.

Smith, Jeremy. *Britain and Ireland: From Home Rule to Independence*. Harlow, England: Longman, 2000. This book belongs to the same series as the previous entry and serves much the same purpose for the movement for Irish independence.

8

World War I, 1914–1919

INTRODUCTION

In mid-Victorian Great Britain, there was a distinct sense of antimilitarism. The British people did not like to think of themselves as a military-minded society, and the British army was relatively small and neglected. This attitude began to change in the 1870s as the specter of international threats to British security began to form following the swift Prussian victory in the Franco-Prussian War (1870–1871) and the consequent merging of Prussia with a number of other Germanic states and principalities to form the modern nation of Germany.

Not only was the thought of an external threat new, but also the potential enemy—Germany—was new. History told the British that if there were to be a fight, it would be with the French or, possibly, the Russians. Germany, with its dynastic ties to Great Britain through the House of Hanover, was simply too civilized a country. While there was some economic and colonial rivalry with Germany in the 1880s and 1890s, it was not until the British discovered around 1900 that the Germans were building a navy the equal of Britain's that relations began to deteriorate.

In addition, the Boer War of 1899–1902 exposed the unhappy fact that Great Britain was quite isolated in Europe, and that the British military was probably inadequate to meet a major challenge from a European rival. This

This photograph of British troops bogged down in the mud of the Western Front during World War I illustrates the incredibly difficult conditions under which men had to live and fight. Reproduced from the Collections of the Library of Congress.

led to the movement for National Efficiency, which included the creation of a Committee of Imperial Defence, an Officer's Training Corps, and a General Staff, all designed to improve the professionalism of the military. In addition, other measures were undertaken to increase the physical fitness level of British schoolchildren based on recommendations of the ominously named Inter-Departmental Committee on Physical Deterioration. Lobbying for greater military preparedness from outside Parliament were conservative groups such as the Navy League and the National Service League, which promoted the idea of universal male conscription. This idea was never adopted, however, and the British volunteer efforts in 1914 and 1915 showed that it had not been needed.

After 1900 Great Britain moved out of its long period of "splendid isolation." In the United States, the presidency of Anglophile Theodore Roosevelt (1901–1909) strengthened the bonds between the two largest English-speaking nations. The Anglo-Japanese Alliance of 1902 was, ironically, an attempt to avoid entanglements in the Pacific by leaving that responsibility to Japan, but the Russo-Japanese War of 1904–1905 forced Britain into closer relations with France in order to keep that country, an ally of Russia, neutral. In addition, Britain and France both wanted to ameliorate colonial disputes in North Africa. These events led to the Anglo-French Entente of 1904, which became the Triple Entente in 1907 with the addition of Russia, who was welcomed into the alliance both to lessen colonial rivalries and to provide a counterpoint to an increasingly militaristic Germany.

By 1907, Germany and Great Britain were sliding into an intensive arms race. Germany had spurned British appeals for arms reductions, and a crisis in Bosnia accelerated naval construction on both sides. Responding further to the perceived German threat, the British government organized a ready-response Expeditionary Force of 160,000 men, backed up by 300,000 territorial troops and improved logistical support. The Committee of Imperial Defence began making specific contingency plans for a continental war. In addition, both nations were creating extensive alliance systems. Britain, France, and Russia stood against Germany, Austria-Hungary, and Turkey, with smaller nations such as Belgium, Serbia, and Bulgaria attached to one side or the other.

The assassination of the Austrian archduke Franz Ferdinand and his wife at Sarajevo in June 1914 that triggered World War I ended two years of somewhat improved Anglo-German relations highlighted by their cooperation in keeping the Balkan Wars of 1912–1913 from spreading. After Sarajevo, Lord Grey, the British foreign minister, tried to find a way to do the same thing through a European conference, but to no avail. When Austria-Hungary declared war on Serbia after the assassination, Russia honored its treaty agreement with Serbia, and other European nations, bound by their treaty obligations, felt the chill of oncoming war. Germany declared war on France on August 3 and invaded Belgium the following day, and Britain's hand was forced.

Soon after the outbreak of the war, Lord Kitchener was appointed secretary of state for war, and because the coalition cabinet was politically fragile, Kitchener had free reign to conduct military affairs while the rest of the cabinet adopted a business-as-usual policy for Great Britain. Kitchener correctly assumed that the war would be a long one requiring, literally, millions of troops. The four-hundred-thousand–man British Expeditionary Force was clearly inadequate for the task of securing the British sector of the Western Front, but the manpower need was readily met by millions of volunteers who joined so quickly that the government was unprepared to train and supply them all. Many thousands of additional troops came from Australia, New Zealand, Canada, and South Africa.

Most British and Commonwealth troops, except those from India, fought on the Western Front, where a battle line had stabilized by the end of 1914. It ran from the Belgian coast west of Ostend through western Belgium and northeastern France down to neutral Switzerland. For the next three and a half years this front changed very little. By this time, the industrial revolution had greatly changed the technology of military defense, seen in the much-improved machine gun and impenetrable barbed wire, that governed offensive tactics, making every attack along the Western Front horrifically more costly than any previous war in terms of casualties. To fight this kind of war required immense numbers of men, and by 1917, 4 million had seen service in the British army. Of those who served, some 750,000 were killed and another 1.7 million were wounded, many thousands so severely that they could never again function normally in society.

The low point in the war for the British forces was probably the attack at the Somme River in July 1916. A new British commander-in-chief, Douglas Haig, planned a frontal assault on German positions, hoping to bring about a quick and decisive victory and end the war. It was a tactical disaster. On the first day of the offensive sixty thousand British were killed or wounded, the heaviest one-day loss any army had ever sustained. A similar result occurred at the Battle of Passchendaele the following year. British troops tried to breach German lines, got bogged down hopelessly in the mud, and were easy prey for German machine guns.

Back home, David Lloyd George became prime minister in December 1916, replacing H. H. Asquith. Politicians of all parties felt Lloyd George was best suited to end this seemingly endless war. Lloyd George assembled a coalition government made up of individuals who understood that objective. The new prime minister streamlined decision-making by creating a five-member War Council, which consisted of the Labour and Conservative party leaders; the chancellor of the Exchequer; Lord Curzon, the former Viceroy to India; and Lord Milner, the former British High Commissioner in South Africa. Government authority was extended with the creation of ministries of labor, shipping, and food to go along with the existing ministry of munitions, and some ministerial appointments came from outside politics.

That is not to say that all ran smoothly in London. Lloyd George disliked and distrusted both Haig, his field commander, and Sir William Robertson, the chief of the imperial general staff, and tried to find ways to maximize the effectiveness of Great Britain's resources without letting Haig send too many men to their deaths.

In April 1917, three months after the Germans adopted a policy of unrestricted submarine warfare, the United States, the principal victim of that policy, entered the war. This had a great impact on the British war effort because, even before U.S. troops arrived in France, U.S. money and supplies were much more readily available. Despite large numbers of ships sunk by German submarines, grain and other goods got through in large quantities, especially after a convoy system was established in August 1917. American troops began to reach the Western Front in early 1918, played a role in thwarting German offensives in the spring of that year, and helped the final Allied offensive (launched in August 1918) succeed in forcing the Germans to seek an armistice in November. The end of the war brought great relief to Great Britain and its politicians, and Lloyd George, now credited for having won the war, quickly called for a new general election. It was held just three days after the November 11 armistice, and Lloyd George won on the promise to make Britain "a fit land for heroes to live in."

The Paris Peace Conference, which lasted from January until June 1919, involved delegations from twenty-seven nations and resulted in the Treaty of Versailles. It is usually portrayed in the United States as a hassle-filled affair in which the idealistic U.S. president Woodrow Wilson, striving to make the world safe for democracy by means of a League of Nations, had to deal with the vengeful European leaders, Lloyd George, Georges Clemenceau of France, and Vittorio Orlando of Italy. Historian Peter Clarke maintains, however, that Lloyd George wanted a just peace in Great Britain's interests. His ability to bring that about was complicated by the fact that he knew Britain owed the United States huge amounts of money borrowed during the war. The United States was not willing to forgive these debts, and this forced Lloyd George to look for an arrangement that would satisfy his domestic opponents and provide a means for repayment. Thus astronomical reparations from Germany became an integral part of the peace treaty. Lloyd George might have wanted reparations kept low enough that Germany could realistically make the payments, but France's reconstruction needs and the dominions' (all that fought) demands for their share forced Lloyd George to insist that the indirect costs of war be added to the reparations bill, pushing the total amount well beyond even a healthy Germany's ability to pay. Lloyd George agreed to the arrangement with the hope and expectation that revisions would later be made in the terms, as indeed they were in 1924 and again in 1929. But Germany never recovered enough before the Great Depression of the 1930s to pay more than a small fraction of its reparations obligations.

Apart from reparations, Lloyd George's principal objectives at the peace conference were to end the German naval threat to Great Britain's maritime supremacy, to obtain additional colonies in Africa and the Middle East, and to reassert British economic dominance in many parts of the world. Among other things, this meant normalizing relations with Germany quickly, since Germany had been a valuable trading partner before the war. The prime minister was generally successful in these areas. German naval construction was forbidden and Britain assumed control (through mandates rather than actual annexation) of most of Germany's African territories, including Togo and German East Africa, and of substantial territory in the Middle East that had been part of the crumbling Ottoman Empire, including Iraq, Jordan, and Palestine. Lloyd George's efforts to reassert British economic dominance, however, was blunted by serious economic and labor problems at home, the immense reconstruction costs in Europe, and the emergence of the United States as a major global economic force.

INTERPRETIVE ESSAY
Larry P. Thornton

World War I affected virtually every British citizen so that each man, woman, and child knew without a doubt that they were no longer the same people and Great Britain was no longer the land they once knew. Long before the war's end, Britons called it the "Great War." They recognized its magnitude and were certain that they had never before seen its likes. In this context, *Great* connoted more than big; it was terrible, gruesome, catastrophic, and all-consuming. The war tormented literally millions of people while also opening doors of opportunity, innovation, and liberation, and dramatically altering Britain's place in the world. The Great War ended one era and initiated its successor.

Before 1914 war was a common topic of discussion and widely anticipated. Public figures had long declaimed the virtues of war: it ennobled men and made the empire. War would sustain Great Britain's honor and distract the population from the divisive issues of the day. Most young men had been nurtured on tales of the glory of the wars against Napoleon, in the Crimea, in the Indian subcontinent, or in some other part of the empire. War offered the promise of adventure, career advancement, or simple escape from everyday routine.

Great Britain's recent war experiences had been limited to conflicts in the colonies, small affairs in distant lands. The last major war had ended in 1815 with the defeat of Napoleon. Recent wars (the South African, or Boer, War [1899–1902], the Spanish-American War [1898], and the Russo-Japanese War [1904–1905]) demonstrated the changing face of war, although most saw these conflicts as aberrations. New technologies such as the machine gun and the "flying machine" pitted men against machines in ways disadvantageous to men. Enthusiasm for war persisted, but few people realized that the war they yearned for existed primarily in their imaginations.

Initially in Great Britain, as elsewhere across the European continent, people exhibited an enthusiasm for the onset of war in August 1914 that with hindsight is difficult to understand. They poured into the streets in largely spontaneous demonstrations of patriotic fervor. Since many assumed the war would be brief—"Home by Christmas" was the widely repeated cliché—young men rushed to enlist. They did not want to miss the spectacle.

Two factors brought Great Britain into the war. First, Britain was allied with both France and Russia in what was called the Triple Entente, formed in 1907. The terms of this alliance called on its signatories to assist one another militarily in case of an unprovoked military assault by another state. Germany declared war on Russia on August 1, 1914 and on France two days later. Second, the German attack on France was launched through neutral Belgium, and Belgium's neutrality had been a matter of international law since 1830. The maintenance of Belgian neutrality had been an important plank in British foreign policy throughout the decades. Thus the British government acted in support of Belgium as well as of France and Russia on 4 August 1914 when it declared war on Germany. Lord Grey, the British foreign minister, remarked that the lights were going out all over Europe.

Before the end of August the British Expeditionary Force (BEF), numbering slightly more than one hundred thousand men, joined the French and Belgian armies, seeking to stop the German advance toward Paris. Its deployment was sharply constrained by the fact that the BEF had only one plan of action, drawn up in 1911, and that was to occupy the ground to the "left" (or north) of the French forces. This plan largely determined where the BEF would spend the next four years. The BEF had its first contact with German forces near Mons in Belgium and acquitted itself quite well, firing rifles at a rate of fifteen shots per minute, which persuaded the Germans that they were fully equipped with machine guns when in fact they had only two per battalion. After this initial good showing, German pressure forced the British, French, and Belgian forces into retreat.

Very quickly though, the power of the machines of war produced a stalemate on what came to be known as the Western Front. Neither side was able to assert supremacy, and the sheer firepower of the machine guns and artillery forced soldiers to dig into the ground for some protection from the lead-filled air. Although most prognosticators expected a brief war of movement, within weeks the Great War turned into a war of attrition fought from opposing trenches. Trench warfare introduced a long list of horrors.

Nature tormented the soldiers as much as the war itself. Soldiers lived largely exposed to the elements year-round. Water and mud exacerbated the situation. In the British portion of the line of trenches, the land was very near sea level, which meant that wherever one dug into the ground, one quickly reached water. This area also received considerable rain throughout the year. Water in the trenches was commonly ankle deep, but sometimes soldiers stood for hours in water up to their waists or even their armpits. They could not keep their feet dry, which led to an ailment called trench foot that could turn a foot gangrenous. The mud made walking from one place to another exhausting. The mud was also life threatening. British soldiers frequently drowned in mud so deep that their comrades could not pull them out without the risk of being sucked under themselves. Water seepage also undermined whatever work they had done on the trench system, forcing soldiers to repair their trenches repeatedly.

In addition to the elements of nature, the soldiers had to contend with countless other pests. Accumulated rubbish, urine, and excrement, along with thousands of unwashed men and unburied or partially buried corpses, attracted every sort of vermin and provided an environment in which they thrived. Flies, fleas, and lice brought torment to one and all. Rats were a particular blight. Tens of millions of rats ranged over the trenches getting fat on corpses and even crawling over sleeping soldiers to search their pockets for food.

The daily routine of trench life was an assault on all the senses. Soldiers had to contend with the persistent stench from chloride of lime used to combat infection, creosol to reduce flies, latrine contents, smoke from braziers, sweat, mildew, and decomposing flesh. Even the food took on the taste of these odors. Putrefaction was ever present. Soldiers also endured the sounds and feel of artillery barrages that might drop a few shells over a ten-minute period or drop as many as thirty a minute for hours and hours. Visually, the world of the trenches looked nothing like Earth. The ground was pockmarked with shell holes, strewn with barbed wire, and stripped of most vegetation and life other than pests and soldiers. Those consigned to this alien environment felt the continual discomfort of wet feet, exhaustion from chronic lack of sleep, the endless struggle with the mud, and most of all, fear.

As if all this were not bad enough, there was the war itself. The trench system featured roughly parallel trenches facing each other across a no-man's-land covered with barbed wire and other obstacles. The average distance between the opposing trenches was two to three hundred meters (the distance varied, but an important rule of thumb was that the barbed wire had to be at least a grenade's throw away from one's own trenches). Behind the front trenches was a complex network of connecting trenches for moving reinforcements or replacements and supplies. In 1915 the French estimated they had twenty miles of trench for each mile of the line; thus the entire Western Front on the Allied side had perhaps as much as fifteen thousand miles of trenches. Another indication of the scale of the trenches is the statistic that the BEF issued 10,638,000 shovels and spades to its soldiers on all fronts during the war.

With respect to combat, both small-scale and large-scale offensives revolved around the principal tactic of the frontal infantry assault. Some attacks were largely localized, lasting a few hours or, at most, several days, whereas others were along a longer section of the line and continued for weeks or even months. The senior officers in all armies generally believed that human will was the most important weapon of war, and they were convinced that a glorious charge would strike fear in the enemy so that they would surrender or break ranks and run. Many of the generals described the frontal assault in terms of its "beauty" or "moral" superiority.

The strategists and tacticians in the Great War ignored the implications of the technological advances in weaponry. Machine guns and rifles gave an overwhelming advantage to the defenders, especially when the attacking forces had to struggle with the mud, barbed wire, and other obstacles of no-man's-land before they could get close enough to inflict any harm. The new technologies of war were the dominant force on battlefield, but those who drew up the battle plans and deployed the soldiers persisted in their belief in men *en masse*. Few, if any, senior officers learned any of the lessons provided by the American Civil War (1861–1865) or other more recent wars. Ignoring the implications of these weapons brought gains measured in only a few meters at best while producing huge casualty rates.

One side sought to use artillery barrages to break through the obstacles of no-man's-land and to "soften up" the opposing trenches, thus reducing the advantages of the defenders. Intense bombardments introduced a new malady, shell shock. The noise and pounding took its toll on men huddled in underground bunkers for hours and hours. (The British fired more than 170 million artillery rounds during the war.) As the bombardment ended, the attacking infantry went "over the top" into no-man's-land and the defenders emerged from their trenches to man their machine guns and rifles. These assaults were deadly. At the Second Battle of Ypres (April 1915) entire brigades were almost annihilated; the 149th Brigade lost 75 percent of its officers and men and the 10th Brigade almost ceased to exist, losing 73 officers and 2,346 men of other ranks. In the first two hours at Loos, the BEF lost more men than would be lost by all services on all of D-Day (June 6, 1944) in World War II. On the second day at Loos 10,000 soldiers launched another assault and 285 officers and 7, 861 men were lost in three and a half hours. On the first day of the Battle of the Somme in 1916, the 8th Division lost 218 of its 300 officers and 5,274 out of 8,500 enlisted men, while their German foes lost fewer than 300. Although these battles were meticulously planned at headquarters with clearly defined objectives, the "beauty" of the frontal infantry assault degenerated into chaos once the show began.

To suggest that the frontal assault characterized the war experience is somewhat misleading. Soldiers passed considerable time without contact with the enemy. Their time was filled with night patrols, dusk and dawn "stand-tos" (during which everyone manned the parapets in case of assault), trench repair, inspections, and assorted other tasks. Between night patrols and daytime assignments, soldiers suffered from a chronic lack of sleep. The normal sequence involved service in the front line, a period of time in reserve positions somewhat behind the front line, and then a short period of rest. There was no set system of rotation. In some places units spent two eight-day terms on the line followed by one eight-day period in support and one in rest, but there are also examples of extremely long assignments at the front. In 1915 one Scottish battalion spent thirty-eight consecutive days and another battalion passed seventy days out of ninety in the front trenches. Even when the fighting was light, life was miserable and death ever present.

There were many different ways to die in this war. Approximately half of the officers and men in the BEF were casualties (118,941 officers and 2,571,113 men killed, wounded, or missing). Although many were killed in the big battles, many others succumbed to the work of snipers or the effects of living in wet, exposed trenches. Death also came from badly aimed shells from one's own guns, what came to be called "friendly fire" in the Vietnam War (1959–1975).

Poison gas was one of the most insidious weapons used in this war. Dispensed by cylinders and artillery shells, it worked more slowly than bullets, grenades, or bombs. First used in 1915, chlorine gas slowly asphyxiated its victims, sometimes taking days to produce death. Most gas casualties, however, came from mustard gas. Initially there were no obvious effects as the gas assaulted the body internally. Then skin and eyes blistered, followed by nausea and vomiting as the gas attacked the bronchial tubes and the mucous membranes. All of this was extremely painful, but death might not come for a month. Many of those who survived mustard gas attacks were blinded and plagued by respiratory problems for the rest of their lives.

Gas proved to be indiscriminate though, as likely to attack one's own soldiers as the enemy's, and incapable of breaking the stalemate. In the search for something that *would* break it all armies sought to employ the new weapons. Researchers were employed to harness science and technology, but the new weapons frequently were not used to their greatest effect by those officers wedded to the frontal assault. For example, tanks had the capacity to assault trenches with an effectiveness that the infantry lacked, but their deployment evenly throughout the regiments limited their impact. Toward the end of the war tanks played increasingly important roles but their fuller impact would not be realized until World War II. Airplanes initially competed with hot-air balloons and zeppelins for observing enemy activities. In time the pilots began to shoot at one another and drop explosives but their planes lacked the capacity for sustained firepower. The Germans periodically sent zeppelins across the English Channel on bombing raids, but neither side waged concerted war against civilians. During the Great War various motor vehicles, flame-throwers, and the radio were also introduced.

Life in the trenches changed those who fought there as well as the women who worked in hospitals and other facilities close to the fighting to such an extent that they struggled with psychological problems upon their return home. Feeling ill suited for civilian life, many soldiers experienced a strange pull back to the trenches. For years after the war many veterans had a sense of permanent alienation, seen in the title of Robert Graves's memoir, *Goodbye to All That*. They came to be called the "Lost Generation," a reference to those actually dead or relegated to institutional care for the rest of their lives as well as those who were so disillusioned that they turned against conventional society.

Although the fighting may be the most obvious manifestation of war, World War I also significantly affected noncombatants who labored and sacrificed to sustain and supply the war effort. In Great Britain, the Great War challenged many traditional assumptions, in particular, assumptions about the role of women and the nature of the economy. Although a vocal minority of women had for decades been calling for the right to vote and an expansion of opportunities for women, their situation, determined largely by socioeconomic class distinctions, had not changed much. Upper-class women were primarily acculturated to do nothing of value, although some of the professions were just beginning to open to them. Many women had never held paid employment of any kind. Working class women were kept out of skilled trades, earning their wages in domestic service, agricultural work, dressmaking, and other low-wage positions.

When Great Britain entered the war, women joined in the enthusiasm. Most suffragettes replaced their calls for the vote with calls for national unity and patriotism. As men flocked to the recruiting stations and issued calls for all citizens to contribute to the war effort, British women wondered what their role would be in this crusade. Initially they were counseled to knit garments and engage in other traditionally female activities, a reflection of the conservatism of the authorities as well as their misunderstanding of the demands of modern war. Few men or women had any sense of the possible contributions women might make. Most people's perspectives were governed by the fundamental assumption that most tasks connected to the war effort exceeded the capacity of women.

As it became clear that the war would continue past Christmas 1914 and that the BEF needed more and more men, the British began to move slowly toward the employment of women in industry and agriculture in order to release men for military service. In March 1915 government officials announced the formation of a registry of women who were willing to do industrial, agricultural, and clerical work. Women responded immediately and enthusiastically, but applicants did not find many employers willing to engage them. In July 1915 about thirty thousand women demonstrated in London on behalf of women's "right to serve." Gradually the demands of production compounded by labor shortages overcame prejudice and conservatism. After the introduction of conscription in 1916 the employment of women increased by leaps and bounds.

In July 1914 the munitions industries employed approximately 212,000 women. This number increased slightly over the first year of the war, but by July 1916 it had more than doubled to 520,000. More than 800,000 women were employed in the munitions industry by July 1917 and at least 100,000 more joined their ranks before the war ended in 1918. In industry in general, the numbers of girls over ten and women working in the industrial sector increased from 2,179,000 to 2,971,000 during the war. Banking and finance, the bastions of British conservatism, employed more than six times as many women by 1917 (63,700) as in 1914 (9,500). The only areas where the number of women working decreased were in the low-paying factory jobs, the dressmaking trades, and domestic service.

By the end of the war, working women seemed to be everywhere. Women served as train or bus conductors, clerks, drivers, milk deliverers, window cleaners, ticket takers, and factory workers. They ran canteens to aid departing or returning soldiers. They served as nurses in hospitals near the front lines and in recuperation stations in Great Britain. Men were profoundly surprised by women's capacity to do both physical and mental work. Most observers recognized the importance of women's work to the war effort. In 1915 David Lloyd George, the future prime minister, said, "Without women victory will tarry and the victory which tarries means a victory whose footprints are footprints of blood." Later in the war, Minister of Munitions E. S. Montagu noted that "our armies have been saved and victory assured by the women in the munitions factories." War provided the opportunity for women to demonstrate abilities that advocates for women's rights had repeatedly asserted they possessed.

Buoyed by their wages, women began to exercise more independence. Prior to the war, many social constraints, such as parental or spousal authority, limited women's public life. For many women, the war provided an independent income for the very first time, and this economic independence fostered increasing social independence. In the absence of men, women felt more comfortable dining out, either alone or with another woman. Unescorted women even spent time in public houses. In many circles smoking in public was considered shocking behavior for a woman, but it became more commonplace during the war. With their new sense of status, women became just what conservatives feared—independent.

Fashions for women also changed dramatically during the war. Prewar dress wrapped women in layers and layers of garments from chin to toe. Such encumbered dress reflected the widely held assumption that women, especially of the middle and upper classes, were not doing anything practical. People were amazed as hemlines left the floor, revealing ankles. Women also donned trousers in the workplace and even after work. Observers noted that the use of cosmetics increased dramatically during the war. Prior to the war, respectable women had largely eschewed heavy use of makeup. Concern for appearance is nothing new, but many women had more disposable income than ever before. Another less visible but lasting change came as the brassiere replaced the camisole.

Increased sexual activity was another manifestation of growing independence for both men and women. Sex without benefit of marriage was not unusual in the working classes, but before the war, parents of middle- and upper-class young women carefully supervised their daughters and sought to limit not only their social activities but also their access to information about sex. Chaperones accompanied young women everywhere. During the war many chaperones were otherwise occupied, and young women were increasingly free to make their own way. In addition to increased freedom for young women, there was a pervasive sense of the fragility of life that undercut conventional morality. It was obvious to one and all that young men might go away, never to return. For many men and women, waiting until the war's end made less and less sense.

Although sex came earlier and was more precious for many couples, sex also seemed insignificant to many others during the war. Observers all across Great Britain recognized that sexual activity during the war differed from the prewar situation. Some suggested that women starved for masculine company aggressively pursued any man in uniform. There is evidence that many people reached out for comfort or distraction in this stressful time. In the areas near military bases, birth rates increased dramatically. During the war some suggested that these "war babies" were necessary "replacements" for the casualties, while others sought to sustain conventional standards, wringing their hands over the crisis of immorality.

More important than fashion and manners, the war service of British women undercut the long-standing opposition to women's suffrage. Many men had opposed granting women the right to vote on the grounds that women could not help defend the country and thus were unqualified to participate in political decision-making. Two famous examples of heroic war service effectively disposed of that assumption. In 1915 Dr. Elsie Inglis's offer to form a women's ambulance corps was rebuffed by an official in the War Office who said, "My good lady, go home and sit still." Ignoring his advice, she led a staff that established the Scottish Women's Hospitals, which performed admirably in war-torn Serbia. And in 1915 military authorities in German-occupied Belgium executed Red Cross nurse Edith Cavell for aiding the escape of Allied prisoners. These highly publicized stories as well as the examples of women doing vital work closer to home overcame the prejudices of many men and the fears and hostilities of many women. The British Parliament enacted legislation in February 1918 granting women over age thirty and all adult males the right to vote.

In addition to these challenges to conventional thinking, the demands of the war brought into question Great Britain's commitment to the hallmarks of *laissez-faire* economics, free trade, free currency, and free enterprise. Initially government officials and businessmen proclaimed business as usual would sufficiently provide for both the military forces and the civilian sector. Even so, the government took control of the railroads, requisitioned 20 percent of the merchant ships, and sought to exercise control over strategic materials in the early days of the war. Gradually it became obvious that the war would last longer than expected and demand an unprecedented production of war supplies and a complex organization that "business as usual" could not satisfy. Slowly, fitfully, the British government took a greater and greater role in running the economy to support the war. Over the course of the war, government spending multiplied by a factor of six. Although many staunch free-market advocates were not convinced, necessity required that pre-war economic assumptions be set aside.

Curiously enough, one early program to stimulate industrial production focused on alcohol. Excessive alcohol consumption negatively affected industrial production, according to some analysts, and a campaign against alcohol was launched. Although few people inside or outside government followed his example, King George V pledged to abstain from alcohol for the duration of the war. Government regulations remodeled the liquor-licensing system, restricted hours, and increased prices. Other regulations limited alcohol content and, later, affected the supply by restricting the cultivation of hops.

Over the course of the war, these and other actions transformed Great Britain from a land where drunkenness was commonplace among most classes to a land where excessive drinking was more the exception. Whether this campaign had any effect on industrial production is difficult to prove.

Shortages of essential material forced the government to move away from business as usual in 1915. Efforts to increase production and distribution brought the government into the midst of a myriad of philosophical and practical private-property and labor issues. Over the next two years the government faced significant disapproval of its efforts to cope with the problems of war. Shortages of artillery shells imperiled the lives of the men in uniform. It became obvious that there was a growing public expectation that the state be more active in directing the economy. Increasingly the state sought to direct labor and restrain rising prices, but by 1918 the government owned more than 250 factories.

A ministry of munitions was established in 1915, and this agency struggled to organize labor and production without resorting to conscription. The government ruled that no employee could leave a place of employment without the employer's consent. Not surprisingly, union officials and working people objected to this loss of freedom. There were numerous efforts to protect skilled workers from military service while, at the same time, to get as many men into uniform as possible. A national registry of all persons aged fifteen to sixty-five was established to replace the myriad of local programs. Still, virtually every sector of society opposed conscription.

Necessity sometimes makes for strange partnerships. The war heightened long-simmering labor issues, but British government officials and union leaders worked together in unprecedented ways to address these issues as well as others raised by the demands of the war. Labor leaders formed partnerships with officials in the government ministries and the owners of the factories and mines to establish policies and limit conflicts. Labor agreements were modified to open the skilled trades to unskilled and semi-skilled workers as well as to women.

Even in the midst of a patriotic cause, workers were concerned that they were carrying an unfair portion of the burden. With the declaration of war, prices for many essential goods began to rise. Wages also rose, but not as fast. The Board of Trade estimated that the cost of living for an unskilled worker rose 81 percent and for a skilled worker 67 percent over the course of the war. Obviously the workers appreciated higher wages more than higher prices for food, rent, and other necessities. They called attention to examples of profiteering and sought to protect their gains in the face of inflation. As the union leaders were increasingly bound by the partnership with government and management, shop stewards became more powerful. In 1915 shop stewards led local strikes over wages and restrictions of workers' freedom of mobility. Other labor activists called for protection of particular trades, of the right to strike, and against increased rents. Tensions and occasional conflicts persisted throughout the war.

The Great War consumed manpower, and the authorities repeatedly struggled to satisfy the demands of the military as well of industry. In 1915 Lord Derby was appointed director-general of recruiting. His task was to increase the number of recruits in the face of considerable opposition to conscription. In fact, the Derby Scheme provided the foundation for conscription while seeking to avoid it. The scheme divided all men into annual classes eligible for military service. Married men were not to be considered until after all eligible unmarried men had been taken. Once the eligible men had been identified, however, there was no compulsion. Derby's program relied upon moral persuasion because it aimed at getting every man to "attest" that he was willing to serve if and when called. Roughly half the eligible men attested their willingness to serve. Women invoked considerable moral persuasion; men of military age who appeared in public in civilian dress risked being given a white feather, which implied cowardice.

However, the effort to avoid conscription failed. Parliament debated several bills before enacting universal conscription in May 1916. This legislation is very important in the social history of the war. Conscription greatly exacerbated the labor shortage, so that employers increasingly—and frequently with great reluctance—turned to women to fill the shortages. As a result of conscription, approximately one-third of Britain's adult population had some direct experience of the war. For a century Britain's war experiences had been far removed from its population, but no longer.

There were people who not only objected to conscription but refused to comply with the system. The conscription legislation allowed individuals with objections to military service to appeal to local boards for individual consideration. A new term emerged—*conscientious objector*. The local boards rarely sympathized with the often incoherent arguments raised by pacifists and others seeking to avoid military service, but they did assign many to non-combatant service or labor camps. Others were drafted, and the military had the authority to imprison or execute those who refused to follow orders.

Approximately 16,000 Britons earned the designation of conscientious objector in the mist of a war frequently deemed a defense of civilization. About 3,300 served as noncombatants and almost 7,000 drove ambulances or engaged in alternate service deemed in the national interest, but more than 6,000 conscientious objectors went to prison at least once. Some 1,500 refused to recognize the authority of the state to conscript its citizens or to accept any alternate employment, and they remained imprisoned. Close to 100 died in British prisons. Throughout the ages, conscientious objection has been controversial, but democratic societies guard the right of individual judgment even in the face of mass disapproval. Those brave individuals who opposed the war deserve mention for their contributions to the history of human rights.

Perhaps it was unavoidable in a struggle of this magnitude, but all sides waged this war as though it were a crusade in defense of civilization itself. It became the "War to End All Wars." The enemy became the embodiment of evil. Stories of German atrocities against Belgian civilians mixed fact with invention. At times, hostility toward the enemy lurched into hysteria. After the first zeppelin raids, Londoners attacked people with German-sounding names and destroyed their property. Clergymen fulminated about the righteousness of the cause, and the government limited freedom of speech and manipulated people to support the cause.

During the twentieth century, people have become wiser (or perhaps more cynical) and may view the efforts in the 1914–1918 war as amateurish, but the propaganda and censorship of that era represented a dramatic change in the relationship between the state and its citizens. The classic British military recruiting posters sent messages loaded with guilt and moral obligation. One featured Minister of War Kitchener pointing his finger at the viewer and urging him to enlist. A more emotionally charged poster showed a worried young man pondering how to answer his daughter's question, "Daddy, what did you do in the Great War?" A third example clearly aimed its message at both the men and the women of Great Britain. Under the caption "Women of Britain say 'Go'," two women and a child watch men in uniform march away.

Perhaps not since the *levée en masse* of 1793 in France had a state sought to order its population to such an extent. In the process the people changed and Great Britain itself changed. Winston Churchill said, "This is no ordinary war, but a struggle between nations for life and death. It raises passions between nations of the most terrible kind. It effaces the old landmarks and frontiers of our civilization." Britain had traditionally been a nation with a large navy, befitting its island identity, but it had rarely maintained a large army. Nineteenth-century British foreign policy celebrated "splendid isolation" from the affairs of the continent. The country departed from that long-standing policy when it joined the Triple Entente. A large land force was needed, with huge amounts of supplies and soldiers. Feeding the war machine compelled the government to abandon its traditional values. As it turned out, however, the Great War exceeded Britain's capacity to wage war. By its end, it was clear that Britain could no longer win a European war without outside help, which came when the United States entered the war in 1917.

Even though Great Britain was on the winning side, its victory was Pyrrhic. By many measures the Great War was a catastrophe for almost every nation that participated. Almost a million young men were killed, and many of those who survived were physically, mentally or emotionally scarred. Thousands languished in institutions for years after the war ended. There is no standard to measure these costs to the men, their loved ones, or society.

The Great War accelerated Great Britain's economic decline. Rationing of meat continued until 1919 and of butter and sugar until 1920. Britain suffered severe economic difficulties for much of the 1920s and 1930s. Domestic unemployment rose from 3 percent during the war to almost 14 percent by 1922. Because of the war some markets were lost completely, and Britain faced new competitors in others. Oil increasingly replaced coal as the fuel of choice, and this change meant further unemployment. The outmoded British shipbuilding industry fell on very hard times after the war without prospect of recovery. In the face of these and other economic woes, many looked to the government for assistance. Britons had seen what could be accomplished by state intervention, and they urged the government to address the postwar poverty and economic dislocation.

The Great War also extracted considerable political cost. Within days of its start, the government enacted the Defence of the Realm Act, which empowered government officials to put in place any regulations deemed necessary to wage the war. Such a dramatic expansion in the power of the state would have been unimaginable and unacceptable just a few days earlier. The war also increased the strain of holding together the British Empire. The Irish rose in rebellion on Easter Sunday 1916 and assumed independence shortly after the war ended. Other parts of the empire also edged closer to separation. All of these trends existed before the war, but the war weakened Britain's vitality, hastening disintegration.

The Great War marked the end of one era and the beginning of another. Many people who lived through it no longer saw the world in the same way. Transitions are never so neat and tidy; change is gradual. However, 1914–1918 is a definite line of demarcation. It is easy to see the increasing opportunities for both women and men and the emergence of new technologies that are so familiar to us today. But one must also count innocence among the casualties of the Great War.

SELECTED BIBLIOGRAPHY

Books

Brittain, Vera. *Testament of Youth*. London: Virago, 1978. The author worked as a nurse near the front lines and in 1933 wrote this memoir of her disillusionment.

Eksteins, Modris. *Rites of Spring: The Great War and the Birth of the Modern Age*. Boston: Houghton Mifflin, 1989. This discussion begins with prewar cultural developments and weaves in the war and postwar politics and culture, culminating in 1945.

Ellis, John. *Eye-Deep in Hell: Trench Warfare in World War I*. London: Croom Helm, 1976; New York: Pantheon, 1976. This book summarizes trench warfare in text, illustrations, and photographs.

Fussell, Paul. *The Great War and Modern Memory*. New York: Oxford University Press, 1973. The author connects the experience of the trenches with literature.

Graves, Robert. *Good-bye to All That*. 1929. Reprint, Providence, RI: Berghahn Books, 1993. This memoir by the renowned British writer describes his experiences and his decision to leave Great Britain after the war.

Hart, B. Liddell. *History of the First World War*. London: Cassell, 1970. Probably the best overall history of the war by the distinguished British military historian.

Keegan, John. *The First World War*. New York: Knopf, 1998. A thorough and accessible narrative of the war by one of the most prolific writers on modern warfare.

Lane, Arthur E. *An Adequate Response: The War Poetry of Wilfred Owen and Siegfried Sassoon*. Detroit: Wayne State University Press, 1972. A discussion of the war poetry of two British poets who served in the trenches.

Macdonald, Lyn. *Somme*. London: M. Joseph, 1983. Macdonald details the horrific casualty rates of the Battle of the Somme as the crucial event that forced Great Britain to move to conscription.

Marwick, Arthur. *The Deluge: British Society and the First World War*. New York: Weston, 1970. A discussion of the impact of the war on British society.

Sassoon, Siegfried. *Memoirs of an Infantry Officer*. London: Faber and Faber, 1930. Better known for his war poetry, Sassoon also wrote this fine war novel.

Sheffield, Gary. *Forgotten Victory: The First World War Myths and Realities*. London: Headline, 2001. This study of British military performance asserts that strategy and tactics gradually became more effective as the war went on, thus challenging an older argument that characterized the British war effort as wholly inept.

Films

All Quiet on the Western Front. 35 mm., 123 min. Universal Films, Hollywood, 1930. Directed by Lewis Milestone (1930). Adapted from the novel by Erich Maria Remarque, this film focuses on the life of a German soldier, but the story is universal, not partisan. A restored version was released in 1987 by MCA Home Video.

A Room with a View. 35 mm., 115 min., Curzon, London, 1985. Directed by James Ivory (1985). Visually stunning, this film illustrates genteel life in 1910 Britain, where people are beginning to struggle with some of the issues of modernity but are woefully ill prepared for the crisis of 1914.

Paths of Glory. 35 mm., 87 min, Directed by Stanley Kubrick (1957). This film tells the true story of a court-martial of French soldiers, but its strength is in its portrayal of soldiers coping with the difficulties of trench warfare on the Western Front. Released on video disc by Voyager, 1989.

9

World War II, 1939–1945

INTRODUCTION

Great Britain faced many problems during the 1930s, but the massive economic breakdown known as the Great Depression was clearly the most important one. Triggered by the October 1929 collapse of the U.S. stock market, the Depression soon became a global economic and financial disaster. Britain, whose economy and finances had never really recovered from World War I, experienced serious hardship. By 1933 more than 3 million British workers were unemployed; as late as 1939, as Britain rearmed and prepared to shift to a war economy, the figure stood at 1.6 million workers. In 1931 the British government reluctantly abandoned its cherished gold standard which linked the British currency—the pound sterling—to that precious metal.

In the face of such a profound domestic crisis, Great Britain's leadership placed international matters on the back burner. Unfortunately for Britain, European dictators, especially Germany's Adolf Hitler, who had taken control in 1933, were in no mood to accommodate London. As Hitler became more secure in Germany he pursued an ever more aggressive foreign policy. The British prime minister since 1937, Conservative politician Neville Chamberlain, responded to the growing German threat with a policy of appeasement.

British Prime Minister Winston Churchill surveys the ruins of Coventry Cathedral after a particularly ferocious German bombing attack. By the summer of 1940, Great Britain stood alone against the Nazi onslaught; however, Britain subsequently formed the Grand Alliance with the United States and the Soviet Union, and in 1945 emerged victorious from the ordeal of World War II. Reproduced from the Collections of the Library of Congress.

At its heart, appeasement seeks to defuse real and potentially dangerous disputes through negotiation, compromise, and concession. Under different circumstances this might have been a wise policy for Chamberlain and Great Britain to follow, but Hitler was determined to expand Germany at the expense of his neighbors, and British appeasement simply reinforced the German dictator's conviction that Britain was weak and that he could act with impunity.

Until Hitler overplayed his hand, most Britons endorsed Chamberlain's approach. Fixated on the Depression and its debilitating effects, the average Briton wanted little or nothing to do with foreign matters. Furthermore, a substantial portion of Great Britain's political and economic elite had concluded that the 1919 Treaty of Versailles, which formally ended Germany's participation in World War I, had been unfair to that country, and they supported revisions to the treaty in Germany's favor. A smaller number of the elite endorsed the alleged stability and sense of order and discipline that fascist dictators such as Hitler and Italy's Benito Mussolini had brought to their respective countries. Most important, perhaps, vivid memories of the horrors of World War I remained etched in the minds of the people. Thanks to the disasters of that war, pacifism enjoyed great support in Britain. This was dramatically demonstrated in 1933 when the Oxford Union debating society overwhelmingly endorsed the proposition that "this House will in no circumstances fight for its King and Country." That Chamberlain would go to great lengths to keep the peace suited the wishes of most Britons.

Neither Hitler, nor Mussolini, nor the Spanish general Francisco Franco for that matter, was interested in peace. Throughout the 1930s international crises provoked by the dictators roiled the waters. From Japan's 1931 invasion of Manchuria through the 1935 Italian attack on Abyssinia (Ethiopia), the 1936 outbreak of the Spanish Civil War, and the 1938 German annexation of Austria, the forces of fascist aggression were on the move. Instead of alarming Chamberlain, this movement only served to strengthen his resolve to find a peaceful resolution to any and all problems that might arise. The climax of Chamberlain's policy of appeasement occurred in September 1938 at the Munich Conference, during which Great Britain and its ally France reneged on their real and implied commitments to defend Czechoslovakia. Instead they capitulated to Hitler's demands that Germany be allowed to annex the Sudetenland, Czechoslovakia's mountainous boundary region that separated it from Germany, although without its Sudetenland fortifications Czechoslovakia had no way of defending itself from its strong and expansionist neighbor. Chamberlain, dismissing the problem as "a quarrel in a far away country between peoples of whom we know nothing," returned from Munich a relieved man and announced to a grateful Britain that he had secured "peace for our time."

Six months later, appeasement crumbled when Hitler violated his promise to Chamberlain by seizing the Czech capital, Prague, and dismembering the Czechoslovak state. Great Britain responded by signing an alliance with Poland, obviously the next country on Hitler's hit list. At home, measures for rebuilding Britain's armed forces were undertaken, and for the first time in Britain's peacetime history conscription was introduced. Nevertheless, Britain was woefully unprepared for war when Hitler invaded Poland on September 1, 1939, thereby beginning World War II in Europe.

Although pledged to defend Poland, Great Britain and France found it impossible to send direct aid to the beleaguered Poles. Moreover, rather than relieve German pressure on Poland by launching offensive operations from France against Germany's western flank, the western Allies chose to assume a defensive posture. Poland quickly succumbed to superior German arms, although its demise was hastened when the Soviet Union, allied with Germany since August 1939, invaded Poland in mid-September.

Following Poland's defeat, a period of military inactivity sometimes referred to as the "phony war" set in. At home, Chamberlain shook up his cabinet and Great Britain moved to a war footing. The relative calm was shattered in spring 1940 when the Germans went on the offensive in the west. Rapidly overrunning Denmark and Norway, they prepared to launch a massive attack on the Netherlands, Belgium, and France, where a small British Expeditionary Force was stationed. The German successes destroyed what little support Chamberlain enjoyed in the House of Commons, and on May 10, 1940, he resigned in failure.

The Conservative politician Winston Spencer Churchill succeeded Chamberlain as prime minister. At age sixty-five, Churchill had already spent his entire adult life in politics and government service. His experiences ranged from soldier to holder of several cabinet posts. Brilliant, articulate, self-assured, innovative, and controversial, Churchill had gradually moved from left to right on the political spectrum, abandoning friends and convictions along the way. Although a Conservative, he had spent the 1930s as an isolated parliamentary backbencher severely criticizing fellow Conservative Chamberlain's policy of appeasement. Now, in his maiden speech to the House of Commons, Churchill noted that "I have nothing to offer but blood, toil, tears, and sweat." However, he also added, "You ask what is our policy: It is to wage war, by sea, land, and air, with all our might.... You ask, what is our aim? I can answer in one word: Victory, victory at all costs, victory in spite of all terror; victory, however long and hard the road may be; for without victory, there is no survival."

Churchill, of course, proved to be correct, and he was also right in concluding that much sacrifice would precede ultimate victory. Within weeks of his taking office, the Nazis brought France to its knees. Moreover, they barely missed annihilating the shattered British Expeditionary Force, which was withdrawn from its exposed position on the beaches of the French town of Dunkirk by a hastily assembled, ragtag flotilla of naval vessels, fishing trawlers, tugboats, and pleasure craft. Great Britain now lay virtually defenseless against the German onslaught. Had it not been for the English Channel and the German failure to master the trick of walking (or marching) on water, Britain most certainly would have fallen.

In preparation for what of necessity would be a risky amphibious invasion, Hitler and his subordinates determined to bomb Great Britain into submission. The resulting Battle of Britain commenced in July 1940 and continued furiously for several weeks. Sometimes as many as 1,800 German planes joined in a single attack. On the night of September 7, 1940 German bombers set London afire. However, British defenses took a massive toll of German planes and pilots, and by the beginning of October Hitler suspended his invasion plans. Speaking of the British fliers who won the Battle of Britain, Churchill noted that, "never in the field of human conflict was so much owed by so many to so few."

While Germany had been repulsed and the threat of invasion lifted, the Nazis and their allies nevertheless remained in control of virtually the entire European continent, and Great Britain stood alone. But Churchill and the British were neither helpless nor friendless. The resources of the great British Empire lay at their disposal, and troops from as far afield as Canada, Australia, South Africa, and India soon began to appear at English and Scottish bases. There they found dedicated foreign soldiers who had escaped from European countries overrun by Hitler's troops. In particular, the sometimes difficult but patriotic French officer Charles de Gaulle had established a Free French movement on British soil that inspired effective resistance to the Nazi occupiers of France. Clearly the United States provided the greatest support to Britain in its hour of need. The U.S. president, Franklin D. Roosevelt, repeatedly defied isolationist sentiment at home to provide aid for the beleaguered British. The most important U.S. contribution came in the form of the March 1941 Lend-Lease Act, which allowed Roosevelt to direct significant amounts of war supplies to Britain.

World War II in Europe took a decisive turn in 1941 when Nazi Germany first invaded its erstwhile ally, Soviet Russia, and then declared war on the United States. By the start of 1942 a Grand Alliance consisting of Great Britain, the Soviet Union, and the United States confronted Hitler and his European allies, the most important of which was Mussolini's Italy.

In December 1941 Great Britain and the United States had established a Combined Chiefs of Staff Committee, which coordinated their military activity. Beginning in that year and extending well into 1943, the British army—later joined by U.S. units—dueled with German and Italian armored forces in North Africa. Under British commanders Harold Alexander and Bernard Montgomery and U.S. generals Dwight Eisenhower and George Patton, the Anglo-American forces finally emerged victorious. This victory was quickly followed by the Allied seizure of Sicily and the invasion of Italy. The Italian campaign featured extended and difficult fighting for the remainder of the war.

While its army slogged through the Mediterranean theater, the British fleet combined with its U.S. counterpart to establish control over the sea-lanes leading to Great Britain. This was vital to the British war effort because Britain's survival depended upon the importation of food for its people and raw materials for its factories. German submarines posed a serious threat, but Anglo-American forces relied on the convoy system, superior firepower, and more sophisticated technology to overcome the German challenge.

As the war ground on, German air attacks on Great Britain dwindled but never ceased. More than sixty thousand British civilians lost their lives to German bombs. To marshal all available resources to prosecute the war, Britain quickly moved to a total war footing. Politics-as-usual receded into the background for the duration of the conflict, and the government strictly controlled the supply of essential items such as food, labor, and raw materials. Inspired by Churchill's eloquence, many Britons believed that the war really was a life and death struggle between the forces of good and evil, and they acted accordingly. Volunteerism reached an unprecedented level as Britons shouldered unpleasant wartime obligations and endured extensive rationing with both determination and good humor.

Thanks to Japan's aggression, Great Britain was also at war in Asia; but as was the case with the United States, Britain relegated the Pacific front to a secondary role behind the drive for victory in Europe. In June 1944 a combined Anglo-U.S. force launched a cross-channel invasion against the Nazi-held Normandy coast of France. The success of this amphibious attack signaled the start of the final phase of the European war. British and U.S. forces steadily moved eastward, crossing the Rhine River into the heartland of Germany in March 1945. At the same time, the Soviet Union's Red Army pushed westward into Germany. Hitler committed suicide on April 30 and two days later Berlin fell to the Soviets. Germany's formal surrender occurred the following week. A few months later the United States dropped atomic bombs on the Japanese cities of Hiroshima and Nagasaki, effectively putting a halt to World War II in Asia. After almost six years and at a cost of 370,000 lives, Great Britain once again was at peace.

INTERPRETIVE ESSAY
George P. Blum

Following within twenty years of the Great War, or World War I, World War II came to Great Britain in 1939 as an unwanted challenge to its way of life and national existence. Britons faced a test as never before in modern history. The war and its outcome made a lasting impact upon Britain's economy, society, and international standing. The British government, supported by large segments of the public, attempted to stave off war by a policy of negotiation and compromise during the 1930s. This policy was prompted by the belief that Germany had been treated vindictively in the peace settlement of World War I, the memories of the horrors of the bloody trenches and battlefields of the Great War, and the fear that war would ruin Britain's economy and bring the loss of its empire. Germany and Italy, under Nazi and Fascist dictators, welcomed the opportunity to alter the terms of the peace settlement through border changes and territorial expansion—peacefully if possible, militarily and violently if necessary. While Germany's Adolf Hitler aimed to expand in Europe and Italy's Benito Mussolini eyed North Africa, Japan embarked as early as 1931 on a path of relentless territorial expansion in Asia. In March 1939 Hitler seized the rest of the hapless state of Czechoslovakia after obtaining its Sudetenland at the Munich Conference of 1938 with the help of Britain and France. At this point, Prime Minister Neville Chamberlain of Britain reluctantly decided that the German ruler could not be trusted to remain content with the territorial possessions he had annexed either unilaterally or in concert with Britain and France. As a warning to the aggressive German dictator, he pledged a guarantee of support to Poland, Romania, and Greece if their independence was threatened. It was Chamberlain's assurance to Poland that dragged Britain into the war on September 3, 1939.

Hitler launched his invasion of Poland with an overwhelming strike on September 1, 1939, supported by tanks and airplanes. Within two days Britain and France presented ultimatums to Germany and, after their expiry, declared war. However, Poland's western allies could not save it from utter military defeat at the hands of the superior German forces. Moreover, on September 17 Soviet forces occupied the eastern part of Poland to claim their share of Polish territory as secretly agreed upon in the Nazi-Soviet Nonaggression Pact of August 1939. While Poland was being destroyed in less than four weeks of *Blitzkrieg* (lightning war), Britain and France waged a strange *Sitzkrieg* (sitting war), or "phony war," with Germany in the west that lasted for eight months. Neither Anglo-French nor German forces engaged in notable military encounters on land. Only at sea did German U-boats (submarines) inflict some painful losses on the Royal Navy. Several British divisions were moved to the European continent as promised, but British and French military leaders agreed on a defensive strategy that relied on the protection of the fiercely fortified Maginot Line along the French border from Switzerland to Belgium. The Maginot Line did not extend to the Franco-Belgian frontier.

Hitler, who despite British warning signals was surprised by the British and French declarations of war, made a peace overture to London and Paris in October 1939 and repeated peace offers in 1940. Even though a few British leaders at first were inclined to favor a compromise settlement in order to avoid all-out war, the British and French governments were not ready to accept anything less than the restoration of Czechoslovakia and Poland as a condition of peace. Obviously Germany was in no mood to give up the gains that it had won, and thus any cessation of hostilities was unlikely. Prime Minister Chamberlain and others hoped that a naval blockade would strangle Germany's economy and force her to abandon any further aggression. Many British civilians experienced annoying disruptions of normal life but not undue hardship during this lull. This uncertain interlude came to a sudden end in spring 1940.

On April 9 German forces occupied Denmark in five hours, but their effort to gain control of Norway, the campaign's most important strategic objective, proved more difficult. Hitler was intent on securing the delivery of Swedish iron ore, which he considered vital to Germany's war economy. During the winter, the iron ore needed to be transported by rail to Narvik, Norway, and then shipped along the Norwegian coastline to Germany. On the day before the German invasion, British destroyers mined Norwegian waters around Narvik. Anglo-French forces were sent to secure Norwegian central and northern coastal strongholds, including Narvik. However, German military units were too strong, and after weeks of fierce fighting the Allied troops withdrew.

The Allied military disaster in Norway triggered severe questioning of Chamberlain's conduct of the war. Discredited by his prewar appeasement policy, Chamberlain had failed to form a coalition cabinet when an electoral truce was announced in September 1939. But two Conservative antiappeasers, Winston Churchill and Anthony Eden, joined the reorganized government. Paradoxically, as first lord of the admiralty Churchill had been even more responsible for the failure in Norway than Chamberlain, who was being censured for it. Only a few days before the German attack on Scandinavia, the beleaguered prime minister imprudently declared that Hitler, in failing to exploit his superior advantage in attacking France, had "missed the bus." Chamberlain was now being skewered for lacking fighting spirit, daring, and administrative and economic resolution to achieve victory. Even though he won a contentious vote of confidence in the House of Commons, he resigned on May 10, 1940 when the Labour Party refused to enter a coalition government under his leadership. It was this very day that Hitler started to march his armies into the Netherlands, Belgium, Luxembourg, and France. On Chamberlain's advice, the king sent for Winston Churchill to become the new prime minister.

Churchill had been a controversial political personality throughout much of his career. He was sixty-five years old when he assumed the admiralty, a position he had earlier held in World War I, after being out of ministerial service for a decade. Supremely confident, brilliant as a speaker and writer, resolute and daring, he had extensive experience as a soldier and newspaper correspondent before entering parliamentary and governmental service early in the twentieth century. He mustered the qualities of a war leader and saw himself as a man "walking with Destiny"—as he related in his early postwar memoirs—to lead a crusade against Germany to save democracy from totalitarianism. At the same time, he was astute enough to retain Chamberlain and Edward Wood, Lord Halifax, the latter as foreign secretary, among the fellow Conservatives in his early war cabinet even though he had bitterly castigated them for their appeasement policies in the preceding years. In addition, leading members of the Labour Party and the Liberal Party joined what became a national government.

Within a few days of assuming office, Churchill came before the House of Commons and, ignoring Great Britain's precarious strategic position, declared that "our aim ... is victory, victory at all costs, victory in spite of all terror, victory, however long and hard the road may be; for without victory, there is no survival." These were not only bold words to bolster public morale, but also a position that Churchill held when Chamberlain and Halifax recommended in the cabinet that Britain explore a compromise peace in the weeks that followed. Some revisionist historians have been critical of Churchill's adamant stance, but they seem to underestimate Hitler's determination to persist in his aggression on the Continent despite his repeated calls for peace with Britain.

When German forces invaded the Netherlands and Belgium, British and French armies attempted to bolster the beleaguered Dutch and Belgian troops. There had been no coordinated military planning by the Dutch and Belgians with the Anglo-French military leadership before the German attack, however. With a surprise strike of armored divisions through the hilly and wooded Ardennes region of Belgium and Luxembourg that then turned northward toward the Channel ports, the German forces drove a wide corridor between the British, French, and Belgian forces in the north and the rest of the French armies in the south. In the confusion, the Anglo-French military leadership failed to counterattack and most of the British armies were trapped near Dunkirk in northern France. Bad weather and the Royal Air Force kept the German *Luftwaffe* (air force) from annihilating the concentrated Allied troops during the critical days of May 29 to June 3. A hastily assembled flotilla of regular naval vessels, ferry boats, fishing craft, private yachts, and motorboats succeeded in evacuating 338,200 Allied troops, including 139,000 French, to England. The operation saved men but not their guns, ammunition, and motor vehicles, which remained strewn on the land and beaches of Dunkirk. Even though Churchill admitted that Dunkirk was "a colossal military disaster," he defiantly declared on June 4: "We shall defend our Island, whatever the cost may be . . . we shall never surrender." But would there have been the will to continue fighting if the British Expeditionary Corps had not been saved?

Within two weeks after Dunkirk, the French armies collapsed, and the French government sued for an armistice on June 21. The resulting agreement between France and Germany divided France into a German-occupied northern and western zone and a central and southern zone left under a pliant French government seated in the resort town of Vichy. Churchill desperately tried to keep France in the war, and when that failed he ordered the destruction of the French fleet in Oran, French Algeria, to keep it from falling into German hands. This cost the lives of 1,300 French seamen.

In a radio broadcast on June 18, Churchill announced: "The Battle of France is over. I expect the Battle of Britain is about to begin. . . . Hitler knows that he will have to break us in this Island or lose the war." Great Britain stood alone at this point and could count only on the support of its dominions—Australia, New Zealand, Canada, and South Africa. The United States continued to maintain neutrality in what was seen as a European war, even though there was much sympathy with the democracies. The Soviet Union was meanwhile occupying the Baltic States, and Mussolini joined Hitler in the war by seizing the southeastern part of France bordering on Italy.

Hitler expected Great Britain to come to terms within a matter of weeks and renewed his offer of peace, only on conditions of his choosing. But the British leadership, prodded by Churchill's defiant stand, remained obstinate, and by mid-July the Führer issued secret orders to his general staff to prepare plans for an invasion of England. At this threat, Britain mobilized its manpower resources and stepped up its armament and home food production, pointing toward a total war economy. With the adoption of a cash-and-carry arrangement, America eased its neutrality and enabled Britain to restore much of the arms and equipment lost in the evacuation of Dunkirk.

Before an invasion could be launched, Hitler knew that air supremacy had to be established; therefore he ordered the Luftwaffe to achieve control of British air space and to destroy coastal defenses, factories, and airfields. The Battle of Britain raged from July to October with often daily attacks by German bombers and fighter planes. The British Royal Air Force, supported by radar communication and an accelerated production of new airplanes, heroically defended England and kept the Germans from gaining air superiority. German intelligence failures and strategic errors further lessened the chances of Nazi victory. The Germans failed to discover and destroy many of the British coastal radar networks. Nevertheless, by late August and early September the Luftwaffe appeared to be gaining a definite advantage by concentrating its attacks on airfields, aircraft factories, and radar installations. But on September 7 it shifted its bombing target to London, continuing the "blitz" on the capital for the next seventy-six nights. Heavy bombing of selected other cities persisted as well until May 1941. Some cities suffered severe devastation and loss of lives. In London alone, well over ten thousand people were killed. But Great Britain's war production was not seriously damaged, nor did public morale collapse. In mid-September Hitler postponed invasion plans and one month later ruled out a land attack until at least spring 1941.

The British had managed to break the German military cipher and were thus able to read intercepted military messages. From these Churchill knew that Great Britain was safe from invasion for a time. However, German U-boats in the Atlantic caused heavy losses to transports that were bringing food and raw materials to the beleaguered island throughout 1940 and into the first half of 1941. In September 1940 the Italians attacked British forces in Egypt, threatening Britain's position in the Mediterranean. The Italian armies were routed in early 1941, but the British soon faced much more formidable German forces under General Erwin Rommel. It was not until spring 1943 that they were defeated. Soon after the Italian attack in Egypt, Mussolini launched an ill-fated invasion of Greece and again had to be rescued by the Germans. After British troops were forced to withdraw from Greece in April 1941, German planes and paratroopers launched an assault on Crete and conquered the island in May. On a more hopeful note, when Britain's credit in dollar exchange in the United States was exhausted by January 1941, the British leadership was assured that the American Lend-Lease aid, enacted in March 1941, would enable Britain to carry on the war. Since there were some signs in the late spring that Germany was preparing to invade the Soviet Union, even more relief was expected. When this invasion came about, the path leading to the Grand Alliance was opened. But before turning to that aspect, it is important to consider the impact of the war on Britain's domestic life.

For the duration of the war, the total mobilization of Great Britain became imperative. All facets of British government, economic production, and social and cultural life were affected. Chamberlain's war cabinet of 1939 did not include any leaders of the Labour and Liberal Parties. Churchill, however, added to his inner war cabinet of Conservatives Clement Attlee, the leader of the Labour Party; Arthur Greenwood, its deputy leader; and Ernest Bevin, the most important trade-unionist leader of the day, as minister of labor and national service. Max Aitken, Lord Beaverbrook, a politically independent press baron, assumed the all-important ministry of aircraft production and also joined the war cabinet. The breadth of the national coalition government was further extended by the appointment of prominent Labourites and Liberals to various service ministries and departments. By broadening the representation of the national government with leading appointees from the important parties, Churchill greatly reduced opposition in the House of Commons and the country. Churchill himself kept the most important reins of government in his own hands; in addition to being prime minister he also served as minister of defense and conducted foreign affairs. During the war the powers of the central government were almost limitless as defined by the Emergency Powers Acts of 1939 and 1940. Even though the acts retained the right of Parliament to rescind regulations, they granted government very wide powers to conduct the war efficiently and to maintain public safety and order. What kept Churchill from becoming an outright dictator was his respect for constitutional tradition and Parliament.

To make a centrally organized war government effective, it became necessary to establish a centrally managed economy in which government officials directed practically all activity. This conversion of a mainly free-market economy to a centrally directed one was achieved in Great Britain over a period of more than two years. Rearmament was begun quite late in the 1930s and greatly stepped up at the war's outbreak, resulting in high airplane and ship production. But full mobilization of manpower and materials production for the war effort began only under Churchill's cabinet. Conversion to a "total war economy" was brought about not so much by compulsion as by consent. Ownership of industry generally remained in private hands and only basic industries and services, such as railroads and harbors, were under government control. However, government exercised firm direction by fixing prices centrally, allotting raw materials and labor, issuing licenses for capital equipment, and adjusting taxes. Human and material resources were channeled into war production at the expense of civilian goods production. Rationing of foodstuffs and consumer goods helped ensure the stabilization of living costs and the availability of basic necessities on a fairer basis for all the population. Bread and potatoes remained unrationed. Alcohol and tobacco were also not rationed, but increased prices on these consumer items helped to subsidize food products.

Massive government investment in war-related production financed huge expenditures between 1939 and 1945. Female labor largely supplied the workforce that the war effort demanded. By 1943, 7.75 million women held paid positions. At that time some 1.5 million more women were employed in industry and transportation than in 1939; a similar number held jobs in commerce and government and served in the armed forces.

The following selective figures illustrate both industrial and agricultural growth under the demands of war. In armament production, there was an eightfold increase in the output of various kinds of ammunition between 1939 and the end of 1943. The production of machine carbines jumped from 6,400 units in 1941 to over 1.5 million, and tank production rose from 969 to 8,600 in one year alone. In 1939 Great Britain manufactured 7,900 aircraft of all types; this output more than tripled to almost 26,500 in 1944. Only 6 submarines were produced in 1939, but 39 in 1943. Imports of food before the war accounted for 70 percent of British needs; increase in domestic food production reduced this figure to 60 percent during the war. When arable acreage expanded during the war years, it brought crop advances of 81 percent for wheat, 92 percent for potatoes, 30 percent for vegetables, and 27 percent for fodder.

One of the greatest challenges to the British government was how to finance the war. It adopted strict financial policies in order to avert financial disaster. The basic income-tax rate was increased from 9 percent to 50 percent, personal exemptions were reduced, and sales taxes were raised from 60 percent to 100 percent. Personal consumption was reduced to 79 percent of the prewar level. However, only 54.2 percent of government expenditure in 1944–1945 could be met from current revenue. Quite early in the war, Great Britain depleted its gold and hard-currency reserves and exhausted most of its overseas assets. Only when U.S. Lend-Lease became available in March 1941, which gave Britain access to U.S. products without immediate monetary settlement, was the British government sure it would be able to carry on the struggle. By the end of the war, Britain had received $27 billion of goods in Lend-Lease aid.

Even though British civilians never suffered an invasion by enemy forces, the war disarranged, narrowed, and diminished their lives. Sixty-three thousand British civilians died in the bombings and many more were injured. At the outset of the war, about 1.5 million schoolchildren with their teachers and infants with their mothers were evacuated from major cities to rural areas; individuals moved even more of their family members in order to ensure their safety. During the "phony war" many drifted back to their homes, but with the onset of the Battle of Britain many more children were separated from their parents as they moved away from threatened cities to the countryside. Problems arose especially when host families and evacuees were mismatched socially. Slum children horrified many of their middle-class hosts when they came with head lice, scabies, dirty habits, and foul language. There were also families who less than welcomed children of African, Caribbean, Chinese, or Roman Catholic background.

Conscription was another aspect of war that disrupted family life and brought the separation of husbands, wives, sons, and daughters, often throughout the entire war. By 1945 more than 4.6 million persons served in the armed forces, close to 440,000 of whom were women. About one-third of working-age men were in uniform away from home. Since half of them were married, this translated into 2.1 million married women who missed their husbands' support. When young husbands and fathers served in the military, thousands of wives and dependents were impoverished since an ordinary soldier's wife received only very modest government support. When women went to work, they still earned lower wages than men. Also, prewar limitations, especially on employment of married women, were merely suspended during the war. The war did not destroy traditional male-female relationships, but it strained marriages through long separations that tempted some partners to establish extramarital liaisons. Out-of-wedlock births and cases of venereal disease increased markedly. When U.S. servicemen appeared in Great Britain—1.5 million of them by the time of the Normandy invasion—they were met with mixed feelings. Some Britons regarded them as "over-paid, over-fed, over-sexed, and over here," and others welcomed them for their luxury goods. By the end of the war, 60,000 British women had married G.I.s.

Despite bombings, loss of lives and homes, dislocation and separation, blackouts, and sharp increases of property and sex crimes in some areas, public morale did not falter during the war years. There was no hysteria, no mass panic, no defeatism. At worst there were times of malaise as the war wore on, but never of very long duration. To alleviate the tedium, the British government provided an array of entertainment on the radio. In addition to news, the British Broadcasting Corporation (BBC) broadcast music, comedies, and even intellectual discussions of science and philosophy. Movies enjoyed great popularity during the war years and weekly movie theater attendance reached twenty-five to thirty million. Though feature length inspirational documentaries paying tribute to servicemen were well received, escapist feature films enjoyed the greatest acclaim. The most popular film during the war was Hollywood's *Gone with the Wind*. For the average citizen, the government offered school meals, food subsidies, free vaccinations; very basic medical services were extended to help the most needy, but there was little prospect of permanent social reform. In 1944 Parliament passed a major education reform bill that secured the right of free secondary education for all. More auspicious was the Beveridge Report of 1942, which proposed a comprehensive public insurance system for all Britons from the cradle to the grave, protecting them against sickness, poverty, and unemployment, and in old age. It received only lukewarm governmental support during the war, but its popular ideas came to form the foundation of the postwar British welfare state.

Before any concrete plans could be laid for peacetime, however, the war needed to be won. When Hitler attacked the Soviet Union on June 22, 1941, Churchill, a staunch anticommunist, immediately offered full support to the Soviets. He remarked in private that if the Nazi leader invaded hell, he would have something friendly to say about the devil. In December Japan launched a surprise attack on Pearl Harbor. The United States immediately declared war on Japan and so did Great Britain. In turn, a German and Italian declaration of war against the United States followed. Britain no longer stood alone but was now a part of the Grand Alliance. Churchill later was to write: "to have the United States at our side was to me the greatest joy.... after seventeen months of lonely fighting.... we had won the war." The close personal friendship that Winston Churchill and Franklin D. Roosevelt had formed even before the two countries became formal allies helped facilitate British ties with the United States. To win the war in Europe, the U.S. and British leadership decided that the defeat of Germany would take precedence over the defeat of Japan.

But throughout most of 1942 victory remained elusive. In the Far East Japan quite quickly occupied Hong Kong, Malaya, Burma, Singapore, the U.S.-controlled Philippines, hundreds of small Pacific islands, and the Dutch East Indies. In North Africa, Axis forces captured Tobruk (in present-day Libya) and drove British forces back into Egypt. In the Battle of the Atlantic German submarines sent Allied ships to the bottom of the ocean faster than British and U.S. shipyards could replace them. The transfer of part of the U.S. fleet to the Pacific to fight the Japanese reduced the convoys in the west, while the Germans increased their production of submarines. As a result, about 1,600 Allied vessels were lost in 1942 alone, creating the most serious Allied shipping crisis of the war.

With U.S. production volume expanding on everything one could imagine and armed forces steadily growing in numbers, the tide turned late in 1942. In the Far East, in Russia, and in North Africa the Allies went on the offensive. The U.S. recapture of Guadalcanal in the Solomon Islands commenced the liberation of the Pacific islands from the Japanese. The surrender of the German army at Stalingrad in early February 1943 gave the Soviets the initiative on the eastern front. The British general Bernard Montgomery turned Rommel's forces back at El Alamein, Egypt, in October 1942, forcing them into a westward retreat. Finally, in November 1942 Anglo-U.S. forces under General Dwight Eisenhower landed in French North Africa and began to drive the Axis armies eastward. By May 1943 the combined drives of Montgomery and Eisenhower culminated in the defeat of the Axis forces in Tunisia.

After the capture of Tunisia, Anglo-U.S. forces invaded Sicily in July, thereby triggering the collapse of Mussolini's fascist regime. Italy's surrender followed the Allied invasion of the Italian mainland in September, but quick German rearguard action and the mountainous Italian terrain frustrated the Allied advance. Rome did not fall to the Allies until May 1944 and German forces defended northern Italy until early 1945.

Joseph Stalin protested the Anglo-U.S. decision to invade Italy for it further postponed the creation of a second front in northwest Europe, which he had repeatedly demanded of the western Allies since 1941 to give the Soviets relief. If successful, an early invasion of France—urged by the U.S. military leadership—would very likely have ended the war sooner and saved parts of eastern Europe from Soviet domination. But Churchill and his chiefs of staff resisted a premature cross-Channel attack—in which the British would have carried the brunt—as too risky and too costly and prevailed upon Roosevelt to defer it. In a way, the joint invasion of French North Africa served as a temporary substitute for a second front. However, the United States overruled Churchill's idea of an Allied attack on the Balkans to head off a Soviet occupation of eastern Europe. By 1943 the United States had mobilized sufficient armed forces and resources to consider itself the senior in the Anglo-U.S. partnership and it dominated strategy and command.

Under the code name Operation Overlord, the invasion of Normandy led by Eisenhower was finally launched on June 6, 1944, with a massive landing of troops and matériel. At the time the Allies stormed the Normandy beaches, Hitler believed that the main attack would actually come in the Pas-de-Calais region of France and held the largest German army back from Normandy for several weeks. By the beginning of July, one million Allied troops had been deployed in France. In August Paris was liberated and in another month, all of France. A Soviet offensive begun on June 22 swept with a massive thrust toward Warsaw, Bucharest, and Sofia. In January 1945 Soviet forces began their final drive into Germany, conquering Berlin in late April and early May.

Despite enormous German losses, many Nazi leaders, fearing execution if captured, were resolved to fight to the death rather than surrender. Goebbels's propaganda exploited the Allies' insistence on unconditional surrender and tough plans for postwar Germany as a way to sustain the war morale of the German populace. He also claimed that secret wonder weapons would save Germany from defeat. The "vengeance weapons"—the V-1 flying bomb and the V-2 rocket—that Germany employed from summer 1944 to early 1945, mainly against London, killed nine thousand Britons and resulted in considerable damage. The sporadic but persistent German bombing attacks since 1941 caused much more devastation in the British Isles. A temporarily successful German counterattack through the Ardennes in December 1944—the Battle of the Bulge—surprised the Allies but was repulsed within two weeks with losses that Germany could not sustain. In March 1945 the Allies crossed the Rhine River and on May 7, one week after Hitler had committed suicide and Mussolini had been shot by Italian partisans, the German high command surrendered unconditionally at Eisenhower's headquarter in Reims, France. The war in the Pacific continued through the summer until the United States dropped two atomic bombs on Hiroshima and Nagasaki, bringing about Japan's precipitous surrender in mid-August 1945.

In the end, the might of the human and material resources of the United States and the Soviet Union won the war. But Great Britain played a critical role between the summer of 1940 and the fall of 1941 when it stood alone and deprived Hitler of his victory in Europe. It was the greatest endurance trial for Britain in modern history. Several considerations explain Britain's ability to carry on the war when the odds of prevailing appeared extremely slim. Geographically, the United Kingdom was fortunate to be separated from the European mainland by a gigantic moat: the English Channel. It abruptly stopped marching German armies. Churchill became prime minister at the most critical juncture. His dogged determination to resist Hitler when some of his colleagues advised compromise with Germany, and his superb charismatic leadership throughout the war, assured the perseverance and unity of his beleaguered people. The dramatic increase in British airplane production starting in 1940 proved extremely decisive. It gave the brave airmen of the Royal Air Force the wherewithal to keep the Luftwaffe from attaining air superiority and thwarted German strategy. Finally, the formation of the Grand Alliance in 1942 guaranteed ultimate victory.

The effects of World War II on the British people and nation were manifold, and the price of victory was high. Great Britain lost about 370,000 people, 272,000 of them in the armed forces, 35,000 merchant seamen, and 63,000 civilians killed in air raids. About 600,000 more were disabled. Surprisingly, this toll was lighter than that of World War I. Grievous though the human losses were to families, greater damage was done to Britain's economy, which limited the nation's capacity to play the role of a great power. The struggle of supplying the war effort left Britain's industry and economy exhausted and the country burdened with a £25 billion national debt, making it a debtor nation for the first time in modern history. Britain was dependent on imports for food and raw materials but no longer commanded enough export industries to finance such trade. Cities had been destroyed as never before in war. Harbor facilities and railroads were in disrepair. Destruction of homes enormously exacerbated the housing shortage. The hardships that many British citizens endured during the war, following years of Great Depression austerity, made the enactment of the social reforms proposed in the Beveridge Report a popular expectation after the war had been won. Britain had no choice but to turn to Washington for economic and strategic support in the postwar era, as it had during much of the war, confirming that Britain was now a permanent junior partner of the United States. Britain's days as an independent great power in Europe were over, and the advance of national movements in its colonies hastened the dissolution of the British Empire.

SELECTED BIBLIOGRAPHY

Addison, Paul. "Churchill and the Price of Victory, 1939–1945." In *From Blitz to Blair: A New History of Britain since 1939*, edited by N. Tiratsoo, 53–76. London: Weidenfeld and Nicolson, 1997. Concludes that without Winston Churchill "the British war effort might have petered out in faction, intrigue and defeatism in the summer of 1940."

———. *The Road to 1945: British Politics and the Second World War*. London: Quartet Books, 1975. Political history that examines the shift from Conservative politics to Labour politics, culminating in the 1945 Labour victory.

Calder, Angus. *The People's War: Britain, 1939–1945*. New York: Pantheon Books, 1969. Very readable account that describes the effect of the war on civilian life.

Chapman, James. *The British at War: Cinema, State, and Propaganda, 1939–1945*. London: I. B. Tauris, 1998. Examines how films were used as effective weapons of propaganda during the war to boost public morale.

Churchill, Winston. *The Second World War.* 6 vols. Boston: Houghton Mifflin, 1948–1953. Memoir history by Great Britain's greatest statesman of the twentieth century, who was also a superb master of the English language.

Donnelly, Mark. *Britain in the Second World War.* London and New York: Routledge, 1999. Concise history of the political, economic, social, and media developments in the war with consideration of some of the historical debates on these issues.

Douglas, Roy. *The World War, 1933–1945: The Cartoonists' Vision.* London: Routledge, 1990. Political cartoons drawn from Allied and a few Axis newspapers provide a commentary on some events and personalities of the war.

Fielding, Steven. "The Good War, 1939–1945." In *From Blitz to Blair: A New History of Britain since 1939*, edited by N. Tiratsoo, 25–52. London: Weidenfeld and Nicolson, 1997. Argues the war did not eliminate social differences and prejudices but gave people the notion of a common interest in fighting Hitler and supporting Labour.

Gilbert, Martin. *Churchill: A Life.* New York: Henry Holt, 1991. A readable one-volume distillation of the author's massive eight-volume biography of Winston Churchill.

Havighurst, Alfred F. *Britain in Transition: The Twentieth Century.* Chicago: The University of Chicago Press, 1979. Contains an interesting chapter on Great Britain in World War II that can serve as a starting point for further study.

Langmate, Norman, ed. *The Home Front: An Anthology of Personal Experience, 1938–1945.* London: Chatto and Windus, 1981. Reports of ordinary civilians on their experiences during the war.

Lewin, Ronald. *Churchill as Warlord.* New York: Stein and Day, 1973. Offers a good descriptive portrait of Winston Churchill at war.

Marwick, Arthur. *The Home Front: The British and the Second World War.* London: Thames and Hudson, 1976. A social history of Great Britain in World War II.

McKay, Robert. *The Test of War: Inside Britain, 1939–45.* London: University College London, 1999. The best recent account of domestic developments in Britain during the war.

Milward, Alan S. *The Economic Effects of the Two World Wars on Britain.* London: Macmillan, 1984. Discusses the economic changes that Great Britain experienced as a result of the wars and attributes them to international consequences rather than domestic transformations.

Morgan, David, and Mary Evans. *The Battle for Britain: Citizenship and Ideology in the Second World War.* London: Routledge, 1993. Looks at the impact of the war on British ideology and social policy from the perspective of the Thatcher era in the 1970s and 1980s.

Pelling, H. *Britain and the Second World War.* London: Fontana, 1970. Largely a political and military history of Great Britain during the war.

Ruggiero, John. *Neville Chamberlain and British Rearmament: Pride, Prejudice, and Politics.* Westport, CT: Greenwood Press, 1999. Asserts that Chamberlain had a strong personal inclination to avoid war and did not support rearmament to prepare for it.

Smith, Harold S., ed. *War and Social Change: British Society in the Second World War.* Manchester: Manchester University Press, 1986. Somewhat specialized essays that examine the impact of the war on social classes and political parties.

Taylor, A.J.P. *English History, 1914–1945.* New York: Oxford University Press, 1965. Chapters 13–16 offer a lively commentary on Great Britain in World War II based on early research.

Taylor, Philip M., ed. *Britain and the Cinema in the Second World War.* London: Macmillan, 1988. Essays by historians interested in film on the variety of themes covered by British cinema in World War II.

10

The Thatcher Era, 1979–1990

INTRODUCTION

Despite its membership in the victorious coalition in both World War I and World War II, Great Britain experienced a marked decline during the twentieth century. Part of this decline was due to the tremendous expenditures in terms of both men and money that the two wars required; part of it was due to the loss of empire, the world's largest for many decades; part of it was due to the aging and eventual collapse of the country's industrial infrastructure; and part of it was due to frequent periods of uninspired and sometimes incompetent leadership.

It can be argued that Britain's fortunes touched bottom during the 1970s. At that time, an economy in decline featured incessant strikes, raging inflation, and a worrisome level of unemployment. The obsolete nature of Britain's industrial economy manifested itself, and plans for modernization never materialized. Social services took an increasing share of the government's budget, while powerful unions resisted efforts to impose fiscal restraints. Racial discord reared its ugly head in many cities, and a virtual state of civil war prevailed in Northern Ireland. The country's prime ministers, Harold Wilson and James Callaghan of the Labour Party and Edward Heath of the Conservative Party, appeared weak and unable to reverse the

In December 1979, Margaret Thatcher paid a visit to Washington, D.C., where she was hosted by President and Mrs. Jimmy Carter. Thatcher's commitment to free market economics and her harsh, anti-Soviet rhetoric made Great Britain's first woman prime minister a more compatible partner for Carter's successor, President Ronald Reagan. Reproduced from the Collections of the Library of Congress.

decline. To some observers, a debilitating malaise seemed to pervade the country.

For a number of years, the Conservative Party had issued rhetorical attacks against the growth of the welfare state and its socialist origins. However, in practice it seemed quite clear that the party was not inclined to act on its purported convictions; rather, it tended to "go along to get along," never really challenging the basic direction that British society had followed since the end of World War II. This would change when the Conservative Party chose Margaret Thatcher as its leader on February 11, 1975. Henceforth, the party would pursue a more traditionally conservative and significantly less accommodationist set of goals.

Margaret Hilda Roberts was born on October 13, 1925 in Grantham, a quiet town in central England. Her father was a small businessman and local politican with a conservative bent whose no-nonsense approach to life and dedication to hard work greatly influenced his daughter. After schooling in Grantham, she went off to Oxford University, where she studied chemistry and actively participated in the Conservative Party's student organization. Upon graduation she worked as a research chemist, but politics was her passion. In 1951 she married Denis Thatcher, a prosperous businessman, and two years later she gave birth to twins. In the meantime, she embarked upon a career as a lawyer and entered Conservative Party politics. In 1959 she was elected to Parliament representing Finchley, a staunchly Conservative district.

Thatcher's rise through the ranks of British conservatism was fairly rapid. In 1961 she received her first government appointment, joining Prime Minister Harold Macmillan's government in the minor post of parliamentary secretary at the Ministry of Pensions. When Harold Wilson and Labour won the 1964 election, Thatcher lost her governmental post, but Finchley returned her to Parliament by a comfortable majority. In opposition, Thatcher's move to the front bench, or leadership ranks of the Conservative Party, reflected her growing importance. Her fellow Conservatives selected her for a number of posts in their shadow cabinet, including fuel and power, transport, and education.

In the election of 1970, the Conservatives returned to power under Edward Heath, who selected Thatcher to be his secretary of state for education and science. She was the only woman in his cabinet. During her four-year tenure, Thatcher gained a reputation for being intelligent, focused, and industrious; she was also viewed as unnecessarily abrasive, ambitious, and self-righteous. Thatcher received much notoriety when she ended the free-milk program for schoolchildren aged eight to eleven. Her Labour opponents quickly dubbed her "Thatcher the Milk Snatcher."

The elections of 1974 saw the defeat of the Conservatives and the return to power of Wilson and the Labour Party. In opposition, Thatcher was first shadow minister of the environment and then shadow spokesman for treasury affairs. Most important, however, on February 11, 1975 the Conservatives unexpectedly elected her to replace the unpopular Heath as party leader. For many years, Great Britain's Conservative Party had essentially accepted the post–World War II growth of the welfare state and its socialist implications. It is even possible to say that what most distinguished the Conservatives from Labour was their different views on the rate at which the welfare state was to grow. By the 1970s grassroots elements within the Conservative Party started to challenge the general tone of Conservative politics. Led by figures such as Keith Joseph, a rising star in the party and formerly Heath's minister for Social Services, a small but growing number of Conservatives called for the downsizing if not the outright abandonment of the welfare state and a new emphasis on private property, individual initiative and responsibility, and a market economy. Originally, Thatcher did not play an important role in this movement within the party; in fact, she indicated a slight preference for the "wets"—those who would continue the now traditional post–World War II policies of the Conservatives. By the time she assumed leadership of the party her conversion was well underway, however, and as leader and, subsequently, prime minister she clearly and forcefully moved the Conservative Party to the political right.

On May 3, 1979, thanks to the perceived incompetency of the Labour government and its inability to deal with a declining economy, militant trade unionism, violence in Ulster, and a feeling of malaise, the Conservatives won a comfortable electoral victory and Margaret Thatcher became the first woman prime minister in British history. Initially, Prime Minister Thatcher turned her attention to economic and social issues. Reflecting her growing belief that government should play a reduced role in the lives of individuals and that personal responsibility was the keystone to national revival, in June 1979 Thatcher's Conservatives restructured Great Britain's tax system. The Value Added Tax (VAT), a form of sales tax, was almost doubled, while income taxes, especially for the wealthy, were substantially reduced. At the same time, government expenditures were cut for perhaps the first time in memory. Also in 1979, Thatcher lifted all remaining controls on the exchange rate and allowed the minimum lending rate, the equivalent of the U.S. prime rate, to hit 17 percent. The results were a mixed bag: The value of the pound rose dramatically and the rate of inflation was cut in half; but almost one million Britons lost their jobs in 1980 alone. The number of unemployed hit 2.1 million that year, and Britain's aging heavy industry collapsed. Faced with an economic recession, in 1981 Thatcher raised taxes

The Thatcher Era

and further cut government spending. Clearly Keynesian economics—the ideas of renowned economist John Maynard Keynes which had dominated British economic policy since the end of World War II—was dead.

Thatcher also took on the trade unions. The prime minister was convinced that the growing power of the unions and their seemingly endless demands and willingness to resort to strikes not only sapped Great Britain of its economic vitality but also threatened Britain's political stability. The result was the Employment Act of 1980. Among other things, this legislation limited picketing during strikes, expanded the right of the rank and file to determine whether it wished to strike or not, and weakened the closed shop, or the requirement that all workers in a specific shop or factory belong to a union. Fed up with the antics of the unions, most of the country supported Thatcher's initiative. Ironically, she was also aided by the high unemployment rate, which served to make Britain's workers more cautious than their leaders. At the same time that Thatcher whittled away at the power of the unions, she introduced legislation that won her a degree of popularity with Britain's lower classes. The 1980 Housing Act made it easier for a resident of council (public) housing to purchase the home in which he or she lived. The prospect of becoming a home owner proved quite popular with the working class.

In concentrating on domestic matters, the "Iron Lady" (a nickname given to Thatcher because of her energetic but inflexible style) placed foreign affairs on a back burner. In the Cold War, she continued Great Britain's long-standing role of Robin to the United States' Batman, although she much preferred the spirited anticommunism of President Ronald Reagan, a fellow conservative, to the earlier tepid and conciliatory approach of the Jimmy Carter administration. Northern Ireland, more a domestic problem than a foreign one, continued to fester. Thatcher did achieve a signal foreign policy success with the November 1979 Lancaster House agreement that peacefully settled the question of black rule in Rhodesia (Zimbabwe).

In spring 1982 foreign issues unexpectedly grabbed the prime minister's attention when Argentina's military dictatorship seized the Falkland Islands, an isolated and underpopulated British possession in the South Atlantic Ocean. In a campaign lasting more than two months, British forces regained the islands at the cost of 255 British lives.

Victory in the Falklands helped to rescue Thatcher and the Conservatives from increasing unpopularity with the British voters and to set the stage for a Conservative electoral victory in June 1983. Helped also by a fractured Labour Party that had taken a sharp turn to the left, Thatcher and the Conservatives won a 144-seat majority in the House of Commons, a margin that encouraged the prime minister to continue her neoconservative initiatives.

After purging her cabinet of the remaining wets, Thatcher embarked upon a series of privatization measures designed to turn over economic assets held by the British government to individuals and corporations. In other words, Thatcher set out to destroy one of the most important pillars upon which British socialism rested. In 1984 British Telecom was privatized; this was soon followed by British Gas (1986), British Airways (1987), and the electricity and water utilities (1990).

Thatcher also dealt a heavy blow to the unions. In 1984 the miners, the most unreconstructed, leftist trade union, went on strike. Thatcher met the challenge head on. She refused to compromise—going so far as to call the miners the "enemy within"—and outlasted her opponents in the course of a bitter strike that lasted almost one year and resulted in a complete victory for Thatcher's government.

During this period, Prime Minister Thatcher became more prominent on the global scene. Together with her U.S. counterpart, President Reagan, she engaged Mikhail Gorbachev, the new Soviet leader, in a series of discussions and meetings that helped put an end to the Cold War. She also renegotiated downward Great Britain's contribution to the European Community's budget at the 1984 Fontainebleau Agreement. That December her government successfully negotiated an agreement providing for the 1997 return of Hong Kong to China. Northern Ireland continued to be a major headache for Thatcher, and in October 1984 the IRA detonated a bomb in the Bristol hotel where she was staying that came perilously close to killing her.

The 1987 general election returned Thatcher and the Conservatives with a 102-seat majority, but time in office was beginning to take its toll on the Prime Minister. She had rubbed a number of people in her own party the wrong way and these unhappy Conservatives, including former prime minister Heath, began to oppose Thatcher more forcefully. Furthermore, a series of questionable policy decisions carried out with her usual brusque inflexibility undermined the Iron Lady in the eyes of her Conservative colleagues.

Thatcher's attempt to substitute a poll tax, or a tax on each individual, for a property tax to finance local government drew heated opposition and provoked rioting in central London in March 1990. Interest rates skyrocketed beyond 15 percent and the rate of inflation exceeded 8 percent, clear indications that Great Britain's economic health was not as sound as Thatcher would have the electorate believe. The much loved National Health Service, Britain's unique form of socialized medicine, found itself in chaotic conditions for which Thatcher was blamed. The problems of Northern Ireland continued unabated.

But it was Thatcher's ambivalence about Great Britain's role in the European Community that brought the rising discontent to a head. In 1988 at Bruges, Belgium, Thatcher made a speech highly critical of some aspects of the European Community, especially its envisioned political and economic union. A first step toward the latter was the Exchange Rate Mechanism (ERM) that would move Europe toward a single currency. Thatcher agreed to Britain's joining ERM only after two of her closest advisors, Foreign Secretary Geoffrey Howe and Chancellor of the Exchequer Nigel Lawson, threatened to resign if she did not. When Lawson subsequently resigned over continuing policy disputes with Thatcher and Howe followed suit with a bitter farewell speech in the House of Commons, the ranks of those within the Conservative Party opposed to Thatcher swelled. In 1990 open revolt broke out, and on November 28 of that year Margaret Thatcher left Number Ten Downing Street, bringing to a close the longest continual tenure of a twentieth-century British prime minister.

INTERPRETIVE ESSAY
Richard A. Leiby

Margaret Thatcher entered Number Ten Downing Street as prime minister for the first time on May 4, 1979, having soundly defeated James Callaghan's Labour Party in general elections the night before. At the time, the most profound importance many observers attached to the election was the fact that she became Britain's first female prime minister. However, by the time Thatcher resigned in 1990, oblique references to her gender were supplanted by comparisons to the greatest political figures of modern Great Britain. Her eleven years of uninterrupted rule was second only to that of Robert Banks Jenkinson, Lord Liverpool, who governed from 1812 to 1827. She would inaugurate the most sweeping reforms to British government and society since the creation of the welfare state under Clement Attlee's postwar Labour government. And she would lead Great Britain through war and on to victory, prompting comparisons to David Lloyd George and Winston Churchill.

Such superficial comparisons are flattering, but Margaret Thatcher's tenure as prime minister defies direct comparison with those of the past. She will stand alone in twentieth-century history, both for her unique approach to politics (which many have dubbed "Thatcherism") and for her dogged persistence in pursuit of her social and economic goals. Even now, more than a decade after the end of her administration, Thatcher remains one of the most controversial political figures of the past century.

Margaret Hilda Roberts was born in 1925 in the town of Grantham in Lincolnshire, and while her family life and upbringing are fairly indistinguishable from that of many English children of her time, the circumstances of her childhood do give some insights into the development of her political thinking. Perhaps the greatest influence on her life was her father, Alfred, who worked his way up from managing a grocery store during his teenage years to owning one. His impact on his daughter's life cannot be overestimated. From his strict Methodist demeanor, Margaret learned to distinguish right from wrong and to value integrity above all else. His involvement as church alderman, town mayor, and justice of the peace helped introduce Margaret to civic responsibility. From the example of his life, she derived her belief in entrepreneurship and the faith that one is rewarded for hard work, thrift, and ingenuity. Having Alfred as a father had other, more tangible, benefits since his success as a shop owner also helped to insulate his family from many of the hardships of the Great Depression. Although no one could escape the ravishes of the "slump" completely, the Roberts' middle-class background afforded Margaret a childhood more fortunate than those of many working-class children her age. If she experienced any privation as a youth, it was because of her father's parsimony, not because of any lack of family income.

As important as her upbringing may have been for her political development, the (accidental) timing of her birth also helps explain why her politics differed from many of those who later became her parliamentary contemporaries. Born in 1925, Margaret was still young when Great Britain plunged into the depths of the Great Depression. Although she was already a precocious political activist, Margaret was only fourteen when Britain went to war against Nazism. Consequently, much of her young adult life was spent coping with the wartime realities of rationing, privation, and Germanophobia. These experiences might account for why she chose the ideological path she took. Whereas older politicians cut their teeth in a time of soup kitchens and unemployment lines, Margaret's generation found itself dominated by patriotism, a sense of duty, and wartime sacrifice. Her conservative leanings grew during the war, and they blossomed after the war's end. For a young college student raised in a petit bourgeois environment of thrift and hard work, the creation of the social welfare system under Attlee's Labour government must have been something of a shock.

The Thatcher Era

The future prime minister did not enter politics immediately. Following her time at Oxford University, where she earned a degree in chemistry, she worked in industry and then took the bar in 1953 to become a tax lawyer. She was first elected to Parliament in 1959 and spent much of her tenure in and out of the shadow cabinets of the 1960s. Conservative party elders began to notice her earnestly in 1968 after she delivered a speech, entitled "What's Wrong with Politics," outlining her approach to conservativism. In it, she urged her party to champion the practices of budgetary restraint and fiscal responsibility and argued that the best government is one that stays out of the affairs of its citizens. It would not be long before she got the chance to put her philosophy into action. Her first forays into cabinet politics occurred when the Conservatives, led by Edward Heath, were returned to power in the elections of June 1970, having vowed to reverse Labour policies and tend to Great Britain's economic decline. Thatcher accepted Heath's offer of a cabinet position as secretary of state for education and science.

Unfortunately for those in positions of power, the 1970s was a cruel decade. Industrialized nations across the globe were rudely shocked by OPEC's oil embargo in 1973, and the attendant energy crisis sent ripples of economic distress throughout the West. Nowhere was this crisis more acute than in Great Britain, where the economy was already reeling from more than a decade of subpar productivity and low growth rates. As the price of oil rose, so too did the rate of inflation. The value of the pound sterling, once the symbol of world monetary stability, declined concomitantly. Suddenly, the British government was faced with a growing budgetary deficit, forcing Whitehall to borrow more and more money just to meet the funding needs of its ever-growing public sector entitlement programs. Heath soon found it difficult to manage simultaneously both a struggling economy and an ever-more-militant labor movement that did its best to resist any changes that might weaken its economic bargaining position. In less than two years, Heath had to abandon his principles twice in order to make salary concessions to striking workers. Such U-turns angered many, both within his party and in the public at large, and reinforced the appearance that the labor unions, not Parliament, were running the country. That perception cost the Conservatives the election of 1974.

In this climate of electoral defeat and ideological stagnation, a group of Conservatives led by William Whitelaw, Keith Joseph, and Thatcher combined their efforts to launch an internecine challenge to Heath's leadership. Out of their efforts emerged a movement some have called the "new right." At the risk of oversimplifying what was a complex set of assumptions, the "Thatcher-wing" program was built on a bedrock belief in the greatness of Great Britain. This once proud nation, at one time the "workshop of the world" and a victor of two world wars, was now in the throes of decline, and the political system needed to halt and reverse that trend. As much as these ideas were the foundation of Thatcher's politics, they were not at all new in the Conservative Party. What separated the Thatcherites from past leaders was the belief that the Conservative party had made a fundamental mistake after 1945 when it acquiesced to the welfare state. Although the postwar Conservative Party had been fundamentally opposed to the socialization that Attlee's revolution brought about, its leadership considered it politically ill advised to reverse it once they returned to power. Thus began the trend for Conservatives to "govern from the middle"; that is, to seek consensus with the Labour movement and to rule more or less jointly. The end product of this acquiescence was that the welfare state's continued existence became the unassailable "third rail" of British politics; to touch it meant certain political death. Thatcherites rejected that premise. Attributing much of the contemporary economic turmoil to the excesses of the postwar socialist experiment, they rejected consensus politics, reviled the welfare state, and even occasionally spoke in terms of "killing off" socialism entirely.

Although the new right movement can be seen as a reaction to the excesses of the twentieth-century welfare state, the theory supporting it comes straight out of classical nineteenth-century liberalism. Its centerpiece is the belief that governments and interest groups should do nothing to interfere with the marketplace (*laissez-faire*, as the eighteenth-century French Physiocrats first described it), for when they do, they adversely affect the general economic balance. It follows then that governments cannot, and should not, attempt to solve every social or economic problem. In practical terms, this meant that Parliament needed to be serious about rolling back expenditures and controlling the public debt, even if it meant making cuts in the welfare state and abandoning the notion of full employment. That would include dealing harshly with those institutions (read: labor unions) that still held that the primary function of government was to create and safeguard jobs.

Since Heath had shown neither the ability nor the will to pursue such a revolutionary course, the stage was set for a leadership showdown. Whitelaw, the most logical candidate, vacillated when asked to oppose Heath, and Joseph chose not to enter the contest at all. Taking a chance, Thatcher allowed her name to be advanced and (to the surprise of many) beat Heath on the first ballot. Subsequent ballots confirmed the initial result: Thatcher had won the leadership of the party—almost by accident. In some ways, it was a Pyrrhic victory. The Conservatives were badly divided between those who still supported Heath and those who had helped to unseat him. Consequently, Thatcher was forced to spend a good deal of her time putting out fires within her own party membership.

In other ways, the timing of Thatcher's accession to leadership was fortuitous. By the end of 1975, the inflation rate had reached a staggering 28 percent. By 1978, prices had doubled from only four years before. The dire economy forced even the Wilson-Callaghan Labour government to abandon its principles and resort to expenditure-cutting legislation. Then, between November 1978 and March 1979, during what many called the "winter of discontent," a series of strikes led at first by truck drivers but soon supported by public-sector employees crippled an already exhausted economy. In the opinion of many observers, the unions had gotten out of control. Overseas, the country had become notorious for its inability to deal with strikes (a malady often called "the British disease"). Suddenly the Labour government seemed no better at finding solutions than the Heath government had been. The loyal opposition saw this as a propitious moment to bring a vote of "no confidence" against Callaghan's government, thereby forcing an election for spring. Thatcher could now position herself as a relatively complete outsider, opposed to Labour's ineffective policies but also sufficiently distanced from the failures of Heath's ministry. By calling for immediate action to stop inflation and legislation to curb union abuses, Thatcher quickly became the candidate of radical change. Her dogged persistence in search of new solutions made Callaghan's pleas to stay the course seem out of touch with reality. The voters agreed with Thatcher and on May 3, 1979 gave her a working majority in the House of Commons. Hers was a negative victory. Voters were not opting for a new ideology as much as they were rejecting the status quo.

Mrs. Thatcher now had to put this experiment into motion, and the means she employed were often more controversial than the ends she sought to accomplish. It is her leadership style, as much as her message, that has become known as Thatcherism. To outsiders, she was distant, cold, and heartless. Even her closest supporters and fellow party members felt that she preferred to be aloof from them. Her personality spilled over into her legislative style. When asked if she would make her cabinet representative of the disparity of views within the Conservative movement, she answered that she "couldn't waste time having any internal arguments." Once forced by expediency to bring centrists into her government, she often did not allow for cabinet debate of proposed legislation, leading many to see her style as heavy-handed or even authoritarian. She justified this approach by reminding everyone that hers was a "conviction government," and participants needed to accept those convictions or stand aside. To close supporters, the question "Is he/she one of us?" was Thatcher's way of identifying those who shared her convictions; to detractors, it was a further indication of her autocratic manner and closed-mindedness. What may appear as personality failings to some people can be seen by others as evidence of determination, tempered by a sense of what is right and proper. At any rate, personality notwithstanding, it is fair to categorize her government as one with a distinct ideological bent, led by an ideologue with a no-nonsense approach to getting things done.

The Thatcher government tackled the economy head-on, and it is in this realm that the most far-reaching changes took place. At the heart of the problem (according to the Thatcherites) was Keynesian economic thinking, which dictated that governments should step in to expand the supply of money in an effort to promote employment across society. While it is arguable that Keynesian economics served the West well in the decade of the Great Depression, Thatcherites considered such direct intervention in the marketplace outmoded, and in large part responsible for the double-digit inflation of the 1970s. Thatcher sought to make Keynesianism obsolete by changing the paradigm to "monetarism," which calls for government to restrict the money supply and work toward fiscal responsibility. Budgets had to be cut, public sector borrowing needed to be reduced, and overall spending had to decrease.

The easiest way to accomplish these goals while at the same time striking a blow against the welfare state was to sell off—or privatize—many of Great Britain's nationalized industries. Despite the government's good intentions, its practice of purchasing nonprofitable industries in order to "prop them up" and save jobs had led to considerable unwanted consequences. For one thing, government agencies proved no better at running ailing industries than private operators. In the worst cases nationalization led to waste, and stories of absurdities within the system—such as workers being paid for doing no work—abounded. These investments were also a massive drain on the treasury, and Thatcher recognized that a sell-off would accomplish two ends. Not only would it rid the government of a budgetary burden, it would broaden the base of the economy by encouraging ordinary citizens to become investors. Among the first industries to be sold were British Aerospace and National Freight, followed by Jaguar and British Telecom, British Gas, British Airways, Rolls-Royce, and British Petroleum. By 1989 almost 40 percent of industries run by the state only ten years earlier had been transferred to private ownership. In addition to reinstituting private initiative in the supply side of the economy, the Thatcher government also aimed at stimulating the demand side through tax cuts.

The economic effects of these changes are clear. After a two-year recession at the beginning of Thatcher's term, the gross domestic product of

Great Britain started to recover. By 1988 it was roughly one-quarter higher than the recessionary trough of 1981. Public-sector borrowing rates had fallen, and the dreaded inflation rate soon came in line as well. Following its peak at nearly 22 percent (in August 1980), the rate of inflation declined steadily and stabilized between 3.7 and 5.5 percent (in May 1983). Such figures seemed to validate the "Thatcher experiment." However, a closer look at the social effects gives pause. While the constriction of the money supply did get inflation under control, millions of jobs were lost in the process. Unemployment rates, which heretofore had been the bête noire of every British government, went through the roof. When Thatcher took office in May 1979, the unemployed numbered a fraction over one million. Within two years that figure had doubled and by July 1986 it had almost tripled. Similarly, the tax cuts and privatization efforts produced a mixed bag of effects. Tax rates for the average citizen were cut from 33 percent to 30 percent, but for the highest socioeconomic groups rates were cut from 83 percent to 60 percent, making the average tax cut much more substantial for the wealthy. The disparity was exacerbated by the fact that much of the income shortfall was made up by hiking indirect taxes, such as the value added tax and prices on medical prescriptions, both of which affected the poorer classes more directly than the wealthy.

Privatization, too, had curious effects. While the sale of government-held stocks did increase the number of individual shareholders in British industry from three million in 1979 to nine million in 1989, the statistic is somewhat misleading as most private citizens had very small stakes, many in just one company. The true winners of the privatization sell-off were investment banks, insurance companies, and those already heavily invested in the stock market. Clearly, not everyone benefited from the Thatcher revolution equally. In fact, the very lowest cadre of wage earners saw their real income drop in Thatcher's first six years (primarily due to rising unemployment), and the number of people living at the poverty level rose to nearly 17 percent of the population. Such disparities prompted some observers to remark that British society was divided into three groups; the "haves," the "have-nots," and the "have lots." Not surprisingly, Thatcher gained a reputation as politician unfeeling toward the plight of the lower classes of society, an opinion she only exacerbated by referring to those who did care as suffering from "bourgeois guilt."

To be sure, Thatcher's programs did not go unchallenged, even within her own ranks. However, dissenting voices in her cabinet were systematically silenced or forced to acquiesce. The labor unions, on the other hand, were in no mood for acquiescence. Having had a long history of striking in order to effect changes in government policy, unions chose to make an issue of the government's financial austerity measures and rising unemployment rates. Their ploy played right into Thatcher's hands. Believing that the unions had deviated from their true purpose and had become political tools of their leaders, she made "giving the unions back to the workers" a mantra of her administration. Over the course of her ten years as prime minister, Thatcher introduced and passed through Parliament a myriad of laws designed to curb union excesses. They focused not on the existence of the unions per se but on the right to strike. In 1980 secondary strikes became illegal. Two years later, unions became legally liable for any damages that resulted from unlawful acts. The centerpiece of the new legislation mandated that union leadership could call strikes only after authorized to do so by a decision of the rank-and-file membership through a secret ballot. This law pulled the teeth of union leaders with a penchant for calling out work stoppages for political reasons. Ultimately, this law was extended to allow union members to sue their union in court if its leadership called them out on strike without first holding a ballot. Similarly, the laws struck at mandatory union membership. Restrictions were placed on closed shops, and unions could be forced to compensate workers who were dismissed because they refused to become union members.

The defining moment of the struggle with labor came shortly after the 1983 elections returned Thatcher to power. Arthur Scargill, a Marxist and leader of the Mine Workers Union, managed to call out his membership on strike without a ballot after the government announced plans to close the least profitable pits. Thatcher had bowed to the mine workers once before, but now in summer 1984 there was enough coal stockpiled and sufficient legislation in place for her to take on the union directly. The strike went badly from the start. To Scargill's chagrin, not every mine wished to strike (most notably, the profitable ones in Nottinghamshire), thereby giving Thatcher the opportunity to send police to keep militant pickets from disrupting production. By autumn some local unions attempted to test the legality of the strike by suing the national union under the new statutes. Scargill continued his crusade, but by the end of the year his battle was all but lost. In March 1985 he called off the devastating strike—devastating not to the British economy, but to the unity of the mine-workers union. Thatcher's resolve, combined with the restrictive legislation, had cured the "British disease."

By besting the unions and getting inflation back on track, Thatcher took a giant step toward reviving Great Britain's image overseas and reviving economic pride at home. As fate would have it, the greatest impetus for a national revival came not from any legislation or labor dispute but from an armed attack against British territory. In 1982 the military dictatorship then ruling in Argentina invaded the Falkland Islands, which it claimed as Argentine territory. That Thatcher chose to go to war to defend the islands is not surprising. No nation can accept aggression toward its soil without suffering in the court of world opinion. What was surprising was Thatcher's persistent refusal to accept less than complete Argentine withdrawal. Doubtless drawing from her memories of Churchill's resolve against Adolf Hitler, she saw the Falklands crisis as "an issue of dictatorship versus democracy" and insisted that as long as British subjects were deprived of their right of self-determination, her government would seek to dislodge the invaders by any means necessary. As she said in Parliament, "I'm standing for our people. I'm standing for international law. I'm standing up for all those territories . . . who, if someone doesn't stand up and say to an invader 'enough, stop' . . . would be at risk." Her intransigence set her at odds not only with Britain's international allies but with many in her own inner circle who urged compromise. Once committed to complete victory, Thatcher ordered a military task force to the South Atlantic to face an enemy more than eight thousand miles from home. It was an incredible gamble, and sending men and women into harm's way must have been the toughest decision of her ministry. Fortunately, Port Stanley (the capital) was retaken after several weeks of fighting, effectively ending the conflict. Thatcher had again taken a stand and prevailed. In a speech, she placed the victory in perspective. Rather than bask in the personal glory of victory, she took time to reflect on its meaning for her country. For the time being, Britain "ceased to be a nation in retreat."

By 1988 Thatcher had many victories to tout, both domestic and foreign. One might expect her status with the voters to be at its zenith. In truth, British public opinion had been drifting steadily away from Thatcherism as the 1980s wore on. Though the electorate continually returned the Conservatives to office, voters still said they preferred to see the welfare state expand, even if it meant higher taxes. The economic prosperity of the first half of the decade had slowed, and by 1989 the inflation rate was again approaching double digits. What remained of Thatcher's public popularity was lost following passage of a poll tax, which was so ill received that it spawned violent demonstrations across Great Britain. Ten years after her election, the term *Thatcherism* had become a pejorative for most people, and Thatcher's satisfaction rating with the electorate was lower than any other postwar prime minister save Heath. As one contemporary observer put it, "it is as if the public recognizes that society has changed over the decade, but does not much like what it sees."

Ironically, Thatcher's foreign policy—the very same arena that produced her greatest triumph—would be the source of her undoing. It was particularly her antipathy toward the European unity movement that set her at odds with others in her party and abroad. Thatcher took a "de Gaullist" approach to the idea of "Europe," that it should be a "common market" of sovereign states working in close cooperation with one another. By the late 1970s, however, Eurofederalism was becoming more and more the talk, and many political leaders envisioned an ever closer union of states leading up to the creation of a single authority that might be described as a "United States of Europe." Although Thatcher supported the European Community, she opposed any effort toward political unity that would surrender British sovereignty to a non-British authority. Her first forays into this battle with Europe were her successful attempts to renegotiate downward Great Britain's dues payments to the Common Market treasury. Later in her ministry, she balked at Britain's entry into the European Monetary System (EMS) until finally in 1985, at the urgency of cabinet members Douglas Hurd, John Major, and others, she acquiesced. Her objections to the Draft Treaty of Union led to the passage of a watered-down version called the Single European Act. Even though she helped push its passage through Parliament, she was never a friend of supranationality and repeatedly made her consternation known, much to the displeasure of her pro-European counterparts.

The events of 1989–1990 hastened the fall of an already declining ministry, when a series of foreign policy gaffes hurt her relationships with foreign dignitaries and Conservative party colleagues alike. For a time in the summer of 1989, internal British events were eclipsed by the news of the imminent collapse of communism in East Germany. Indeed, there was a perceived threat: a reunited Germany might strengthen the European unity movement and lead to a further subordination of Great Britain to Germany. As images of the fall of the Berlin Wall were telecast across the world, Thatcher's guarded response seemed too restrained and historically inappropriate. Further, as East Germany's collapse and the potential for German unification increased, Thatcher's government seemed unable to agree with the rest of NATO on how such a unification might proceed. At a meeting of her advisors and experts on German affairs at Chequers, the prime minister's country retreat, Mrs. Thatcher sought advice on how to handle the possibility of a reunited Germany. In the frank discussion, the attendees made a number of unflattering remarks stereotyping the Germans as obstinate, insensitive, and self-absorbed. When notes from the meeting leaked to the press, Thatcher was criticized again for being Germanophobic and behind the times. The matter might have blown over had it not been for the remarks of cabinet minister Nicholas Ridley, who in an interview with *The Spectator* made comments about German unity that could be construed as comparing Chancellor Helmut Kohl's efforts to those of Hitler. Although his indelicacy led to his resignation, Ridley's comments did nothing to change the growing perception that the Thatcher government was hopelessly outdated. In the end, Thatcher called for a gradual coming together of the two Germanys, perhaps over ten to fifteen years' time. Britain's demands for slowing the pace of German reunification went unheeded, and Britain once again found itself relegated to the role of "former great power."

The final act of this drama played out in the parliamentary debates on the Maastricht Treaty, which aimed at deepening European unity. Faced with mounting pressure from within her own party, Thatcher had no intention of surrendering any more British authority to the union. Her refusal led to Foreign Secretary Geoffrey Howe's resignation from the cabinet, an action that was seen as a signal that the Conservative Party might be better off going into the next elections with a leader other than Thatcher. In October 1990 Michael Heseltine, a former cabinet minister who had been dismissed years before, decided to stand against Thatcher for leadership of the party. Although she most likely could have withstood this attack, she decided to resign instead. After more than eleven years in office, the "Iron Lady" was no longer prime minister.

Assessing the importance of the "Thatcher Revolution" can be a daunting task. Was it truly a "revolution?" For the most part, it was not. Thatcher's goals were not terribly unlike those of her Conservative predecessors; what was different was the way she went about accomplishing them. Her supporters would disagree and would cite her dogged persistence in pursuit of her goals as evidence of a definite program and plan of action. However, a closer look at the accomplishments of her ministry reveals a number of paradoxes that bring the notion of a distinct "program" into question. For example, government-held industries were sold in part to promote competition, yet a few industries that had been government monopolies were allowed to retain their monopoly status once sold. Similarly, while encouraging the average citizen to become a stakeholder in society, the government wound up selling most of its assets to institutions and to the wealthy. One can even discern inconsistencies in the government's expenditure policy. Although Thatcher made expenditure cuts and tax rollbacks the focus of her efforts to end inflation, the average yearly spending on defense increased throughout her time as prime minister. And despite the government's pledge to roll back the welfare state, expenditures on the national health service increased each year. These inconsistencies suggest, as journalist Peter Riddell has written, that Thatcherism was not a clear-cut program at all, but a political mission based on fairly vague notions of antisocialism and the value of private initiative.

Neither were the ideas embodied in the Thatcher experiment peculiar to Great Britain. Anyone who lived in the United States during the 1980s will readily recognize in Thatcherism much of what was dubbed "Reaganomics." Indeed, analogous situations can be found in the contemporary histories of West Germany, Norway, Sweden, and France. Thatcher's impact is perhaps best understood as part of a larger, international reaction against the economic shocks attendant to the energy crisis of the 1970s. As the supply of oil dwindled, industrial economies everywhere could no longer sustain prior levels of spending. Contraction, not expansion, was the order of the day. Suddenly, larger nations found themselves beholden to smaller ones, the powerful bowing to the meek. For nations that had known and coveted "great power" status, such kowtowing was extremely unpalatable. Thatcher was part of a broader political trend to reverse that feeling of decline and to revive the "greatness" that once existed.

To be sure, British political reality has been changed forever. There is a new spirit of economic enterprise in Great Britain. Foreigners no longer talk of the "British disease," as unions do not exert the political muscle they once did. Westminster will think twice before buying up ailing industries, as the government remains trimmer and more efficient. But the one foundational goal that lay under these changes—the revival of Britain's international prestige—remains illusive. Victory in the Falklands notwithstanding, Britain entered the twenty-first century very much a second-class power. Thatcher may be remembered as the last Conservative prime minister to attempt to reverse the ebbing of British national prestige that began with World War I. Perhaps those who compared her to Churchill had it right. Churchill fought Nazism to revive Britain's hegemony as a world power; Thatcher battled socialism to revive its glory as an economic power. Both ministers won their share of victories, but the struggle to make Great Britain truly great again remains unsolved.

SELECTED BIBLIOGRAPHY

Campbell, John. *Margaret Thatcher*. Vol. 1, *The Grocer's Daughter*. London: Jonathan Cape, 2000. Excellent exhaustive biography of Thatcher's early years, ending with the election of 1979.

Dale, Ian. *Memories of Maggie: A Portrait of Margaret Thatcher*. London: Politico's Publishing, 2000. Personal reminiscences of Thatcher from nearly one hundred of her political and personal associates.

Dellheim, Charles. *The Disenchanted Isle: Mrs. Thatcher's Capitalist Revolution*. New York: W. W. Norton, 1995. Approaches the Thatcher decade by concentrating on the interplay between economic culture and a revolution of capitalism. Written by a cultural historian for an American audience.

Evans, Brendan. *Thatcherism and British Politics, 1975–1999*. Gloucestershire: Sutton Publishing, 1999. A valuable overview of the Conservative ascendancy from 1979 to 1997. The final two chapters review the interpretations of the Thatcher phenomenon and its impact on subsequent British history.

Evans, Eric J. *Thatcher and Thatcherism*. London. Routledge, 1997. Part of the publisher's series Making of the Contemporary World; a good brief introduction.

Gamble, Andrew. *The Strong Economy and the Free State: The Politics of Thatcherism*. Durham, N.C.: Duke University Press, 1988. An interesting look at the Thatcher phenomenon from a left-wing perspective. Views the Thatcher decade as the British response to changes in the world's balance of political and economic might and the West's loss of its traditional hegemony.

Harris, Kenneth. *Thatcher*. Boston: Little Brown, 1988. Probably the most readable and comprehensive account of Thatcher's career. A flattering account, lacking a discussion of her last years as prime minister.

Jenkin, Simon. *Accountable to None: The Tory Nationalization of Britain*. London: Penguin, 1996. A close look by a columnist for *The Times* and *The Spectator* at nationalization in the Thatcher/Major era; contends that Thatcherism, through its control of budgets and retreat from local democracy, has actually continued rather than diminished the trends toward bureaucratic centralization.

Jenkins, Peter. *Mrs. Thatcher's Revolution: The Ending of the Socialist Era*. Cambridge: Harvard University Press, 1988. Despite its presumptuous title and overbearing style, this biography deserves study.

Kavanagh, Dennis. *Thatcherism and British Politics: The End of Consensus?* Oxford: Oxford University Press, 1990. A useful book that attempts to explain the Thatcher movement's place in the overall context of postwar British politics.

Krieger, Joel. *Reagan, Thatcher, and the Politics of Decline*. New York: Oxford University Press, 1986. Explains the politics of the two world leaders as a response to the then-prevailing climate of declining prestige and economic stagnation in much of the Western, democratic world.

Letwin, Shirley Robin. *The Anatomy of Thatcherism*. New Brunswick, NJ: Transaction Publishers, 1992. An attempt to define Thatcherism as the promotion of what the author calls the "vigorous values," which include thrift, self-sufficiency, and adventurousness. The book advances an interesting thesis, but its effect is dulled by an overly philosophical, ponderous, and preachy style.

Minogue, Kenneth, and Michael Biddiss. *Thatcherism: Personality and Politics*. New York: St. Martin's Press, 1987. A collection of essays delivered as papers at a London School of Economics conference in 1986. A varied look at the era from historical, political, economic, and sociological perspectives.

Riddell, Peter. *The Thatcher Era and its Legacy*. Oxford: Basil Blackwell, 1991. Revised version of Riddell's earlier works, including *The Thatcher Decade* (1989), updated to include an assesment of her eclipse in 1990. Written by the political editor of *Financial Times* during the 1980s, this book is an excellent, well-balanced assessment of the economic, social, and political effects of the Thatcher years on Great Britain.

Sharp, Paul. *Thatcher's Diplomacy: The Revival of British Foreign Policy*. New York: St. Martins Press, 1997. Careful analysis of the Falklands crisis and policy toward the United States and Europe. Especially valuable for its discussion of Thatcher's approach toward Europe and Germany.

Skidelsky, Robert, ed. *Thatcherism*. Oxford: Basil Blackwell, 1988. A collection of academic lectures delivered at the University of Warwick in 1988.

Thatcher, Margaret. *The Downing Street Years*. New York: HarperCollins, 1993. Thatcher's autobiography of her years as prime minister; volume covering her life leading up to her election in 1979 was published in 1995.

———. *The Path to Power*. New York: HarperCollins, 1995. The second volume of Thatcher's autobiography, covering her life leading up to her election in 1979.

Thatcher, Margaret, and Christopher Collins. *Margaret Thatcher: Complete Public Statements, 1945–1990*. Oxford: Oxford University Press in association with Chesham Place Associates, 1999. An indispensable reference tool for the serious researcher; contains over seven thousand entries.

Young, Hugo. *One of Us*. London: McMillan London, 1989. Thorough, well-researched biography of the prime minister by the political correspondent for the *Sunday Telegraph* and the *Manchester Guardian*. Suffers only from the lack of a chapter on her resignation from office.

Appendix A: Glossary

Anne, Queen of England (1665–1714). The second daughter of Roman Catholic James II and the younger sister of Mary II, the Protestant Anne married Prince George of Denmark in 1683 and bore seventeen children, none of whom lived past the age of twelve. She succeeded William III in 1702 and was the last Stuart monarch.

Barnardo, Thomas John (1845–1905). Born in Dublin, Barnardo became an evangelistic minister, preaching in the slums of London. In 1867, he began founding homes for destitute children, and in the 1880s, he fostered emigration programs to Canada for these children.

BBC. British Broadcasting Corporation, the state-owned radio and television broadcasting network. Converted from a private radio company in 1927, the BBC began television broadcasting in 1936, suspended it during World War II, and added BBC2, a second channel, in 1964. BBC Radio managed five national stations and produces a large amount of overseas shortwave programming.

Bonnie Prince Charlie (1720–1788). The Scottish name for Charles Edward Stuart, grandson of James II. Bonnie Prince Charlie is best known for his leadership of the Jacobite rebellion of 1745–1746 that attempted to restore the house of Stuart to the English throne; his forces were routed at the Battle of Culloden in January 1746.

Boycott, Captain Charles Cunningham (1832–1897). During the land struggles in Ireland in the 1880s, Charles Stewart Parnell urged the Irish to shun or ostracize those who took land from evicted farmers. Irish partisans first applied the idea to Captain Boycott, an English land agent whose name subsequently became attached to the practice.

Burke, Edmund (1729–1797). An English author and politician, Burke first gained notice for his support of the American Revolution, portraying the rebellious colonists as defenders of traditional English rights. His greatest fame came from *Reflections on the Revolution in France* (1790), a work that condemned the French Revolution and set down the principles of modern conservatism.

Butler, Josephine (1828–1906). An English reformer who promoted education for women and campaigned against the Contagious Diseases Acts (1862–1870), which made women thought to be prostitutes liable to mandatory physical examination. Because of her efforts, the acts were repealed in 1883.

Butt, Isaac (1813–1879). Irish-born politican and M.P. who was an early leader in the struggle for Home Rule in Ireland.

Chamberlain, Joseph (1836–1914). A wealthy industrialist from Birmingham, Chamberlain became a prominent politician in the 1880s, leading the opposition to Irish Home Rule. Later he was an ardent supporter of tariff reform and imperial preference, a system of tariff concessions available only within the British Empire. His son, Neville, was prime minister at the beginning of World War II.

Chartist Movement. A working-class movement that originated in England about 1837, based on a so-called charter, listing specific political reforms that would bring greater democracy to the nation. Active as a mass movement for more than ten years, Chartism never achieved its goals, many of which, however, came to frution after the movement collapsed.

Collins, Michael (1890–1922). A leader in the Sinn Fein and Irish Republican Army campaign for Irish independence, Collins spent time in prison for his part in the Easter Rising (1916). In 1921 he helped negotiate the treaty creating the Irish Free State, and in 1922, he was assassinated by partisans who wanted a fully independent Ireland.

Congress of Vienna (1814–1815). Meeting in the Austrian capital at the conclusion of the Napoleonic Wars, the Congress of Vienna redrew the map of Europe and defined European political orthodoxy from the perspective of those who had defeated Napoleon and the French Revolution. France was treated as an equal.

Crimean War (1854–1856). A war fought in and around the Crimean peninsula on the Black Sea in Russia that pitted Russia against Turkey, Great Britain, and France. The war grew out of fear of Russian expansionism in the region, and after indecisive fighting, it ended with the Treaty of Paris (1856) that simply postponed outstanding issues.

Glossary

Curragh Mutiny (March 1914). An incident involving 56 British military officers stationed at Curragh, a base near Dublin, who refused to go to Ulster to enforce acceptance of Home Rule. The war office in London subsequently announced that the officers would not have to take action against the Ulster resistance.

de Valera, Eamon (1882–1975). A leader in the struggle for Irish independence, de Valera was involved in the Easter Rising and in Sinn Fein activities but opposed the treaty creating the Irish Free State in 1921 for not providing total independence. Later, he served as prime minister of Ireland from 1932–1948, 1951–1954, and 1957–1959.

dominion. An autonomous community within the British Commonwealth with the authority to repeal British statutes and block new Parliamentary legislation affecting it. Dominion status was legalized in the Statute of Westminster (1931). Canada, Australia, and New Zealand are among the dominions today.

Easter Rising (1916). An effort by Irish nationalists in April 1916 to win independence for Ireland at a time when Great Britain was preoccupied with World War I. Some 1,500 men occupied the General Post Office and other buildings in Dublin but were quickly routed by British forces. Also referred to as the *Easter Rebellion*.

Elizabeth I (1533–1603). Queen of England from 1558 to 1603, Elizabeth I was the last Tudor to occupy the throne. She reigned during an era of substantial commercial and territorial expansion and oversaw a great increase in English power and prestige.

Engels, Friedrich (1820–1895). The German-born Engels lived most of his adult life in England. He met Karl Marx in 1844 and collaborated with him on *The Communist Manifesto* (1848). After Marx's death in 1883, Engels edited and translated Marx's writings.

Ferdinand, Prince of Brunswick-Wolfenbuttel (1721–1792). Prussian general field marshal and (until 1766) close friend of Frederick the Great; best known for defeating the French at the Battle of Minden (1759).

Franco-Prussian War (1870–1871). War between Emperor Napoleon III's France and a combination of German-speaking states led by Chancellor Otto von Bismarck's Prussia. It resulted in a decisive victory for Prussia and led to the formation of the German Empire in January 1871.

Frederick the Great (1712–1786). King of Prussia (1740–1786), he was involved in a long series of European wars, most of which increased Prussian power and influence. In his domestic policy, he was an able administrator and a generally fair and just ruler. Also known as *Frederick II*.

G.I. Term commonly used to describe a U.S. enlisted man (or veteran). Dating from World War II, it may derive from the term *government issue*, referring to anything distributed by or through the government.

Glorious Revolution (1688). The Glorious Revolution marks the overthrow of James II, the last male Stuart to rule England. James and his family went into exile in Louis XIV's France, while in England the revolution settled the lengthy struggle between Parliament and a divine-right monarchy in favor of the former. Following the revolution, William III and Mary II (the older daughter of James II) became king and queen of England.

Goebbels, Joseph (1897–1945). Adolf Hitler's Reich Minister for Public Enlightenment and Propaganda. As World War II drew to a close, Goebbels remained at Hitler's side and encouraged the Nazi dictator to resist surrender.

Grand Alliance. The name given the World War II coalition joining the United States, Great Britain, and the Soviet Union.

habeas corpus. A Latin phrase meaning "you have the body." In judicial matters, the right of habeas corpus means that prisoners must be produced before a court of law in a timely fasion to determine if they should stand trial or be set free. The right of habeas corpus helps prevent illegal detention or imprisonment.

Habsburgs. The ruling house of Austria from 1267 until 1918; also served as Holy Roman Emperors from 1438 to 1806.

Irish Republican Army (I.R.A.). In January 1919, the Irish Republican Army was formed by Irish nationalists who felt that war against the British was the only way Irish independence could be achieved. Sinn Fein leader Michael Collins was the commander of the I.R.A., which received much money from Irish-Americans and armed itself with leftover World War I weapons and ammunition. The I.R.A. remains today as an important element in the continuing conflict in Northern Ireland.

Keynes, John Maynard (1883–1946). British economist and Labour Party politician, Keynes believed that state spending on such things as public works could revive a depressed economy.

Kitchener, Lord [Horatio] (1850–1916). Irish-born, Kitchener was a career military officer who saw action in Egypt and Sudan in the 1880s and 1890s and was chief of staff to Lord Roberts in the Boer War (1899–1902). Appointed secretary of state for war in 1914, he modernized the British army and foresaw a long war. He died in 1916 when a ship he was on sank after striking a German mine.

laissez-faire. In economics, the theory of *laissez-faire* postulates that the economy will perform most effectively when the state refrains from interfering in economic life.

levée en masse. Instituted in 1793 during the French Revolution's Reign of Terror, the *levée en masse* was a form of conscription. It required all able-bodied Frenchmen to defend the country and its revolution.

Luddites. Working-class people in England who suffered in the economic hard times during the latter years of the Napoleonic Wars (1811–1813). Deriving their name from the signature "Ned Ludd" that appeared on letters denouncing the appearance of industrial machinery, the Luddites destroyed textile machines in various parts of England in 1812; they were quickly suppressed by military forces.

Mafeking, siege of (October 1899–March 1900). Mafeking was a British military outpost in southern Africa near the Orange-Free State-Transvaal border. Boer forces besieged it, but British forces, under the command of Lord Robert Baden-Powell, held out against superior numbers for seven months until other British troops broke the siege.

mercantilism. Mercantilism is an economic doctrine dating to the sixteenth and seventeenth centuries that subordinates individual and corporate economic activity to the state's desire for self-sufficiency. The doctrine maintains that a state's power and prosperity are enhanced by building wealth through a favorable balance of trade achieved by high tariffs and the accumulation of gold. In the eighteenth century (and subsequently), *laissez-faire* challenged mercantilism.

Munich Conference (1938). A meeting of Neville Chamberlain, Edouard Daladier, Adolf Hitler, and Benito Mussolini in September 1938 at which the participants signed an agreement allowing Hitler important concessions in Czechoslovakia. Designed to prevent war in Europe, it failed to do so and became a symbol for appeasement.

NATO. North Atlantic Treaty Organization, a military alliance created in 1949 to contain the expansion of communism. Membership today includes the United States, Canada, the United Kingdom, and many other European nations.

Nazi-Soviet Nonaggression Pact (1939). Treaty between Germany and the Soviet Union pledging each country to remain neutral in a conflict involving the other. It also provided for a division of Poland if war did come. The German invasion of the Soviet Union in June 1941 effectively nullified the treaty.

Newtonian Revolution. A major reconsideration of how mankind views the physical universe. This revolution is attributable to the work of Isaac Newton (1642–1721), an English-born physicist and mathematician who discovered the laws of gravity and motion and advanced knowledge in the area of light that led to the invention of the reflecting telescope.

Number Ten Downing Street. The name and the address of the official residence of the British prime minister.

OPEC. Organization of Petroleum Exporting Countries, a cartel created by oil-rich nations to regain control over their resources from the various oil companies that had earlier received favorable concessions. In the 1970s OPEC worked to raise prices and nationalize foreign-owned production facilities.

Oxford Union. Oxford University's undergraduate debating society. In 1933 it voted for the proposition that its members would never fight for "King and Country."

Parliament Act (1911). An act that significantly reduced the power of the House of Lords by specifying that a money bill could become law in one month even if the Lords had not assented to it.

Redmond, John (1856–1918). A leader in the Irish independence movement and of the Irish Nationalist Party, Redmond succeeded Charles Stewart Parnell as the leading proponent of Irish causes. He worked for Home Rule before World War I, but his efforts were eclipsed by the war and the Easter Rising.

Reign of Terror (1793–1794). At the height of the French Revolution, the most radical revolutionaries gained control of the state and introduced the Reign of Terror, which sought to crush all signs of opposition to the revolutionary government. During this period, thousands of people were executed.

reparations. Payments made by the loser or losers of a war to the victor or victors to "repair" damages done by the former to the latter. At the Paris Peace Conference ending World War I, this definition was stretched to make Germany liable for virtually the entire cost of the war, thereby creating fiscal chaos in Europe.

Rhodes, Cecil John (1853–1902). Born in Great Britain, Rhodes moved to Natal in southern Africa in 1870 and made a huge fortune in gold mining. He entered politics in 1881, served as prime minister of the Cape Colony from 1890 to 1896, and extended British authority northward into what was known as Rhodesia. His fortune endowed the Rhodes Scholarship program.

Ripon, Lord [George Frederick Samuel Robinson] (1827–1909). Long-term Liberal M.P. who was appointed viceroy of India (1880–1884) and distinguished himself by his sympathy to the Indian people's cause.

Roberts, Lord [Frederick Sleigh] (1832–1914). British military leader in the late nineteenth century who was involved in the Indian Mutiny (1857–1858) and the Second Afghan War (1878–1879) and served as commander-in-chief in India (1885–1893) and Ireland (1895). He capped his career as commander-in-chief in the Boer War (1899–1902).

Royal Society of Arts. A British cultural organization, founded in London in 1754; dedicated to the encouragement of the arts, manufactures, and commerce. It played a major role in the organizing and staging of the Crystal Palace Exhibition. Sometimes referred to as the *Society of Arts*, without "Royal."

Russo-Japanese War (1904–1905). Grew out of Japan's perception that expansionist Russian moves in the area of Manchuria and Korea were a threat to its security. The fighting lasted a little over a year, with Japan prevailing. U.S. President Theodore Roosevelt mediated the peace negotiations, resulting in the Treaty of Portsmouth (1905), which generally restored the balance of power to the western Pacific.

Rye, Maria (1829–1903). One of the first social reformers to send poor British girls overseas to Canada and Australia to escape the poverty and disease rampant in London's slums. To do this, she founded the Female Middle-Class Emigration Society in 1861.

shadow cabinet. The practice of the British political party in opposition of forming a parallel, or shadow, cabinet to the legitimate one from its most prominent members serving in Parliament. This cabinet wields no power, but it helps to set policy for the party and provides the electorate with a vivid contrast to the official cabinet.

Stuarts. Ruling royal family of Scotland from 1371 to 1714 and of England from 1603 to 1714. Famous Stuarts include James I, Charles I, and James II.

"total war economy." Phrase describing the impact of World War II on the British economy; so much money was spent fighting the war that Britain was left with very serious economic problems after the war was over.

Tory. The name given to one of the two major English political parties through the mid-nineteenth century. Tories tended to be resistant to change and inclined to support royal authority. Today this term is sometimes used as a synonym for the Conservative Party.

Tudors. Ruling family of England from 1485 until 1603. Famous Tudors include Henry VIII and Elizabeth I.

Walpole, Robert (1676–1745). Whig leader who became the first British prime minister following the accession of George I in 1714. George I allowed Walpole and Parliament considerable discretion in managing the government.

Westminister Parliament. The name given Parliament at times to distinguish it from the Irish Parliament that met in Dublin prior to 1801.

Whig. From the end of the seventeenth century until the middle of the nineteenth, the name given one of the two major English political parties. Whigs tended to favor change and were inclined to restrict the power of the monarch.

Whitehall. Famous street in London leading off Trafalgar Square. Along Whitehall lies the Cenotaph, a memorial honoring the dead of World War I; the Cabinet War Rooms that Winston Churchill and British military leaders used during World War II; and Downing Street.

William III, King of England (1650–1702). A native of the Netherlands, William became King of England (1689–1702) as a result of his marriage to Mary, the oldest child of James II, and the Glorious Revolution, which drove his father-in-law from power. Staunchly Protestant, William fought a lengthy war against the French that distracted him from concern about the English colonies in North America.

Appendix B: Ruling Houses and Monarchs, 1689–Present

At the start of the eighteenth century, the monarch ruled as king of both England and Ireland. Since 1603, the same family had also ruled as king of Scotland, a separate country. However, in 1707 the Act of Union officially joined England and Scotland. The monarch became king of Great Britain and, separately, remained king of Ireland.

House of Stuart
William III	1689–1702
and Mary II	1689–1694
Anne	1702–1714

House of Hanover
George I	1714–1727
George II	1727–1760

In 1801 the Kingdom of Great Britain, which had been formed in 1707, expanded to become the United Kingdom of Great Britain and Ireland.

George III	1760–1820
George IV	1820–1830
William IV	1830–1837
Victoria	1837–1901
Edward VII	1901–1910

Technically, the House of Hanover ended with Victoria, the last of the Hanoverian line. However, the name *Hanover* continued in common usage despite the fact that Victoria's consort (and father of Victoria's successor), Prince Albert, came from the Germanic House of Saxe-Coberg-Gotha. In 1917, at the height of anti-German hysteria during World War I, the reigning monarch, George V, substituted the more English-sounding name *Windsor* for the Germanic Hanover. Since then the ruling house has been known as the House of Windsor.

House of Windsor

George V	1910–1936
Edward VIII	1936
George VI	1936–1952
Elizabeth II	1952–

Appendix C: Prime Ministers

1721–1742	Robert Walpole, Earl of Oxford
1742–1743	Spencer Compton, Earl of Wilmington
1743–1754	Henry Pelham
1754–1756	Thomas Pelham-Holles, Duke of Newcastle
1756–1757	William Cavendish, Duke of Devonshire
1757–1762	Thomas Pelham-Holles, Duke of Newcastle
1762–1763	John Stuart, Earl of Bute
1763–1765	George Grenville
1765–1766	Charles Watson-Wentworth, Marquis of Rockingham
1766–1768	William Pitt, Earl of Chatham (Pitt the Elder)
1768–1770	Augustus Henry Fitzroy, Duke of Grafton
1770–1782	Frederick North, Earl of Guilford
1782	Charles Watson-Wentworth, Marquis of Rockingham
1782–1783	William Petty, Earl of Shelburne
1783	William Cavendish Bentinck, Duke of Portland
1783–1801	William Pitt (Pitt the Younger)
1801–1804	Henry Addington, Viscount Sidmouth

1804–1806	William Pitt (Pitt the Younger)
1806–1807	William Wyndham Grenville, Baron Grenville
1807–1809	William Cavendish Bentinck, Duke of Portland
1809–1812	Spencer Perceval
1812–1827	Robert Banks Jenkinson, Earl of Liverpool
1827	George Canning
1827–1828	Frederick John Robinson, Viscount Goderich
1828–1830	Arthur Wellesley, Duke of Wellington
1830–1834	Charles Grey, Earl Grey
1834	William Lamb, Viscount Melbourne
1834–1835	Robert Peel
1835–1841	William Lamb, Viscount Melbourne
1841–1846	Robert Peel
1846–1852	John Russell, Earl Russell
1852	Edward Smith Stanley, Earl of Derby
1852–1855	George Hamilton Gordon, Earl of Aberdeen
1855–1858	Henry John Temple, Viscount Palmerston
1858–1859	Edward Smith Stanley, Earl of Derby
1859–1865	Henry John Temple, Viscount Palmerston
1865–1866	John Russell, Earl Russell
1866–1868	Edward Smith Stanley, Earl of Derby
1868	Benjamin Disraeli, Earl of Beaconsfield
1868–1874	William Ewart Gladstone
1874–1880	Benjamin Disraeli, Earl of Beaconsfield
1880–1885	William Ewart Gladstone
1885–1886	Robert A. T. Gascoyne-Cecil, Marquis of Salisbury
1886	William Ewart Gladstone
1886–1892	Robert A. T. Gascoyne-Cecil, Marquis of Salisbury
1892–1894	William Ewart Gladstone
1894–1895	Archibald Philip Primrose, Earl of Rosebery
1895–1902	Robert A. T. Gascoyne-Cecil, Marquis of Salisbury
1902–1905	Arthur James Balfour, Earl Balfour
1905–1908	Henry Campbell-Bannerman

Prime Ministers

1908–1916	Herbert Henry Asquith, Earl of Oxford
1916–1922	David Lloyd George
1922–1923	Andrew Bonar Law
1923–1924	Stanley Baldwin
1924	James Ramsey MacDonald
1924–1929	Stanley Baldwin
1929–1935	James Ramsey MacDonald
1935–1937	Stanley Baldwin
1937–1940	Neville Chamberlain
1940–1945	Winston Spencer Churchill
1945–1951	Clement Richard Attlee
1951–1955	Winston Spencer Churchill
1955–1957	Anthony Eden
1957–1963	Harold Macmillan
1963–1964	Alec Douglas-Home
1964–1970	Harold Wilson
1970–1974	Edward Heath
1974–1976	Harold Wilson
1976–1979	James Callaghan
1979–1990	Margaret Thatcher
1990–1997	John Major
1997–	Tony Blair

Index

Aboukir Bay, Battle of, 40, 44
Act of Union (1801), 63, 113–114
Addington, Henry (Viscount Sidmouth), 40
Afghanistan, 62–64
Africa, 59, 62, 69, 138
agriculture, 1, 7–8, 12–13, 16
Aix-la-Chapelle, Treaty of, 19, 21, 27
Albert, Prince of England, 66, 96, 98, 100, 105
Alexander I, Tsar of Russia, 42
Alexander, General Harold, 158
Althrop, Viscount. *See* Spencer, John Charles
American Civil War, 59, 78, 142
American Revolution, 34, 46–47, 52, 81
Anglo-French Entente, 135
Anti-Corn Law League, 15, 122
appeasement, 153, 155–156, 159–160
architecture, 96–97, 99
Argentina, 177, 187
aristocracy, 3, 15, 52–53, 75, 77, 81–83, 85–87, 90, 102, 185
Arkwright, Richard, 4

Asquith, Herbert Henry (Earl of Oxford and Asquith), 116–117, 126, 136
Atlantic, Battle of the, 167
Attlee, Clement, 164, 179–180, 182
Attwood, Thomas, 84
Auerstadt, Battle of, 41
Austen, Jane, 8
Austerlitz, Battle of, 41
Australia, 49, 59, 61, 69–70, 136, 157, 162
Austria: and the Napoleonic Wars, 39–41; and the Seven Years' War, 21, 25, 28–30; and World War I, 135–136; and World War II, 155
Austrian Succession, War of the, 19, 26

Baden-Powell, Robert, 67
Balfour Declaration, 72
Balkan Wars, 135
Bank of England, 7, 46
Barnardo, Dr. Thomas, 70
Beaverbrook, Lord (Max Aitken), 164

Belgium, 60, 135–136, 139–140, 149, 156, 161–162
Beveridge Report (1942), 167, 170
Bevin, Ernest, 164
"Blacks and Tans," 116
Blenheim, Battle of, 26
Boer War, 59–61, 64–66, 133, 139
Bonaparte, Joseph, 42
Bonaparte, Napoleon. *See* Napoleon I
Bonnie Prince Charlie. *See* Stuart, Charles Edward
Boscawen, Admiral Edward, 23
Boulton, Matthew, 5
Boycott, Captain C. C., 63
Braddock, General Edward, 21, 23, 28–29
Britain, Battle of, 157, 162–163, 166
British Broadcasting Corporation, 167
British East Africa Company, 60
British Expeditionary Force, 136, 139–142, 144, 156–157
British Royal Air Force, 163, 170
Bulge, Battle of the, 169
Burke, Edmund, 39, 49, 53
Bute, Earl of (John Stuart), 31
Butler, Josephine, 125
Butt, Isaac, 63, 114
Byng, Admiral John, 21

Calcutta, 21–23
Callaghan, James, 173, 179, 183
Campbell, Herbert, 67
Campbell-Bannerman, Henry, 126
Canada, 59, 61, 69–70, 136, 157, 162
Cape St. Vincent, Battle of, 40
capitalism, 11–13, 176
Carlyle, Thomas, 8
Carnarvon, Lord (Henry Howard Molyneux Herbert), 120
Carson, Sir Edward, 126–127
Carter, Jimmy, 177
Cartwright, Edmund, 5
Castlereagh, Viscount (Robert Stewart), 43, 57–58
Cat and Mouse Act (1913), 117, 127
Cavell, Edith, 146
Chadwick, Edwin, 14
Chamberlain, Joseph, 64–65, 121

Chamberlain, Neville, 153, 155–156, 159–161, 164
Chandos, Marquess de, 87
Charles VI, Emperor of Austria, 19, 26–27
Chartist movement, 78, 93, 100, 122
Choiseul, Duke of, 23
Church of England, 82, 90
Churchill, John (Duke of Marlborough), 26
Churchill, Winston, 67, 150, 153, 156–157, 160–164, 167–169, 179, 187, 189
Clausewitz, Carl von, 44
Clemenceau, Georges, 137
Clive, Robert, 23
coal, 3, 5, 6, 9
Cole, Henry, 96
Collins, Michael, 128
colonies: in the eighteenth century, 3, 6, 19–35, 42–43; in the nineteenth century, 59, 61–66, 71–72, 108–109; in the twentieth century, 157, 159, 170, 173. *See also names of individual colonies*
Compton, Samuel, 4
Congress of Vienna, 43, 58
Connolly, James, 127
conscription, 148–149, 156, 166
Conservative Party, 78, 114, 120–122, 126–127, 129, 168, 173, 175–178, 181–183. *See also* Tory Party
consumerism, 104–107
Continental System, 42, 48
Convention of Westminster, 21, 29
Cook, Thomas, 101
Cooke, William Fothergill, 95
Corn Laws (1846), 58, 93, 120
Cort, Henry, 6
cotton, 3–5, 10, 28
Crimean War, 58–59, 78, 139
Crystal Palace, 97–102, 104–110
Crystal Palace Exhibition. *See* Great Exhibition of 1851
Cuba, 24, 31, 32
Culloden, Battle of, 27
Cumberland, Duke of, 22
Curragh Mutiny, 115

Index

Curzon, Lord (George Nathaniel Curzon), 137
Czechoslovakia, 155–156, 159–160

Darby, Abraham, 6
d'Aveze, Marquis, 95
Davison, Emily Wilding, 127
Davitt, Michael, 119
de Gaulle, Charles, 157
de Valera, Eamon, 116
democracy, 49, 52–53
Denmark, 25, 41, 156, 160–162
Derby, Earl of (Edward Henry Stanley), 78, 148
design theories, 105–108
Dettingen, Battle of, 27
Dickens, Charles, 13
Diplomatic Revolution, 21, 29
Disraeli, Benjamin, 58–59, 62–63, 66, 78, 114
Dowlah, Surajah, Prince of Bengal, 21, 23
Dunkirk, 162–163

East India Company, 23, 31, 62, 109
Easter Rising, 116, 118, 123–124, 128, 151
Eden, Anthony (Earl of Avon), 160
Edward VII, King of England, 66
Egypt, 40, 63, 71, 163, 168
Eisenhower, General Dwight D., 158, 168, 169
Eliot, George, 8
Elizabeth I, Queen of England, 7, 45
Elizabeth, Empress of Russia, 31
Emergency Powers Acts (1939, 1940), 164
emigration, 61, 69–70
Employment Act (1980), 179
Engels, Friedrich, 11–12, 14, 100
European Community, 178–179, 187–188
European Union. See European Community
evolution, 69
Eylau, Battle of, 41

factories, 6, 10–12

Falkland Islands, 177, 187, 190
fascism, 153, 155
Fawcett, Millicent, 123, 125
Ferdinand, Franz, Archduke of Austria, 135
Ferdinand, Prince of Brunsick-Wolfenbuttel, 30
First Coalition, 39–40
Fisher, Admiral John, 65
Fitzgerald, Desmond, 123
Fontainebleau Agreement, 178
Forbes, General John, 23
Fort Duquesne, 21, 23, 28, 30
Fort Oswego, 21
Fort William Henry, 22
Fox, Charles James, 49–50
France, 57–58, 60, 64, 95, 97; and the Napoleonic Wars, 37–44, 48–54; and the Seven Years' War, 19–35; and World War I, 135, 138–140; and World War II, 155–157, 159, 160–162, 168–169
Franco, Francisco, 155
Franco-Prussian War, 133
Frederick II (the Great), King of Prussia, 19, 21, 24, 27, 29–31, 44
French and Indian War. See Seven Years' War
French Revolution, 34, 37–39, 43, 49–50, 52–53, 75, 81
Friedland, Battle of, 41

Gascoyne, Isaac, 86
George I, King of England, 50
George II, King of England, 22, 24, 27, 50
George III, King of England, 24, 31, 40, 50
George IV, King of England, 84
George V, King of England, 66, 147
Germany, 24, 58, 64, 97, 133–43, 149, 188–189; and the Third Reich, 153, 155–164, 167–169. See also Prussia
Gladstone, William, 63–64, 78–80, 114–115, 119–122
Glorious Revolution, 7, 10, 37, 75
Goebbels, Joseph, 169

Gorbachev, Mikhail, 178
Grand Alliance, 157, 164, 167, 170
Great Depression, 138, 153, 155, 170, 180, 183
Great Exhibition of 1851, 93–110
Great Macdermott, 68
Great Reform Act. *See* Reform Act of 1832
Greece, 159, 163
Greenwood, Arthur, 164
Grey, Earl of (Charles Grey), 75, 77, 83–91
Grey, Viscount (Edward Grey), 135, 139

Haggard, H. Rider, 66
Haig, General Douglas, 136–137
Haldane, Richard Burdon (Viscount Haldane), 65
Halifax, Lord (Edward Wood), 161
Hanover, 21–22, 24–25, 27, 30
Hanover dynasty, 19, 21, 133
Hargreaves, James, 4
Hastenbeck, Battle of, 22
Hawke, Admiral Edward, 23
Hazlitt, William, 50
Heath, Edward, 173, 175–176, 178, 181–183, 187
Henty, G. A., 67
Heseltine, Michael, 189
Hiroshima, 158, 169
Hitler, Adolf, 153, 155–163, 167–169, 187, 189
Hobson, John, 67, 71
Holland, 25, 27, 39. *See also* Netherlands
Home Rule. *See* Ireland
House of Commons, 82–88, 115, 161. *See also* Parliament
House of Lords, 39, 81, 83, 85–89. *See also* Parliament
Housing Act (1980), 177
Howe, Geoffrey, 179, 189
Hubertusburg, Treaty of, 32
Hurd, Douglas, 188

immigration, 32–33
imperialism, 59–72, 109, 129

India, 40, 136, 157; at the Great Exhibition of 1851, 98, 109; in the nineteenth century, 59, 62, 64, 66, 69; in the Seven Years' War, 19, 21, 23–24, 28, 30–32
Indian Mutiny, 62, 67, 69
Industrial Revolution, 1–16, 49, 51–53, 61, 70, 99–102, 136
Inglis, Dr. Elsie, 146
international exhibitions, 95–96, 101–102. *See also* Great Exhibition of 1851; world's fairs
Ireland, 40, 45, 63–64, 72, 79, 81; famine, 114, 118; Home Rule, 114–116, 119–121, 126–129; independence, 113–114, 118–121, 123–124, 128–129. *See also* Northern Ireland
Irish Land War, 118–119
Irish Nationalist Party, 127
Irish Republican Army, 114, 128, 178
Irish Republican Brotherhood, 114
iron, 6, 160
Italy, 57–59, 155, 157–159, 162–163, 167–169

Jafar, Mir, 23
Jameson Raid, 60
Japan, 60, 64, 135, 155, 158–159, 167–169
Jena, Battle of, 41
Jenkins' Ear, War of, 26
Jones, Owen, 97
Joseph, Keith, 176, 181–182

Kay, John, 4
Keynes, John Maynard, 52, 177, 184
King George's War. *See* Austrian Succession, War of the
King William's War. *See* League of Augsburg, War of the
Kingston, H. G., 67
Kipling, Rudyard, 66
Kitchener, Lord (Horatio Herbert Kitchener), 64, 136, 150
Kohl, Helmut, 189
Kruger, Paul, 60

La Hogue, Battle of, 25

Index

Labour Party, 13, 16, 72, 129, 161, 164, 173, 175–177, 183
Lally, Compte de, 31
Lange, Helene, 128
Law, Andrew Bonar, 126
Lawson, Nigel, 179
League of Armed Neutrality, 41
League of Augsburg, War of the, 25
League of Nations, 137
League of the Empire, 68
Leipzig, Battle of, 43
Lend-Lease Act, 157, 164–166
Libel Act (1792), 83, 161
Liberal Party, 78, 114–117, 119–120, 122, 126, 129, 164. *See also* Whig Party
Liverpool, Earl of (Robert Banks Jenkinson), 75, 179
Livingstone, David, 66
Lloyd George, David, 116, 129, 136–138, 145, 179
Louis XIV, King of France, 25, 43
Louis XVI, King of France, 39
Louisbourg, 21, 23–24, 27–28, 30
Low Countries, 39, 161—162. *See also* Belgium
Luddites, 49
Luxembourg, 161–162

Maastricht Treaty, 189
Macmillan, Harold, 175
Macpherson, Annie, 70
Mafeking, Siege of, 67–68
Maginot Line, 160
Mahan, Alfred Thayer, 34
Major, John, 188
Malthus, Thomas, 8
Marengo, Battle of, 41
Maria Theresa, Empress of Austria, 19, 27
Marryat, Captain Frederick, 66
Marx, Karl, 12–13, 100, 104, 106
mercantilism, 3, 62, 70
middle class, 53, 122, 185; in the eighteenth century, 3, 15; at the Great Exhibition of 1851, 100, 102, 105; and political reform, 68–69, 77, 81, 83, 86

Mill, John Stuart, 79, 116, 122
Milner, Alfred (Viscount Milner), 60, 137
Minden, Battle of, 24
Montagu, E. S., 145
Montcalm, Marquis de, 23
Montgomery, Field Marshal Bernard, 158, 168
Montreal, 23, 30
Morris, William, 67, 105–106
Munday, Messrs. Jas. & Geo., 96–97
Munich Conference, 155–156, 159
Mussolini, Benito, 155, 157, 159, 162–163, 168–169

Nagasaki, 158, 169
Napoleon I, 40–48, 50, 52, 139
Napoleonic Wars, 34, 37–54, 57, 70
National Health Service, 178
National Union of Women's Suffrage Societies (NUWSS), 116–117, 123
nationalism, 50, 65, 72, 108
Nations, Battle of the. *See* Leipzig, Battle of
Native Americans, 28–29, 33–34
NATO. *See* North Atlantic Treaty Organization
Nazi-Soviet Nonaggression Pact, 160
Nelson, Admiral Horatio, 40–41, 44
Netherlands, 161. *See also* Holland
New Imperialism, 62, 64
New Zealand, 59, 61, 69–70, 136, 162
Newcastle, Duke of (Thomas Pelham-Holles), 22, 29
Newcomen, Thomas, 5
Nile, Battle of the. *See* Aboukir Bay, Battle of
Normandy, 168–169
North Africa, 158–159, 167–168
North America, 19, 21–31. *See also* Canada; United States
North American colonies, 33–34
North Atlantic Treaty Organization, 188
Northern Ireland, 130, 173, 177–179
Norway, 156, 160–161

O'Brien, William, 121

O'Connell, Daniel, 63, 114
OPEC. *See* Organization of Petroleum Exporting Countries
Orange Free State, 59–60
Organization of Petroluem Exporting Countries, 181
Orlando, Vittorio, 137
Otis, A. W., 107
Ottoman Empire, 62, 72, 138

Paine, Thomas, 37, 39, 49
Palmerston, Viscount (Henry John Temple), 58–59, 78
Pankhurst, Christabel, 116, 123, 125, 127
Pankhurst, Emmeline, 112, 116–117, 122–123, 127
Pankhurst, Sylvia, 116, 123, 125
Paris Peace Conference, 137
Paris, Peace of, 24, 31–34
Parliament, 9, 15, 33, 77–78, 81–90, 164, 181. *See also* House of Commons; House of Lords
Parliament Act of 1911, 115, 126
Parliamentary reform, 75–91
Parnell, Charles Stuart, 63, 114–115, 119–121, 123, 127
Passchendaele, Battle of, 136
Patton, General George, 158
Pax Britannica, 57–72
Paxton, Joseph, 97, 107–108
Peace of Amiens, 41
Peace of Britain. *See* Pax Britannica
Pearse, Padraic, 124, 127–128
Peel, Sir Robert, 58, 86, 90, 114
Peninsular War, 42
Peter III, Tsar of Russia, 31
Pitt, Thomas "Diamond," 22
Pitt, William, the Elder, 22, 24, 29, 31, 33
Pitt, William, the Younger, 39–42, 46, 49, 75
Pittsburgh, 20–21, 28
Plains of Abraham, 23, 30
Plassey, Battle of, 23
Poland, 40, 156, 159–160
Pondicherry, 23–24, 31
Poor Law (1834), 13

Portugal, 26, 42
power loom, 5, 8
Pragmatic Sanction, 19, 27
privatization, 178, 184–185, 189
Prussia, 57; and the Napoleonic Wars, 39, 41; and the Seven Years' War, 19, 24, 28–32, 34; and the War of the Austrian Succession, 27; and the War of the Spanish Succession, 25
putting-out system, 4–5
Pyramids, Battle of the, 40

Quebec, 23, 30, 34
Queen Anne's War. *See* Spanish Succession, War of the
Quiberon Bay, Battle of, 23

Reagan, Ronald, 177–178, 190
Redmond, John, 127
Reform Act of 1832, 3, 53, 77–78, 80–91
Reform Act of 1867, 78–79, 90, 93, 122
Reform Act of 1884–1885, 79–80, 90, 122
Reign of Terror, 39, 52
Rhodes, Cecil, 71
Ricardo, David, 8
Ridley, Nicholas, 188–189
riots, 48–49, 80, 87–88, 178, 187
Ripon, Lord (George Robinson), 59
Roberts, Alfred, 180
Roberts, Earl (Frederick Roberts), 64, 66
Robertson, Sir William, 137
Rommel, Field Marshal Erwin, 163, 168
Roosevelt, Franklin D., 157, 167–168
Roosevelt, Theodore, 135
Royal Society of Arts, 95–96
Ruskin, John, 106
Russell, Earl (John Russell), 76, 78
Russia, 27, 29, 31, 40–43, 58–59, 62, 64, 66; and World War I, 135, 139. *See also* Soviet Union
Russo-Japanese War, 135, 139
Rye, Maria, 70
Ryswick, Peace of, 25

Salamanca, Battle of, 42

Index

Salisbury, Lord (Robert A. T. Gascoyne-Cecil), 60, 64, 80
Savage South Africa, 67
Scargill, Arthur, 186
Schreiner, Olive, 67
Scotland, 12, 27, 78–79, 81
Scottish Women's Hospitals, 146
Second Coalition, 41
Seditious Meetings Act (1795), 39
Semper, Gottfried, 107
Senegal, 24, 31–32
Serbia, 135–136
Seven Years' War, 19–35, 47
Shaw, George Bernard, 119
Silesia, 19, 21, 27–28, 32
Simon, John, 14
Sinn Fein, 114, 116, 127–128
slavery, 26, 28, 31–32, 50–51, 68–69
Smith, Adam, 8
Society of Friends of the People, 83
Somme, Battle of the, 136, 142
Sons of Britannia, 67
South Africa, 59, 60–61, 63–64, 67, 71, 136, 157, 162
South Asia, 62
Southern Unionists, 124
Soviet Union, 156–159, 162, 164, 167–169. *See also* Russia
Spain, 57; and the Napoleonic Wars, 39–40, 42; and the Seven Years' War, 24, 31–32; and the Spanish Civil War, 155; and the War of the Austrian Succession, 27; and the War of the Spanish Succession, 25–26
Spanish Succession, War of the, 25
Spanish-American War, 139
Spencer, John Charles (Lord Spencer), 84, 88–89
Stalin, Joseph, 168
Stalingrad, Battle of, 168
Statute of Westminster (1931), 72
steam engine, 5, 8–9, 11, 100
Stevenson, Robert Louis, 67
Stickley, Gustav, 106
strikes, 173, 177–178, 183, 186
Stuart Restoration, 19, 27
Stuart, Charles Edward, 27
Suez Canal, 62, 64

Sweden, 29, 31, 41

Tawell, John, 9
technology, 3–6, 8–10, 51, 105–109, 139–143
textile production, 3–5, 11
Thatcher, Margaret, 174–190
Third Coalition, 41
Tilsit, Treaty of, 41
Tory Party, 75, 77–78, 82–83, 85–90, 114. *See also* Conservative Party
total war, 44, 158, 164–165
tourism, 101
trade: in the eighteenth century, 3, 6–7, 15, 28, 42, 48, 51; in the nineteenth century 58, 62, 64–65, 70–71
trade unions, 173, 177–178, 181, 183, 185–186
Trafalgar, Battle of, 9, 41, 44
transportation, 5, 9, 51
Triple Entente, 135, 139, 150
Turkey, 41, 135

Ulm, Battle of, 41
Ulster. *See* Northern Ireland
Ulster Loyalist Anti-Repeal Union, 115–116
Ulster movement, 126–127, 130
United States, 4, 59–60, 64, 97, 190; and World War I, 137–138, 150; and World War II, 157–158, 162–170
urbanization, 3, 13–14
Utrecht, Treaty of, 25

Value Added Tax, 176
Versailles, Treaty of, 137, 155
Victoria, Queen of England, 14, 59, 63, 65–66, 90, 93, 96, 104
Viscount Althrop. *See* Spencer, John Charles
Vitoria, Battle of, 42

Wakefield, Edward Gibbon, 70
Walpole, Horace, 24
Walpole, Sir Robert, 24, 47
Wandiwash, Battle of, 31
Washington, George, 21, 28, 33

Waterloo, Battle of, 43
Watt, James, 5
welfare state, 173, 175–176, 179–180, 182, 184, 187
Wellesley, Arthur. *See* Wellington, Duke of
Wellington, Duke of (Arthur Wellesley), 42–43, 45, 84, 89
Whig Party, 48–50, 75, 77–78, 82–84, 86–88, 114. *See also* Liberal Party
Whitelaw, William, 181–182
Wilberforce, William, 50
William III, King of England, 25, 47
William IV, King of England, 84–86, 88–90
Wilson, Harold, 173, 175–176, 183
Wilson, Woodrow, 137
Wolfe, General James, 23, 30
woman suffrage, 79–80, 90, 113, 116–119, 122–129, 144, 146
Women's Social and Political Union (WSPU), 116–117, 123
Wordsworth, William, 37
working class: in the eighteenth century, 3, 8, 8, 11–12, 14–16, 48–50, 53; at the Great Exhibition, 100–102, 104–105; in the nineteenth century, 65–68, 70–72, 79, 83; and woman suffrage, 122–123, 129
World War I, 117–118, 125, 127, 133–151, 153, 155, 159, 173
World War II, 72, 110, 142–143, 153–170, 173, 175
world's fairs, 99, 109. *See also* international exhibitions

Yeats, William Butler, 123
Ypres, Second Battle of, 142

Zulus, 59, 63

About the Editors and Contributors

GEORGE P. BLUM is professor emeritus of history at the University of the Pacific in Stockton, CA. He received his Ph.D. from the University of Minnesota and, in recent years, has published articles and chapters in *Research Guide to European Historical Biography* (1992–1993), *Statesmen Who Changed the World* (1993), *Events That Changed the World in the Twentieth Century* (1995), *The European Powers in the First World War: An Encyclopedia* (1996), and *World War II in Europe: An Encyclopedia* (1999). He is also the author of *The Rise of Fascism in Europe* (1998).

KENNETH L. CAMPBELL received his Ph.D. from the University of Delaware and is currently the Associate Dean of the School of Humanities and Social Sciences at Monmouth University in West Long Branch, New Jersey. He is the author of *The Intellectual Struggle of the English Papists in the Seventeenth Century* (1987) and is currently working on a book on religious nonconformity in England.

JOHN E. FINDLING is professor of history at Indiana University Southeast. He earned his Ph.D. at the University of Texas and has pursued a research interest in world's fairs for nearly twenty years. He is the author of *Chicago's Great World's Fairs* (1995), and with Robert W. Rydell and Kimberly Pelle, *Fair America* (2000). With Frank W. Thackeray, he edited *Statesmen Who Changed the World* (1993) and the *Events that Changed the World* and the *Events that Changed America* series.

RICHARD A. LEIBY is associate professor of history at Rosement College, where he serves as department chair. He received his Ph.D. from the University of Delaware and is the author of *German Unification, 1989–1990* (1998). He teaches courses in post-World War II European history and Nazi Germany. In his spare time, he is a jazz trombonist and an astronomy buff.

THOMAS C. MACKEY is an associate professor and chair of the history department at the University of Louisville. He divides his time between Louisville, Kentucky, and Long Island, New York. He earned his Ph.D. at Rice University and specializes in the areas of constitutional, legal, and political history. He has written several essays for volumes in the *Events That Changed America* series.

DAVID MITCH earned his Ph.D. at the University of Chicago and is currently a member of the department of economics at the University of Maryland, Baltimore County. He is the author of *Rise of Popular Literacy in Victorian England* (1992) and "The Role of Skill and Education in the English Industrial Revolution," in *The British Industrial Revolution: An Economic Perspective* (1999). He was a Fulbright Lecturer at the London School of Economics in 1995.

DIANA J. REYNOLDS earned her Ph.D. from the University of California, San Diego, and is currently assistant professor of history at Point Loma Nazarene University, also in San Diego. She is the author of *Alois Regal and the Politics of Art History: The Exhibitionary Complex of Fin-de-Siecle Vienna*, to be published in fall 2002. She teaches courses in modern European history, imperialism, and women's history.

LOWELL J. SATRE is professor of history at Youngstown State University. He received his Ph.D. from the University of South Carolina and is the author of *Thomas Burt, Miners' M.P., 1837–1922: The Great Conciliator* (1999) and several articles on late Victorian and Edwardian Britain. He is currently working on a book about "Cadbury v. the Standard," a celebrated 1909 British libel trial.

S. J. STEARNS is associate professor of history at the College of Staten Island, City University of New York. He earned his Ph.D. at the University of California, Berkeley, and has published numerous articles in the *Journal of British Studies, Military Affairs, The Historian*, and *Science and Society*, among others. He is currently working on a study of war and politics in early Stuart Britain.

FREDERICK M. STOWELL is a senior editor for Fire Protection Publications at Oklahoma State University and an adjunct instructor in history and political science at Langston University, Tulsa Campus. He has written two books for the Fire Service and is currently writing a third. He has also contributed an essay to *Events That Changed America Through the Seventeenth Century* (2000).

FRANK W. THACKERAY is professor of history at Indiana University Southeast. He received his Ph.D. from Temple University. He is the author of *Antecedents of Revolution: Alexander I and the Polish Congress Kingdom* (1980) as well as articles on Russian-Polish relations in the nineteenth century and Polish-American relations in the twentiety century. With John E. Findling, he edited *Statesmen Who Changed the World* (1993) and the *Events that Changed the World* and the *Events that Changed America* series. He is a former Fulbright scholar in Poland.

LARRY P. THORNTON is professor of history at Hanover College in Hanover, Indiana. He received his Ph.D. from the University of Illinois and contributed an essay to *Events That Changed America in the Twentieth Century* (1996). He teaches a wide variety of courses in modern European history and is currently doing research on student statements about war in the United States and Great Britain between World War I and World War II, and on relief missions to Poland, 1940–1941.

DIXON PUBLIC LIBRARY
DIXON ILLINOIS